Éditions du Layeur
Dépôt Légal : 2020
ISBN : 978-2-915126-86-0
Imprimé chez Peninsula Books S.L.
c / Major 28
08393 Caldes d'Estrac
Barcelona, Spain
T. +34 650 360 759
NIF B02669729
Espagne, en Décembre 2020

Editorial project:
2020 © **booq** publishing, S.L.
c/ Domènech, 7-9, 2º 1ª
08012 Barcelona, Spain
T: +34 93 268 80 88
www.booqpublishing.com

ISBN 978-84-9936-707-1 [EN]
ISBN 978-84-9936-702-6 [DE]

Editorial coordinator:
Claudia Martínez Alonso

Art director:
Mireia Casanovas Soley

Editor:
Francesc Zamora Mola

Layout:
Cristina Simó Perales

Printed in Spain

The long time New York Times art critic Robert Hughes, in his book, *"American Visions: The Epic History of Art in America"*, believes that the best American Art and Architecture expresses the wonder and awe of the geography found on the North American continent when the first settlers arrived in the early sixteenth century. For the next 200 years, these settlers streaked westward across the continent thru a landscape full of natural wonders.

The Colorado Rockies couldn't stop this crowd, nor could the dry endless badlands of Nevada, but the high energy impulse finally met its match in the mighty Pacific Ocean which stopped cold these adventurers.

When these settlers finally stopped and looked around, they found themselves in California: an Eden blessed with natural beauty and benign weather. They also discovered new building forms: the indigenous Mexican and Hispanic adobe construction to the south; from the east across the Pacific, nineteenth-century Asian immigrants brought rich sensibilities of wood construction. The settlers brought the European craft of wood building, brick, and stone masonry. California provided the rich landscape in which all three cultures melded together in one of the more fertile environments for art and architecture.

Nowadays, many architectural styles have spun off these original influences, but two regional expressions remain a constant. Northern California provided large forests that provided lumber and one expression that sprung forth has a visible wood structure with Japanese stick framing, or traditional European heavy-timber, or simple well-done American balloon framing carpentry. Human movement through this architecture is akin to hiking thru the High Sierra Mountains.

Southern California residential design found one influential expression thru the melding of the glass and steel syntax of the early Modern Architecture along with adobe construction of the local Mexican/Hispanic (the famous Case Study houses of Los Angeles). Human movement thru these homes is akin to driving 80 mph (130 km/h) on a raised concrete Los Angeles Freeway with the top down on a warm summer evening. Both regional expressions are different and yet very sensuous.

Nothing is ever absolute in California, and the north and south now share many attributes. What both expressions have most in common is a fascination with the indoor/outdoor living. The best designs blend local construction traditions and imported Pan-Pacific building sensibilities with modern forms and materials to create harmonious and pleasurable residences fused with their immediate landscape thru large openings between the house and garden.

California is this: an incubator for technological, multi-cultural, ecological thought, and a love for the outdoors. It should be no surprise then to see that California architecture embodies these influences in home design. The homes presented in this book demonstrate the rich cultural synthesis found in California and that the influence of the North American continent upon American architecture continues.

Robert Nebolon, Architect AIA

Half Moon Bay, California. Photo courtesy of Francesc Zamora

Der langjährige Kunstkritiker der New York Times, Robert Hughes, äußert in seinem Buch „American Visions: The Epic History of Art in America" die Ansicht, dass die beste amerikanische Kunst und Architektur das Wunder und die Ehrfurcht vor der Geographie ausdrücken, die man auf dem nordamerikanischen Kontinent vorfand, als die ersten Siedler im frühen sechzehnten Jahrhundert ankamen. In den nächsten 200 Jahren zogen diese Siedler durch Landschaften voller Naturwunder westwärts über den Kontinent.

Die Colorado Rockies konnten diese Menschenmenge nicht aufhalten, ebenso wenig wie die trockenen, endlosen Badlands von Nevada, aber der energiereiche Impuls traf schließlich im mächtigen Pazifischen Ozean aufeinander, der diese Abenteurer vor der Kälte bewahrte.

Als diese Siedler schließlich anhielten und sich umsahen, fanden sie sich in Kalifornien wieder: einem Garten Eden, gesegnet mit natürlicher Schönheit und mildem Wetter. Sie entdeckten auch neue Bauformen: im Süden die einheimische mexikanische und hispanische Lehmbauweise; vom Osten über den Pazifik brachten asiatische Einwanderer des neunzehnten Jahrhunderts einen großen Erfahrungsschatz an Holzkonstruktionen mit. Die Siedler brachten das europäische Handwerk des Holz-, Ziegel- und Steinmauerwerks mit. Kalifornien lieferte die reiche Landschaft, in der alle drei Kulturen in einer der fruchtbarsten Umgebungen für Kunst und Architektur miteinander verschmolzen.

Heutzutage haben viele architektonische Stile diese ursprünglichen Einflüsse weiterentwickelt, aber zwei regionale Ausdrucksformen bleiben eine Konstante. In Nordkalifornien gab es große Wälder, die Holz lieferten, und ein Ausdruck, der hervorsprang, ist eine sichtbare Holzstruktur mit japanischer Stockeinrahmung, oder traditionelles europäisches schweres Holz, oder eine einfache, gut gemachte amerikanische Balloneinrahmung. Die menschliche Bewegung durch diese Architektur gleicht einer Wanderung durch die High Sierra Mountains.

Das südkalifornische Wohndesign fand einen einflussreichen Ausdruck in der Verschmelzung der Glas- und Stahlsyntax der frühen modernen Architektur mit der Lehmbauweise der lokalen mexikanisch-spanischen (die berühmten Case Study Houses von Los Angeles). Die menschliche Bewegung durch diese Häuser gleicht dem Fahren mit 130 km/h auf einem erhöhten Beton-Freeway in Los Angeles mit heruntergeklapptem Dach an einem warmen Sommerabend. Beide regionalen Ausdrucksformen sind unterschiedlich und doch sehr sinnlich.

Nichts ist in Kalifornien jemals absolut, und der Norden und der Süden haben heute viele gemeinsame Attribute. Was beide Ausdrucksformen am meisten gemeinsam haben, ist die Faszination für das Wohnen im Innen- und Außenbereich. Die besten Entwürfe vermischen lokale Bautraditionen und importierte pan-pazifische Bausensibilität mit modernen Formen und Materialien, um harmonische und angenehme Wohnungen zu schaffen, die durch große Öffnungen zwischen Haus und Garten mit ihrer unmittelbaren Landschaft verschmolzen sind.

Kalifornien ist dies: ein Inkubator für technologisches, multikulturelles, ökologisches Denken und die Liebe zur freien Natur. Es sollte also keine Überraschung sein, dass die kalifornische Architektur diese Einflüsse im Hausdesign verkörpert. Die in diesem Buch vorgestellten Häuser zeigen die reiche kulturelle Synthese, die in Kalifornien zu finden ist, und dass der Einfluss des nordamerikanischen Kontinents auf die amerikanische Architektur anhält.

Robert Nebolon, Architekt AIA

Ansel Adams Wilderness, Sierra Nevada, California. Photo courtesy of Francesc Zamora

Le critique d'art de longue date du New York Times, Robert Hughes, dans son livre « American Visions : The Epic History of Art in America », estime que le meilleur de l'art et de l'architecture américains exprime l'émerveillement et la crainte de la géographie du continent nord-américain lorsque les premiers colons sont arrivés au début du XVIe siècle. Pendant les 200 années qui ont suivi, ces colons ont traversé le continent vers l'ouest à travers un paysage plein de merveilles naturelles.

Les Rocheuses du Colorado n'ont pas pu arrêter cette foule, pas plus que les badlands arides et interminables du Nevada, mais l'impulsion de haute énergie a finalement rencontré son pendant dans le puissant océan Pacifique, qui a arrêté le froid de ces aventuriers.

Lorsque ces colons se sont finalement arrêtés et ont regardé autour d'eux, ils se sont retrouvés en Californie : un Eden béni par la beauté naturelle et un temps clément. Ils ont également découvert de nouvelles formes de bâtiments : la construction en adobe indigène mexicaine et hispanique au sud ; de l'est à travers le Pacifique, les immigrants asiatiques du XIXe siècle ont apporté une riche sensibilité de la construction en bois. Les colons ont développé l'artisanat européen de la fabrication en bois, en brique et de la maçonnerie de pierre. La Californie a fourni le riche paysage dans lequel les trois cultures se sont fusionnées dans l'un des environnements les plus fertiles pour l'art et l'architecture.

De nos jours, de nombreux styles architecturaux ont émané de ces influences originales, mais deux expressions régionales restent une constante. Le nord de la Californie a fourni de grandes forêts qui donnent du bois d'œuvre et une expression qui a vu le jour a une structure visible en bois avec des charpentes en bâtons japonais, ou en bois lourd européen traditionnel, ou en simple charpenterie américaine bien faite avec des ballons. Le mouvement humain à travers cette architecture s'apparente à une randonnée dans les hautes montagnes de la Sierra.

Le design résidentiel du sud de la Californie a trouvé une expression influente grâce à la fusion de la syntaxe du verre, de l'acier des débuts de l'architecture moderne et de la construction en adobe des maisons mexicaines/hispaniques locales (les célèbres Case Study houses de Los Angeles). Par une chaude soirée d'été, sur une autoroute de Los Angeles surélevée en béton, á une vitesse de 130 km/h, les gents peuvent distinguer que les toits de ces maisons. Ces deux expressions régionales sont différentes et pourtant très sensuelles.

Rien n'est jamais absolu en Californie, le nord et le sud partagent désormais de nombreux attributs. Ce que les deux expressions ont le plus en commun, c'est une fascination pour la vie en intérieur/extérieur. Les meilleurs designs mêlent les traditions de construction locales et les sensibilités de construction importées du Pacifique avec des formes et des matériaux modernes pour créer des résidences harmonieuses et agréables, fusionnées avec leur paysage immédat par de grandes ouvertures entre la maison et le jardin.

La Californie est un incubateur de pensée technologique, multiculturelle, écologique et d'amour pour le plein air. Il n'est donc pas surprenant de constater que l'architecture californienne incarne ces influences dans la conception des maisons. Les bâtiments présentés dans ce livre démontrent la riche synthèse culturelle que l'on trouve en Californie et que l'influence du continent nord-américain sur l'architecture américaine se poursuit.

Robert Nebolon, architecte AIA

Ansel Adams Wilderness, Sierra Nevada, California. Photo courtesy of Francesc Zamora

El crítico de arte del New York Times Robert Hughes, en su libro «American Visions: The Epic History of Art in America», cree que el mejor arte y arquitectura de América expresa la maravilla y el asombro de la geografía que se encuentra en el continente norteamericano cuando llegaron los primeros colonos a principios del siglo XVI. Durante los siguientes 200 años, estos colonos se extendieron por todo el continente hacia el oeste a través de un paisaje lleno de maravillas naturales.

Las Rocosas de Colorado no pudieron detener a esta multitud, ni tampoco las secas e interminables tierras bajas de Nevada, pero el impulso poderoso océano Pacífico detuvo en frío a estos aventureros.

Cuando estos colonos finalmente se detuvieron y miraron a su alrededor, se encontraron en California: un Edén bendecido con belleza natural y clima benigno. También descubrieron nuevas formas de construcción: la construcción de adobe indígena mexicana e hispana del sur; desde el este a través del Pacífico, los inmigrantes asiáticos del siglo XIX trajeron ricas sensibilidades de la construcción en madera. Los colonos trajeron el arte europeo de la construcción en madera, ladrillo y piedra. California proporcionó el rico paisaje en el que las tres culturas se fusionaron en uno de los entornos más fértiles para el arte y la arquitectura.

Hoy en día, muchos estilos arquitectónicos han derivado de estas influencias originales, pero dos expresiones regionales siguen siendo una constante. El norte de California proporcionó grandes bosques que ofrecían madera y estructuras de madera vista, de madera pesada tradicional europea, o simple carpintería americana bien hecha de enmarcado en forma de globo. El movimiento humano a través de esta arquitectura es similar al senderismo a través de las montañas de High Sierra.

El diseño residencial del sur de California encontró una expresión influyente a través de la fusión del vidrio y el acero de la arquitectura moderna temprana junto con la construcción de adobe de los mexicanos/hispanos locales (las famosas casas *Case Study* de Los Ángeles). El movimiento humano a través de estas casas es similar a conducir a 130 km/h en una autopista de hormigón de Los Ángeles con techo solar cerrado en una cálida tarde de verano. Ambas expresiones regionales son diferentes y sin embargo muy sensuales.

Nada es nunca absoluto en California, y el norte y el sur comparten ahora muchos atributos. Lo que ambas expresiones tienen más en común es la fascinación por la vida en interiores y exteriores. Los mejores diseños mezclan las tradiciones locales de construcción y las sensibilidades de construcción importadas del Pan-Pacífico con formas y materiales modernos que crean residencias armoniosas y placenteras fusionadas con su paisaje inmediato a través de grandes aberturas entre la casa y el jardín.

California es esto: una incubadora de pensamiento tecnológico, multicultural y ecológico, y un amor por el aire libre. No debería sorprender entonces ver que la arquitectura de California encarna estas influencias en el diseño de las casas. Las casas presentadas en este libro demuestran no solo la rica síntesis cultural que se encuentra en California, sino también que la influencia del continente norteamericano en la arquitectura americana continúa.

Robert Nebolon, arquitecto AIA

Half Moon Bay, California. Photo courtesy of Francesc Zamora

AB design studio

abdesignstudioinc.com

MID-CENTURY MODERN RESIDENCE

Design Team: Clay Aurell, AIA; Josh Blumer, AIA; Karmen Aurell, Diana Costea, Schuyler Bartholomay, and Joel Herrera

Interior Designer: Karmen Aurell/ AB design studio

Landscape Architect: CommonGround

Structural Engineer: Taylor & Syfan

General Contractor: Nathan Modesette/ BOMO Design

Photographers: Ciro Coelho and Jim Bartsch

QUARRY HOUSE

Design Team: Clay Aurell, AIA; Josh Blumer, AIA; Robert Pester, Joel Herrera, and Amy Tripp

Interior Designer: House of Honey

Landscape Architect: Progressive Environmental Industries

Structural Engineer: Darkmoon Building Design and Engineering

General Contractor: J Weir Masterworks and Jed Hirsch General Building Contractor

Photographers: Jason Rick and Sam Frost

HO:ME 296

Design Team: Clay Aurell, AIA; Josh Blumer, AIA; and Robert Pester

Interior Designer: McFadden Design Group

Landscape Architect: Greens Landscape, Inc.

Structural Engineer: Ashley & Vance

General Contractor: Barber Builders

Photographer: Jason Rick

In 2005, what began as a conversation between two architects about making a difference in the world through architecture organically evolved into a lasting partnership. Together, Clay Aurell and Josh Blumer bring more than 20 years of passion, experience, and creativity to explorative designs that reflect client, context, and history. Whether it is evoking the authentic essence of historic buildings and structures through adaptive reuse or creating a new ground-up commercial office space, AB design studio ensures that each project communicates a strong signature design solution for client and community, resulting in a seamless identity among concept, brand, and space. AB design studio's architecture, interior design, and planning talents are applied to a variety of project types, including cultural, childcare, retail, hospitality, commercial, healthcare, education, multi- and single-family residential, and experimental architypes. Whether new construction, adaptive reuse, renovation, or interior design, AB design studio promotes innovative techniques, responsible material palettes, and sustainable strategies to create architecturally driven, globally conscious environments that inspire and empower.

En 2005, ce qui a commencé comme une conversation entre deux architectes pour faire une différence dans le monde à travers l'architecture a évolué de façon organique vers un partenariat durable. Ensemble, Clay Aurell et Josh Blumer apportent plus de 20 ans de passion, d'expérience et de créativité à des conceptions exploratoires qui reflètent le client, le contexte et l'histoire. Qu'il s'agisse d'évoquer l'essence authentique de bâtiments et de structures historiques par une réutilisation adaptative ou de créer un nouvel espace de bureau commercial, AB design studio s'assure que chaque projet trouve une solution de design à forte signature pour le client et la communauté, résultant en une identité homogène entre le concept, la marque et l'espace. Les talents d'AB design studio en matière d'architecture, de design d'intérieur et de planification sont appliqués à divers types de projets, y compris les projets culturels, de garde d'enfants, commerciaux, d'hôtellerie, de santé, d'éducation, de résidences multifamiliales et unifamiliales et d'architectures expérimentales. Qu'il s'agisse de nouvelles constructions, de réutilisation adaptative, de rénovation ou de décoration intérieure, AB design studio promeut des techniques innovantes, des palettes de matériaux responsables et des stratégies durables pour créer des environnements architecturaux conscients du monde qui inspirent et responsabilisent.

Was 2005 als Gespräch zwischen zwei Architekten begann, um durch Architektur einen Unterschied in der Welt zu machen, entwickelte sich organisch zu einer dauerhaften Partnerschaft. Zusammen bringen Clay Aurell und Josh Blumer mehr als 20 Jahre Leidenschaft, Erfahrung und Kreativität in explorative Designs ein, die Kunden, Kontext und Geschichte widerspiegeln. Ob es die authentische Essenz historischer Gebäude und Strukturen durch adaptive Wiederverwendung oder die Schaffung neuer gewerblicher Büroräume hervorruft, AB design studio stellt sicher, dass jedes Projekt eine starke Signatur-Designlösung für findet der Kunde und die Community, was zu einer homogenen Identität zwischen dem Konzept, der Marke und dem Raum führt. Die Talente von AB design studio in den Bereichen Architektur, Innenarchitektur und Planung gelten für eine Vielzahl von Projekttypen, darunter kulturelle Einrichtungen, Kindergärten, Hotels, Unternehmen, Gesundheitszentren, Bildungseinrichtungen, Mehrfamilienhäuser und Einfamilienhäuser und experimentelle Architektur. Ob Neubau, adaptive Wiederverwendung, Renovierung oder Innenarchitektur - AB design studio fördert innovative Techniken, verantwortungsvolle Materialpaletten und nachhaltige Strategien, um architektonische und global bewusste Umgebungen zu schaffen, die inspirieren und stärken.

En 2005, lo que comenzó como una conversación entre dos arquitectos sobre cómo marcar la diferencia en el mundo a través de la arquitectura evolucionó orgánicamente hasta convertirse en una asociación duradera. Juntos, Clay Aurell y Josh Blumer aportan más de 20 años de pasión, experiencia y creatividad para explorar diseños que reflejen el cliente, el contexto y la historia. Ya sea evocando la esencia auténtica de edificios y estructuras históricas a través de la reutilización adaptativa o creando un nuevo espacio de oficinas comerciales, AB design studio se asegura de que cada proyecto comunique una solución de diseño emblemática para el cliente y la comunidad, dando como resultado una identidad homogénea que engloba concepto, marca y espacio. Los talentos de AB design studio en el campo de la arquitectura, el diseño interior y la planificación se aplican a una variedad de tipos de proyectos, incluyendo instalaciones culturales, guarderías, hoteles, comercios, centros de salud, de educación, edificios multiresidenciales y unifamiliares, y arquitectura experimental. Ya se trate de una nueva construcción, de una reutilización adaptativa, de una renovación o de un diseño interior, AB design studio promueve técnicas innovadoras, paletas de materiales responsables y estrategias sostenibles para crear entornos arquitectónicos y de conciencia global que inspiren y fortalezcan.

MID-CENTURY MODERN RESIDENCE

SANTA BARBARA, CALIFORNIA

Lot size: 24,315 sq ft
Project size: 2,510 sq ft

Literally built "on" the hillside, this project is a classic mid-century modern house built in the mid-1950s. The original house had been designed, built, and occupied by the original architect, Noel Cook, and changed hands in 2006. Our client loved the mid-century modern style and spent eight months in Scandinavia living in the culture that helped spawn the movement. They came to us with three requests. One: update the building to current standards of finish and space; two: add more square footage for themselves and their family, and three: keep the same charm and aesthetic of the original mid-century modern style. The house was reduced to its foundation and floor framing, while most of the walls and roof were reframed. Every room was remodeled and updated, keeping the same post-and-beam aesthetic and, most importantly, the tongue-and-groove roof/ceiling for the upper floor. As opposed to adding a top floor or pushing out the foot, we were able to create a spacious master suite on the lower level maintaining the existing bedrooms above for the family. A number of custom-designed furniture pieces continue the emphasis on modern lines and are a strong reflection of the collaborative efforts of the client, artisan builder, and architect.

Construite littéralement « sur » la colline au milieu des années 1950, cette maison moderne fut conçue, construite et occupée par l'architecte d'origine, Noel Cook, et changea de mains en 2006. Nos clients ont adoré le style moderne du milieu du siècle et ont passé huit mois en Scandinavie immergé dans la culture qui a généré le mouvement. Ils sont venus à nous avec trois souhaits. Un : adapter la maison aux normes actuelles de finitions et d'espace ; deux : augmenter la surface et trois : conserver le charme et l'esthétique d'origine. La maison a été réduite à sa charpente et la plupart des murs et du toit ont été reconstruits. Chaque pièce a été réaménagée et mise à jour, en conservant l'esthétique des poteaux et des poutres et, plus important encore, le plafond à rainures et languettes de l'étage supérieur. Plutôt que d'ajouter un étage ou d'étendre le périmètre de la maison, une spacieuse suite parentale a été créée au niveau inférieur en conservant les chambres existantes à l'étage supérieur pour la famille. Plusieurs meubles conçus sur mesure renforcent les lignes modernes et reflètent l'effort de collaboration entre le client, le constructeur artisan et l'architecte.

Dieses moderne Haus wurde Mitte der 1950er Jahre buchstäblich „am Hang" erbaut und vom ursprünglichen Architekten Noel Cook entworfen, gebaut und bewohnt. 2006 wechselten unsere Gäste den modernen Stil der Mitte der 1950er Jahre Jahrhundert und verbrachte acht Monate in Skandinavien inmitten der Kultur, die die Bewegung hervorbrachte. Sie kamen mit drei Wünschen zu uns. Erstens: Passen Sie das Haus an die aktuellen Standards für Oberflächen und Platz an. Zwei: Vergrößern Sie die Oberfläche und drei: Behalten Sie den ursprünglichen Charme und die Ästhetik bei. Das Haus wurde auf seinen Rahmen reduziert und die meisten Wände und Dächer wurden wieder aufgebaut. Jedes Zimmer wurde umgebaut und aktualisiert, wobei die Ästhetik der Pfosten und Balken sowie, was noch wichtiger ist, die Nut- und Federdecke des Obergeschosses beibehalten wurden. Anstatt eine Etage hinzuzufügen oder den Umfang des Hauses zu erweitern, wurde auf der unteren Ebene eine geräumige Master-Suite geschaffen, die die vorhandenen Schlafzimmer in der oberen Etage für die Familie beibehält. Mehrere maßgeschneiderte Möbelstücke verstärken die modernen Linien und spiegeln die Zusammenarbeit zwischen dem Kunden, dem Bauhandwerker und dem Architekten wider.

Esta casa moderna, construida literalmente «sobre» la ladera a mediados de la década de 1950, fue diseñada, construida y ocupada por el arquitecto original, Noel Cook, y cambió de manos en 2006. A nuestros clientes les encantó el estilo moderno de mediados de siglo y pasaron ocho meses en Escandinavia inmersos en la cultura que generó el movimiento. Vinieron a nosotros con tres deseos. Uno: adecuar la casa a los estándares actuales de acabados y espacio; dos: incrementar la superficie, y tres: mantener el encanto y estética original. La casa se redujo a su estructura y se reconstruyeron la mayoría de las paredes y el tejado. Se remodeló y actualizó cada habitación, manteniendo la estética de postes y vigas y, más importante aún, del techo machihembrado del piso superior. En lugar de añadir un piso o extender el perimetro de la casa, se creó una espaciosa *suite* principal en el nivel inferior manteniendo los dormitorios existentes del piso superior para la familia. Varias piezas de mobiliario diseñadas a medida refuerzan las líneas modernas y son un reflejo del esfuerzo de colaboración entre el cliente, el artesano constructor y el arquitecto.

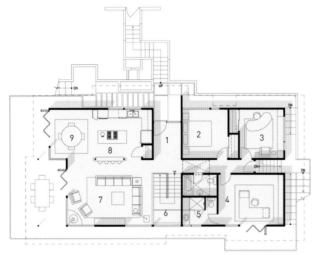

Upper level floor plan

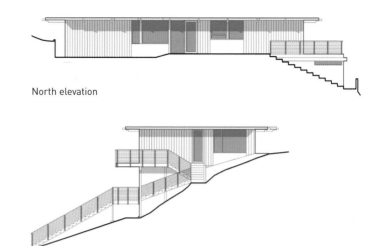

North elevation

East elevation

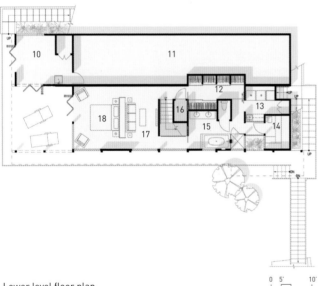

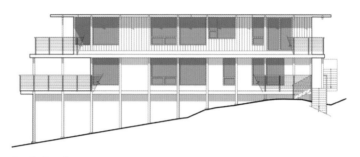

South elevation

Lower level floor plan

0 5'   10'

1. Entry foyer
2. Guest bedroom
3. Study/den
4. Library
5. Library bathroom
6. Interior staircase
7. Living area
8. Kitchen
9. Dining area
10. Art studio
11. Crawl space
12. Master closet
13. Laundry room
14. Sauna
15. Master bathroom
16. Storage closet
17. Sitting area
18. Master bedroom

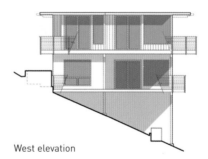

West elevation

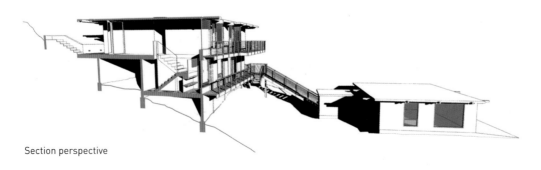

Section perspective

QUARRY HOUSE

MONTECITO, CALIFORNIA

Lot size: 43,585 sq ft
Project size: 2,435 sq ft

The architects worked in collaboration with interior designer Tamara Honey, founder of House of Honey, to modernize a humble 1950s wood cabin set in a rock quarry between the Santa Barbara foothills and Santa Ynez mountain range. Grand boulders surround this single-story residence with an enhanced wrap-around wood deck. A long hallway links both sides of the home, from the remodeled kitchen and living spaces to a new voluminous master suite addition. The creation of a new pavilion-like structure placed along the axis of the existing gabled roof allows for the well-appointed master suite. A second and separate pavilion placed uphill from the main house affords its occupants with a sweeping view of the Pacific Coastline. The placement of these contemporary cubes against the humble mid-century cabin creates a distinct balance between past and present. The Architects intentionally created a living area in the outdoor space between the two pavilion structures. An expansive wrap-around deck and stone stepped pathways join the two structures, creating an opportunity for connection and circulation. The unconventional separation of the buildings creates an expansion of comfortable living space in an otherwise constrained indoor floor plan.

Les architectes ont travaillé en collaboration avec l'architecte d'intérieur Tamara Honey, fondatrice de House of Honey, pour moderniser une humble cabane en bois des années 1950 située dans une carrière entre les contreforts de Santa Barbara et les montagnes de Santa Ynez. De grands rochers entourent cette résidence d'un seul étage avec une terrasse en bois tout autour. Un long couloir relie les deux côtés de la maison, de la cuisine rénovée et des espaces de vie à un nouvel ajout de la suite principale. La création d'une nouvelle structure en forme de pavillon placée le long de l'axe du toit à pignon permet une suite parentale bien aménagée. Un deuxième pavillon séparé offre à ses occupants une vue imprenable sur la côte Pacifique. Le placement de ces cubes contemporains contre l'humble cabane crée un équilibre distinct entre le passé et le présent. Les architectes ont créé un espace de vie à l'extérieur entre les deux structures du pavillon. Une vaste terrasse et des allées en pierre joignent les deux structures, créant une occasion de connexion et de circulation. La séparation des bâtiments crée une expansion de l'espace de vie confortable dans un plan d'étage intérieur autrement contraint.

Die Architekten arbeiteten mit der Innenarchitektin Tamara Honey, der Gründerin von House of Honey, zusammen, um ein bescheidenes Blockhaus aus den 1950er Jahren in einem Steinbruch zwischen den Ausläufern von Santa Barbara und den Bergen von Santa Ynez zu modernisieren. Große Felsbrocken umgeben diese einstöckige Residenz mit einem Holzdeck ringsum. Ein langer Flur verbindet die beiden Seiten des Hauses, von der renovierten Küche und den Wohnbereichen bis hin zu einem Neuzugang der Master Suite. Die Schaffung einer neuen pavillonartigen Struktur entlang der Achse des Satteldachs ermöglicht ein gut ausgestattetes Hauptschlafzimmer. Ein zweiter separater Pavillon bietet seinen Bewohnern einen atemberaubenden Blick auf die Pazifikküste. Die Platzierung dieser zeitgenössischen Würfel gegenüber der bescheidenen Kabine schafft eine deutliche Balance zwischen Vergangenheit und Gegenwart. Die Architekten schufen einen Wohnraum im Freien zwischen den beiden Pavillonstrukturen. Eine große Terrasse und Steinstege verbinden die beiden Gebäude und bieten die Möglichkeit zur Verbindung und Zirkulation. Die Trennung von Gebäuden schafft eine Erweiterung des komfortablen Wohnraums in einen ansonsten eingeschränkten Grundriss.

Los arquitectos trabajaron con la diseñadora de interiores Tamara Honey, fundadora de House of Honey, para modernizar una humilde cabaña de madera de los años 50 ubicada en una cantera entre las colinas de Santa Bárbara y las montañas de Santa Ynez. Grandes rocas rodean esta residencia de una planta con una terraza de madera en todo su alrededor. Un largo pasillo conecta los dos lados de la casa, desde la cocina renovada y las áreas de estar hasta una nueva estructura similar a un pabellón a lo largo del techo a dos aguas dando cabida a un maravilloso dormitorio principal. Un segundo pabellón separado ofrece a sus ocupantes una vista impresionante de la costa del Pacífico. La colocación de estos cubos contemporáneos contra la cabaña crea un equilibrio entre pasado y presente. Los arquitectos crearon un espacio habitable al aire libre entre las dos estructuras del pabellón. Una gran terraza y caminos de piedra unen las dos estructuras, creando una oportunidad para conectar y circular. La separación de los edificios expande el espacio habitable añadiendo confort a una planta interior de proporciones restringidas.

North elevation

West elevation

East elevation

South elevation

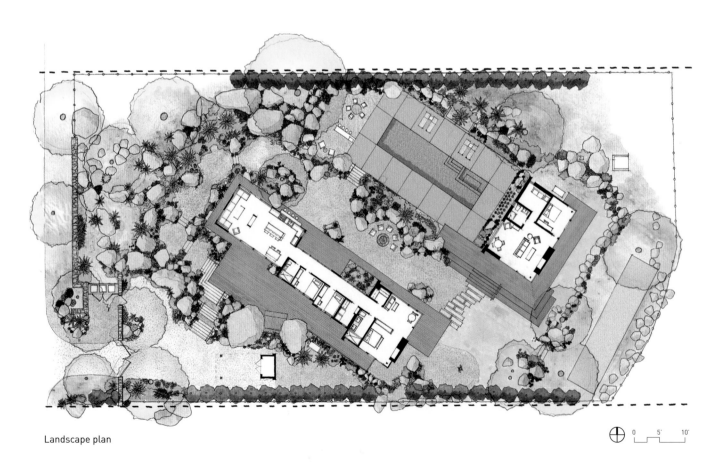

Landscape plan

0   5'   10'

HO:ME 296

SANTA BARBARA, CALIFORNIA

Lot size: 92,270 sq ft
Project size: 2,345 sq ft

Shipping containers seem to be a hot commodity and people want to use them for many solutions. HO:ME 296 integrates ISBUs into a concrete and structural steel residence. HO:ME 296 is nestled into the foothills of Santa Barbara with views of the mountains to the north and the ocean to the south. The Owners, an environmental attorney and fashion stylist, wanted a sustainable and elegant contemporary home that complemented their personalities and occupational passions—and it had to incorporate shipping containers. The result is a two-story, 3-bedroom 3.5 bathroom residence that seamlessly integrates five reclaimed shipping containers. The upper level consists of four 40-foot containers that form the master suite and bedroom spaces, separated by a dramatic central stairwell and corridor with skylight. On an open first floor plan, the architects combined living spaces and kitchen to create a center of activity and area for entertaining. The space's main focal point is an exposed 20-foot shipping container that was transformed into a pantry and scullery.

Les conteneurs maritimes semblent être une denrée très prisée et les gens veulent les utiliser pour de nombreuses solutions. HO:ME 296 intègre les ISBU dans une résidence en béton et en acier de construction. HO:ME 296 est niché dans les contreforts de Santa Barbara, avec vue sur les montagnes au nord et sur l'océan au sud. Les propriétaires, un avocat spécialisé dans l'environnement et un styliste de mode, voulaient une maison contemporaine durable et élégante qui corresponde à leur personnalité et à leurs passions professionnelles. Elle devait intégrer des conteneurs de transport. Le résultat est une résidence de deux étages, 3 chambres à coucher et 3 salles de bain et toilette, qui intègre de façon transparente cinq conteneurs de transport récupérés. Le niveau supérieur est constitué de quatre conteneurs d'environ 12 mètres qui forment la suite principale et les chambres à coucher, séparées par un escalier central spectaculaire et un couloir avec puits de lumière. Sur un plan ouvert du premier étage, les architectes ont combiné les espaces de vie et la cuisine pour créer un centre d'activité et un espace de divertissement. Le point central de l'espace est un conteneur d'expédition exposé d'environ 6 mètres qui a été transformé en garde-manger et arrière-cuisine.

Schiffscontainer scheinen eine heiße Ware zu sein, und die Menschen wollen sie für viele Lösungen nutzen. HO:ME 296 integriert ISBUs in eine Residenz aus Beton und Baustahl. HO:ME 296 liegt eingebettet in den Ausläufern von Santa Barbara mit Blick auf die Berge im Norden und den Ozean im Süden. Die Eigentümer, ein Umweltanwalt und ein Modestylist, wollten ein nachhaltiges und elegantes zeitgenössisches Haus, das ihre Persönlichkeit und beruflichen Leidenschaften ergänzt – und es musste Schiffscontainer enthalten. Das Ergebnis ist ein zweistöckiges Wohnhaus mit 3 Schlafzimmern und 3,5 Bädern, das nahtlos fünf ausrangierte Schiffscontainer integriert. Die obere Ebene besteht aus vier 12 m langen Containern, die die Hauptsuite und die Chambres à Coucher bilden und durch eine zentrale spektakuläre Treppe und ein Couloir mit Puits de Lumière getrennt sind. In einem Plan zur Eröffnung der Hauptbühne kombinieren die Architekten die Räume des Lebens und der Küche, um ein Zentrum für Aktivität und einen Raum für Unterhaltung zu schaffen. Der zentrale Punkt von l'space ist ein 6 Meter langer Container mit Expédition Exposé d'environ, den ich in Garde-Krippe und Arrière-Küche verwandelt habe.

Los contenedores de transporte parecen ser un producto de moda y la gente quiere usarlos para muchas soluciones. HO:ME 296 integra ISBU en una residencia de hormigón y acero estructural. HO:ME 296 está enclavado en las colinas de Santa Bárbara con vistas a las montañas al norte y al océano al sur. Los propietarios, un abogado ambientalista y estilista de la moda, querían una casa moderna, sostenible y elegante que complementara sus personalidades y pasiones, y tenía que incorporar contenedores de transporte. El resultado es una residencia de dos pisos, 3 dormitorios y 3 baños más un aseo que integra perfectamente cinco contenedores marítimos recuperados. El nivel superior consta de cuatro contenedores de 12 metros que forman los espacios de la suite principal y el dormitorio, separados por una dramática escalera central y un pasillo con claraboya. En un espacio diáfano del primer piso, los arquitectos combinaron los espacios de vida y la cocina para crear un centro de actividad y área de entretenimiento. El principal punto focal del espacio es un contenedor de 6 metros expuesto que fue transformado en fregadero y zona de despensa.

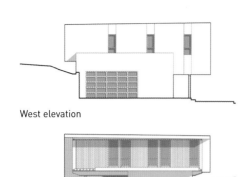

West elevation

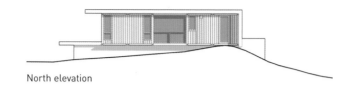

North elevation

East elevation

South elevation

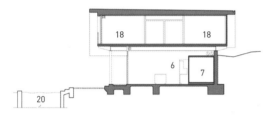

Cross section

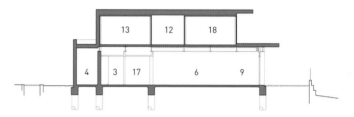

Longitudinal section

Upper floor plan

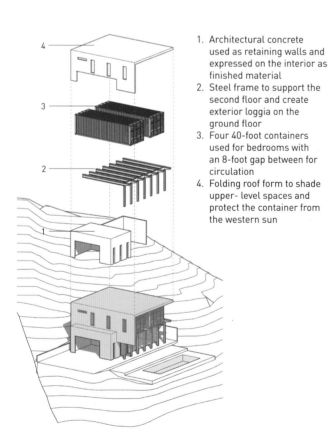

1. Architectural concrete used as retaining walls and expressed on the interior as finished material
2. Steel frame to support the second floor and create exterior loggia on the ground floor
3. Four 40-foot containers used for bedrooms with an 8-foot gap between for circulation
4. Folding roof form to shade upper- level spaces and protect the container from the western sun

Exploded axonometric

Lower floor plan

0   5'   10'

1. Patio
2. Powder room
3. Mud room
4. Bike storage area
5. Garage
6. Kitchen
7. Pantry
8. Living area
9. Dining area
10. Dining patio
11. Equipment area
12. Study
13. Master bedroom
14. Walk-in closet
15. Master bathroom
16. Laundry room
17. Stair hall
18. Bedroom
19. Bathroom
20. Pool

ANX

a-n-x.com

GARDEN HOUSE

Project Team: Aaron Neubert (Principal),
Jeremy Limsenben, Jina Seo, Xiran Zhang,
Khalil Gobir, and Victoria Cuan

Interior Designer: Victoria Pergament, ANX

Landscape Architect: LPO, ANX

Structural Engineer: Craig Philips Engineering

Photographer: Brian Thomas Jones,
Adam Pergament, ANX

TILT-SHIFT HOUSE

Project Team: Aaron Neubert (Principal),
Jeremy Limsenben, Xiran Zhang, and Jina Seo

Interior Designer: Sidonie Loiseleux, ANX

Structural Engineer: Craig Phillips Engineering

Photographer: Brian Thomas Jones

ECHO HOUSE

Project Team: Aaron Neubert (Principal),
Jeremy Limsenben, Xiran Zhang, Jina Seo,
and Sheldon Preston

Interior Designer: Sidonie Loiseleux, ANX

Structural Engineer: Craig Phillips Engineering

Photography: Brian Thomas Jones

The work of ANX begins with a fundamental optimism with regard to the continued value and impact that design and architecture have on our cities and their inhabitants. Our process resists the autonomous and pure in favor of the dependent, messy, and complex possibilities of a poetic inclusion of multiple and often conflicting influences. This process ultimately leads to the intersection of architecture, landscape, and urban networks, and the inherent negotiations necessary to implement a coherent experience respectful of the impact upon the environment.

Our understanding of the capacity for design to organize complex systems with thoughtful intention, environmental appropriateness, and a practical dose of both form and function, is coupled with our belief in the responsibility of the designer to ask questions and challenge assumptions of the built environment. Our ongoing interest in developing experiences that explore space, scale, orientation, light, detail, materiality, and emerging technologies is demonstrated in a wide range of residential, cultural, commercial, and landscape projects that question, and when appropriate, inflect existing paradigms.

Le travail de l'ANX commence par un optimisme fondamental quant à la valeur et à l'impact que le design et l'architecture continuent d'avoir sur nos villes et leurs habitants. Notre processus résiste à l'autonomie et à la pureté en faveur des possibilités dépendantes, désordonnées et complexes d'une inclusion poétique d'influences multiples et souvent conflictuelles. L'intersection de ces processus conduit finalement à l'architecture, du paysage, des réseaux urbains, et aux négotiations inhérentes nécessaires pour mettre en œuvre une expérience cohérente et respectueuse de l'impact sur l'environnement.

Notre compréhension de la capacité de la conception à organiser des systèmes complexes avec une intention réfléchie, une adéquation à l'environnement et une dose pratique de forme et de fonction, est couplée à notre conviction que le concepteur a la responsabilité de poser des questions et de remettre en question les hypothèses de l'environnement bâti. Notre intérêt permanent pour le développement d'expériences qui explorent l'espace, l'échelle, l'orientation, la lumière, les détails, la matérialité et les technologies émergentes se manifeste dans un large éventail de projets résidentiels, culturels, commerciaux et paysagers qui remettent en question et, le cas échéant, infléchissent les paradigmes existants.

Die Arbeit von ANX beginnt mit einem grundsätzlichen Optimismus im Hinblick auf den anhaltenden Wert und den Einfluss, den Design und Architektur auf unsere Städte und ihre Bewohner haben. Unser Prozess widersetzt sich der Autonomie und Reinheit zugunsten der abhängigen, chaotischen und komplexen Möglichkeiten einer poetischen Einbeziehung vielfältiger und oft widersprüchlicher Einflüsse. Dieser Prozess führt schließlich zur Überschneidung von Architektur, Landschaft und städtischen Netzwerken und zu den inhärenten Verhandlungen, die notwendig sind, um eine kohärente Erfahrung umzusetzen, welche die Auswirkungen auf die Umwelt berücksichtigt.

Wir verstehen, dass die Fähigkeit des Designs, komplexe Systeme mit durchdachter Absicht, Eignung für die Umgebung und einer praktischen Dosis von Form und Funktion zu organisieren, mit unserem Glauben an die Verantwortung des Designers einhergeht, Fragen zu stellen und die Annahmen der Umgebung in Frage zu stellen. gebaut. Unser anhaltendes Interesse an der Entwicklung von Erfahrungen, die Raum, Größe, Ausrichtung, Licht, Detail, Materialität und neue Technologien erforschen, zeigt sich in einer Vielzahl von Wohn-, Kultur-, Gewerbe- und Landschaftsprojekten, die herausfordern und gegebenenfalls herausfordern. angemessen, bestehende Paradigmen beeinflussen.

El trabajo de ANX se basa en un optimismo fundamental con respecto al continuo valor e impacto que el diseño y la arquitectura tienen en nuestras ciudades y sus habitantes. Nuestro proceso se resiste a lo autónomo y puro a favor de las posibilidades dependientes, desordenadas y complejas de una inclusión poética de múltiples y a menudo conflictivas influencias. Este proceso conduce en última instancia a la intersección de la arquitectura, el paisaje y las redes urbanas, y a las negociaciones inherentes necesarias para implementar una experiencia coherente y respetuosa del impacto sobre el medio ambiente.

Entendemos que la capacidad del diseño para organizar sistemas complejos con una intención reflexiva, la adecuación al medio ambiente y una dosis práctica tanto de forma como de función, va unida a nuestra creencia en la responsabilidad del diseñador de hacer preguntas y cuestionar los supuestos del entorno construido. Nuestro continuo interés en desarrollar experiencias que exploren el espacio, la escala, la orientación, la luz, el detalle, la materialidad y las tecnologías emergentes se demuestra en una amplia gama de proyectos residenciales, culturales, comerciales y paisajísticos que cuestionan y, cuando es apropiado, influyen en los paradigmas existentes.

GARDEN HOUSE

LOS ANGELES, CALIFORNIA

The desire to fully integrate nature into daily life led to the creation of pavilions across the site, generating varying scales of gardens and allowing landscape elements to visually infiltrate the home's interior. These gardens penetrate an open floor plan, presenting an evolving connection to the site and allowing diffused light to enter the interiors. All the rooms are organized around a central garden, which serves as an exterior living room. Carefully placed apertures are oriented towards the adjacent site features. The bedrooms have lake, meadow, hills, and observatory views, while also looking across the gardens. The pavilions are clad in a Shou sugi ban charred cypress, and the circulation spine is finished in smooth plaster. The gardens and landscape are planted with a variety of native plants and trees that receive a majority of their irrigation through rainwater catch basins located on-site. Thanks to the integration of the gardens and the numerous operable window systems around the perimeter of the home, passive heating and cooling are is achieved throughout the year.

Le désir d'intégrer pleinement la nature dans la vie quotidienne, a conduit à la construction de pavillons sur l'ensemble du site, générant des jardins à différentes échelles et permettant aux éléments paysagers de se fusionner visuellement à l'intérieur de la maison. Ces jardins pénètrent dans un plan ouvert, présentant un lien évolutif avec le site et permettant à une lumière diffuse de pénétrer à l'intérieur. Toutes les pièces sont organisées autour d'un jardin central, qui sert de salon extérieur. Des ouvertures soigneusement placées sont orientées vers les caractéristiques du site adjacent. Les chambres ont une vue sur le lac, la prairie, les collines et l'observatoire, tout en donnant également sur les jardins. Les pavillons sont revêtus d'un cyprès calciné Shou sugi ban, et la colonne centrale est recouverte d'un plâtre lisse. Les jardins et le paysage sont plantés d'une variété de plantes et d'arbres indigènes qui reçoivent la majorité de leur irrigation par des bassins de captage d'eau de pluie situés sur place. Grâce à l'intégration des jardins et aux nombreux systèmes de fenêtres fonctionnels autour du périmètre de la maison, le chauffage et le refroidissement passifs sont réalisés tout au long de l'année.

Der Wunsch, die Natur in den Alltag zu integrieren, führte zur Schaffung mehrerer Pavillons, die verschiedene Größenordnungen von Gärten erzeugten und es den Elementen der Landschaft ermöglichten, das Innere des Hauses visuell zu durchdringen. Diese Gärten dringen in einen offenen Grundriss ein, stellen eine evolutionäre Verbindung zum Gelände dar und lassen diffuses Licht in die Innenräume eindringen. Alle Zimmer sind um einen zentralen Garten angeordnet, der als Wohnzimmer im Freien dient. Die Öffnungen sind auf die Elemente des angrenzenden Geländes ausgerichtet, sodass die Räume Blick auf den See, die Wiese, die Hügel, die Gärten und ein Observatorium bieten. Die Pavillons sind mit einer verkohlten Zypresse (Shou sugi ban) ausgekleidet und der Zirkulationsschacht ist mit glattem Gips versehen. Die Gärten und die Landschaftsgestaltung sind mit einer Vielzahl einheimischer Pflanzen und Bäume bepflanzt, die den größten Teil ihrer Bewässerung durch Regenwassereinzugsgebiete auf dem Gelände erhalten. Dank der Integration der Gärten und der zahlreichen Fenstersysteme rund um das Haus wird das ganze Jahr über passives Heizen und Kühlen erreicht.

El deseo de integrar la naturaleza en la vida cotidiana llevó a la creación de varios pabellones, generando diversas escalas de jardines y permitiendo que los elementos del paisaje traspasen visualmente al interior del hogar. Estos jardines penetran en una planta abierta, presentando una conexión con el terreno y permitiendo que la luz penetre en los interiores. Todas las habitaciones se organizan alrededor de un jardín central, que sirve como sala de estar exterior. Las aperturas están orientadas hacia los elementos del terreno de manera que las habitaciones tienen vistas al lago, al prado, a las colinas, a los jardines y a un observatorio. Los pabellones están revestidos con un ciprés carbonizado (Shou sugi ban), y el eje de circulación está acabado en yeso liso. Los jardines y el paisaje están plantados con una variedad de plantas y árboles nativos que reciben la mayor parte de su riego a través de cuencas de captación de agua de lluvia ubicadas en el solar. Gracias a la integración de los jardines y a los numerosos sistemas de ventanas en todo el perímetro de la vivienda, se consigue la calefacción y refrigeración pasiva durante todo el año.

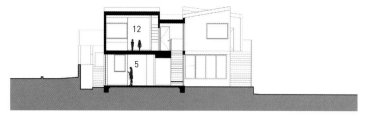

Cross section

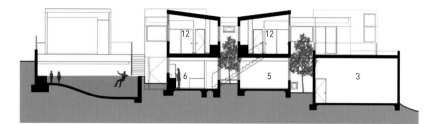

Longitudinal section

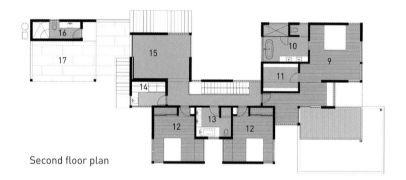

Second floor plan

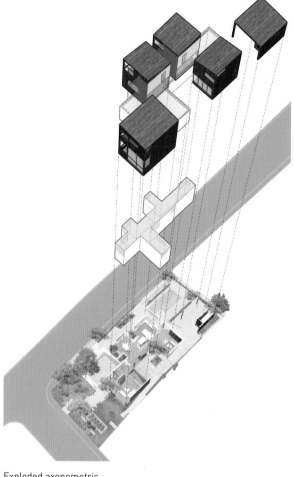

Exploded axonometric

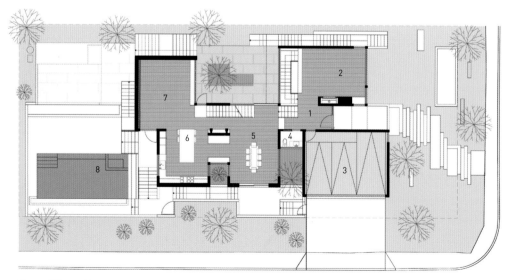

Ground floor plan

1. Entry
2. Living room
3. Garage
4. Powder room
5. Dining area
6. Kitchen
7. Family room
8. Pool
9. Master bedroom
10. Master bathroom
11. Master closet
12. Bedroom
13. Shared bathroom
14. Laundry room
15. Media room
16. Bathroom
17. Pool patio

TILT-SHIFT HOUSE

LOS ANGELES, CALIFORNIA

Lot size: 3,750 sq ft
Project size: 2,100 sq ft

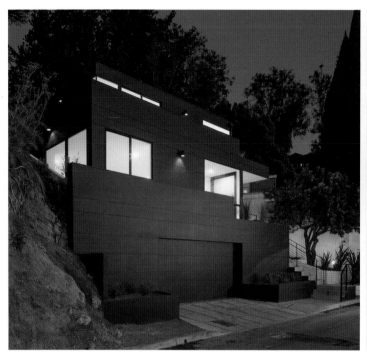 

The project site is an ascending northwesterly facing parcel with panoramic views towards Los Angeles' Silver Lake Hills and Reservoir. The residence is situated adjacent to multiple significant mid-century modern homes, including William Kesling's Vanderpool and Wilson houses, and the Allyn Morris cantilevered duplex. The adjacency of these neighboring properties and the pronounced site slope guided the design of the three-story house, which was conceived as a series of plan shifts, creating numerous exterior living spaces within the volume of the residence. The house, which sits atop an underground garage, has open living spaces engaging the entry and street-facing decks. The bedrooms floor is accessed by a staircase that, in conjunction with the operable windows and skylights, naturally ventilates the residence while providing circulation to all levels. Strategically located apertures, exterior stairs, patios, and decks around the perimeter connect the home to the multiple and diverse landscapes of the site, expanding the usable living space of the compact residence.

Le site du projet est une parcelle ascendante orientée vers le nord-ouest, avec des vues panoramiques sur les collines de Silver Lake et le réservoir de Los Angeles. La résidence est située à côté de plusieurs maisons modernes importantes, construites au milieu du siècle dernier, dont les maisons Vanderpool et Wilson de William Kesling, et le duplex en porte-à-faux d'Allyn Morris. La proximité des propriétés voisines et la pente prononcée du site ont guidé la conception de la maison de trois étages, qui a été conçue comme une série de changements de plan, créant de nombreux espaces de vie extérieurs dans toute la résidence. La maison, se trouve au dessus d'un garage souterrain, comportant des espaces de vie ouverts qui engagent l'entrée et les terrasses qui donnent sur la rue. L'étage des chambres est accessible par un escalier, dont de nombreuses fenêtres et lucarnes ouvrantes, ventile naturellement la résidence tout en permettant la circulation à tous les niveaux. Des ouvertures stratégiquement situées, des escaliers extérieurs, des patios et des terrasses sur le périmètre relient la maison aux paysages multiples et variés du site, élargissant l'espace de vie utilisable de la résidence .

Der Projektstandort ist eine ansteigende, nach Nordwesten ausgerichtete Parzelle mit Panoramablick auf die Silver Lake Hills und das Becken von Los Angeles. Die Residenz grenzt an mehrere bedeutende moderne Häuser aus der Mitte des Jahrhunderts, darunter William Keslings Vanderpool- und Wilson-Häuser sowie das freitragende Doppelhaus Allyn Morris. Die Nachbarschaft dieser Anwesen und die ausgeprägte Neigung des Grundstücks waren ausschlaggebend für die Gestaltung des dreistöckigen Hauses, das als eine Reihe von Planverschiebungen konzipiert wurde, wodurch innerhalb des Volumens der Residenz zahlreiche äußere Wohnräume geschaffen wurden. Das Haus, das auf einer Tiefgarage steht, verfügt über offene Wohnräume, die sich in die Eingangs- und Straßendecks einfügen. Der Boden des Schlafzimmers ist über eine Treppe zugänglich, die zusammen mit den Fenstern und Oberlichtern die Residenz auf natürliche Weise belüftet. Strategisch platzierte Öffnungen, Außentreppen, Innenhöfe und Terrassen rund um den Außenbereich verbinden das Haus mit den vielfältigen und unterschiedlichen Landschaften des Geländes und erweitern den nutzbaren Wohnraum der kompakten Residenz.

El proyecto se construyó en una parcela ascendente orientada al noroeste con vistas panorámicas hacia las colinas de Silver Lake y el embalse de Los Ángeles. La casa está situada junto a múltiples y destacadas casas modernas de mediados de siglo, como la de William Kesling en Vanderpool y Wilson, y el dúplex en voladizo de Allyn Morris. La cercanía con estas propiedades y la pronunciada pendiente del terreno guiaron el diseño de la casa de tres niveles, que fue concebida como una serie de cambios de plano, creando numerosos espacios exteriores. La casa, que se asienta sobre un garaje subterráneo, goza de espacios abiertos conectados a la entrada y a las terrazas que dan a la calle. A la planta de dormitorios se accede por una escalera que, junto con las ventanas y tragaluces, ventilan naturalmente la residencia. Las aperturas estratégicamente ubicadas, las escaleras exteriores, los patios y las cubiertas alrededor del perímetro conectan la casa con los diversos paisajes, ampliando el espacio habitable.

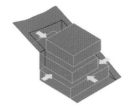

Massing diagram

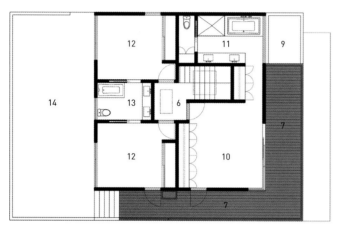

Second floor plan

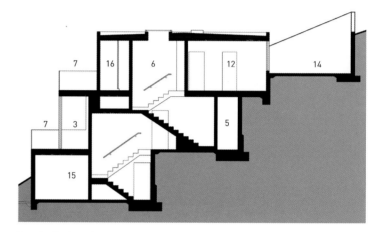

Longitudinal section

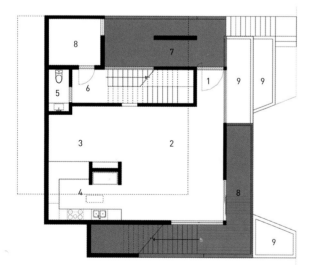

Ground floor plan

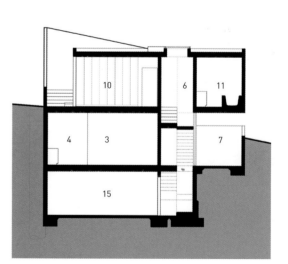

Cross section

1. Entry
2. Living room
3. Dining area
4. Kitchen
5. Powder room
6. Stair hall
7. Deck
8. Office
9. Planter
10. Master bedroom
11. Master bathroom
12. Bedroom
13. Bathroom
14. Patio
15. Garage
16. Closet

ECHO HOUSE

LOS ANGELES, CALIFORNIA

Lot size: 7,450 sq ft
Project size: 3,378 sq ft

This residence and a detached artist studio in the Elysian Heights neighborhood of Los Angeles are oriented to perceptually inhabit an adjacent community garden and present views of the downtown skyline and surrounding hills. To a more intimate level, the compound also carves out an introspective landscape for the enjoyment of the family. The residence, which stands over the utilitarian spaces located at street level, is organized as a staggered sectional volume distributing program over three levels. Living spaces occupy the multi-level second floor with direct access to the outdoors via the front deck and the rear terrace, physically expanding the interior. The third floor, accessed by the expressed scissor stair, consists of the bedrooms and bathrooms. Strategically placed apertures around the residence and studio encourage the spatial reverberation and dialogue between the activities of the home and the multiple and diverse terraces, decks, balconies, and landscapes of the property.

Cette résidence et el studio d'artiste indépendant dans le quartier d'Elysian Heights à Los Angeles sont conçus avec un jardin communautaire adjacent, offrant une vue sur le centre-ville et les collines environnantes. À un niveau plus intime, l'enceinte sculpte également un paysage introspectif pour le plaisir de la famille. La résidence, qui se dresse au-dessus des espaces utilitaires situés au niveau de la rue, est organisée comme un programme de distribution de volumes en sections échelonnées sur trois niveaux. Les espaces de vie occupent le deuxième étage avec un accès direct à l'extérieur par les terrasses avant et arrière, ce qui élargit physiquement l'intérieur. Le troisième étage, auquel on accède par l'escalier en ciseaux express, comprend les chambres et les salles de bain. Des ouvertures stratégiquement placées autour de la résidence et du studio favorisent la réverbération spatiale et le dialogue entre les activités de la maison et les multiples et diverses terrasses, ponts, balcons et paysages de la propriété.

Dieses Wohnhaus und ein freistehendes Künstleratelier im Stadtteil Elysian Heights von Los Angeles sind darauf ausgerichtet, einen angrenzenden Gemeinschaftsgarten wahrnehmbar zu bewohnen und Ausblicke auf die Skyline der Innenstadt und die umliegenden Hügel zu bieten. Auf einer intimeren Ebene bildet die Anlage auch eine introspektive Landschaft zur Freude der Familie. Die Residenz, die über den auf Straßenebene gelegenen Nutzflächen steht, ist als ein gestaffeltes Bauvolumen organisiert, das sich über drei Ebenen erstreckt. Die Wohnräume befinden sich im zweiten Stock mit direktem Zugang ins Freie über das vordere Deck und die hintere Terrasse, wodurch der Innenraum physisch erweitert wird. Die dritte Etage, zu der man über die ausdrucksstarke Scherentreppe gelangt, besteht aus den Schlaf- und Badezimmern. Strategisch platzierte Öffnungen rund um die Residenz und das Atelier fördern den räumlichen Nachhall und den Dialog zwischen den Aktivitäten des Hauses und den zahlreichen und unterschiedlichen Terrassen, Decks, Balkonen und Landschaften des Anwesens.

Esta residencia con estudio artístico independiente en el barrio de Elysian Heights de Los Ángeles están concebidos para habitar un jardín comunitario adyacente y presentar vistas del horizonte del perfil de la ciudad y las colinas circundantes. A un nivel más íntimo, el complejo también esculpe un paisaje introspectivo para el disfrute de la familia. La vivienda, que se levanta sobre unos espacios situados a nivel de la calle, se organiza como un volumen seccional escalonado que distribuye el programa en tres niveles. Los espacios habitables ocupan el segundo piso de varios niveles con acceso directo al exterior a través de la cubierta delantera y la terraza trasera, ampliando físicamente el interior. El tercer piso, al que se accede por una escalera en forma de tijera, consta de los dormitorios y los baños. Las aperturas estratégicamente situadas alrededor de la residencia y el estudio fomentan la reverberación espacial y el diálogo entre las actividades de la casa y las múltiples y diversas terrazas, cubiertas, balcones y jardines de la propiedad.

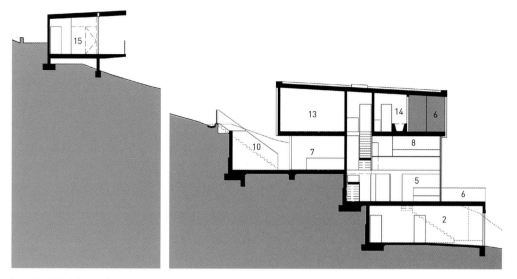

Longitudinal / site section

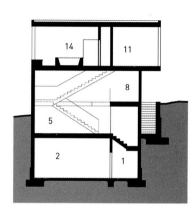

Cross section

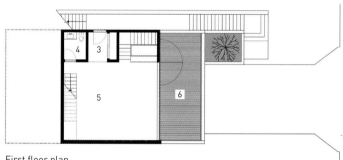

First floor plan

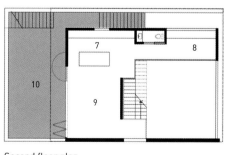

Third floor plan

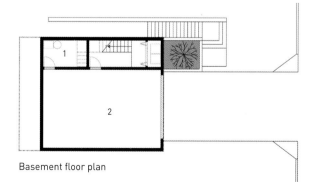

Basement floor plan

Second floor plan

1. Utility room   6. Deck   11. Bedroom
2. Garage   7. Kitchen 12. Bathroom
3. Entry   8. Loft   13. Master bedroom
4. Powder room 9. Dining area 14. Master bathroom
5. Living area   10. Terrace   15. Studio

Arterra
Landscape Architects

arterrasf.com

RURAL RETREAT

Architect: Richard Beard Architects

Builder: Alftin Construction

Photographer: Paul Dyer

SLOT HOUSE

Architect: Feldman Architecture

Landscape Contractor: Douglas Landscape

Photographer: Adam Rouse

TARONGA

Architect: Holdren + Lietzke Architecture

Builder: Vucina Construction

Landscape Contractor: Town and Country Landscape

Photographer: Paul Dyer

Arterra Landscape Architects is a boutique design firm specializing in sustainable, site inspired design. Arterra's collaborative approach yields client-focused results in projects ranging from intimate urban gardens to ranches and estate master plans. Kate Stickley and Vera Gates began collaborating in 1994. After many years at large national firms, they created a practice based on personal relationships with clients and the spirit of the land. In 2003 Arterra was formed, its name derived from the firm's founding concept: Art + Terra (Latin for Earth). Gretchen Whittier joined the partnership in 2011, bringing a strong background in both design and business.

Today, Kate and Gretchen lead Arterra's diverse and creative team in an open studio space that fosters collaboration as they craft outdoor settings of incomparable beauty. Arterra focuses on imaginative solutions, clear communications, and designs that seamlessly integrate landscape with architecture. Whether creating for a rooftop garden or a working ranch, Arterra is committed to building a better world through a meaningful and sustainable landscape legacy.

Arterra Landscape Architects est un cabinet de design spécialisée dans la conception durable et inspirée des sites. L'approche collaborative d'Arterra produit des résultats axés sur le client dans des projets allant des jardins urbains intimes aux ranchs et plans directeurs de domaine. Kate Stickley et Vera Gates ont commencé à collaborer en 1994. Après de nombreuses années dans de grandes entreprises nationales, elles ont créé une pratique basée sur les relations personnelles avec les clients et l'esprit du site. En 2003, Arterra a été créée, son nom dérivé du concept fondateur du bureau: Art + Terra. Gretchen Whittier a rejoint le partenariat en 2011, apportant une solide expérience en design et en affaires commerciales.

Aujourd'hui, Kate et Gretchen dirigent l'équipe diversifiée et créative d'Arterra dans un espace ouvert qui favorise la collaboration tout en créant des environnements extérieurs d'une beauté incomparable. Arterra se concentre sur des solutions imaginatives, des communications claires et des conceptions qui intègrent parfaitement le paysage à l'architecture. Qu'il s'agisse de créer un jardin sur le toit ou un ranch en pleine activité, Arterra s'engage à construire un monde meilleur grâce à un héritage paysager significatif et durable.

Arterra Landscape Architects ist ein Designstudio, das sich auf nachhaltige Projekte spezialisiert hat, die vom Ort inspiriert sind. Der kollaborative Ansatz von Arterra führt zu kundenorientierten Ergebnissen, um Projekte zu erstellen, die von abgelegenen Stadtgärten über Ranches bis hin zu Masterplänen reichen. Kate Stickley und Vera Gates begannen 1994 ihre Zusammenarbeit. Nachdem sie viele Jahre für große nationale Firmen gearbeitet hatten, gründeten sie eine Praxis, die auf persönlichen Beziehungen zu Kunden und dem Geist des Ortes beruhte. 2003 wurde Arterra gegründet, sein Name leitet sich vom Gründungskonzept der Firma ab: Art + Terra. Gretchen Whittier kam 2011 ins Studio und brachte einen starken Hintergrund in Design und Business mit.

Heute führen Kate und Gretchen das vielfältige und kreative Team von Arterra in einem offenen Raum, der die Zusammenarbeit fördert und gleichzeitig Umgebungen im Freien von unvergleichlicher Schönheit schafft. Arterra konzentriert sich auf einfallsreiche Lösungen, klare Kommunikation und Designs, die Landschaft nahtlos in Architektur integrieren. Ob es sich um einen Dachgarten oder eine voll funktionsfähige Ranch handelt, Arterra setzt sich dafür ein, durch ein bedeutungsvolles und nachhaltiges Landschaftserbe eine bessere Welt zu schaffen.

Arterra Landscape Architects es un estudio de diseño que se especializa en proyectos sostenibles inspirados en el lugar. El enfoque colaborativo de Arterra produce resultados centrados en el cliente para crear proyectos que van desde jardines urbanos recónditos hasta ranchos y planes maestros. Kate Stickley y Vera Gates comenzaron a colaborar en 1994. Después de muchos años trabajando para grandes firmas nacionales, crearon una práctica basada en las relaciones personales con los clientes y el espíritu del lugar. En 2003 se formó Arterra, su nombre deriva del concepto fundacional de la firma: Art + Terra. Gretchen Whittier se unió al estudio en 2011, aportando una sólida experiencia tanto en diseño como en negocios.

Hoy, Kate y Gretchen lideran el diverso y creativo equipo de Arterra en un espacio abierto que fomenta la colaboración mientras crean ambientes al aire libre de incomparable belleza. Arterra se centra en soluciones imaginativas, comunicaciones claras y diseños que integran a la perfección el paisaje con la arquitectura. Ya sea para crear un jardín en la azotea o un rancho plenamente funcional, Arterra se compromete a construir un mundo mejor a través de un legado paisajístico significativo y sostenible.

RURAL RETREAT

Understanding the community of Portola Valley was key to designing the Rural Retreat. This small picturesque town, situated on the edge of bustling, high-tech Silicon Valley, cherishes its rural feel and strives to preserve its natural beauty and open space. The straightforward design of the house and site is a direct reference to this heritage. Originally an equestrian lot, the property redesign offered an opportunity to restore the land while creating a home for a family of five. The carefully composed arrival court creates a sense of entry and accommodates a play court for children as well as the required fire truck access and turnaround. Multiple activity areas include gracious lawns, extensive entertaining patios, a tranquil pool, a kitchen garden and orchard, and discovery trails leading throughout the property. Grading, drainage, and surface water management concerns were mitigated with lawn terraces graded to provide capacity for underground water detention. A bosque of crepe myrtle trees adds color and interest throughout the seasons.

Comprendre la communauté de Portola Valley a été la clé pour le design de Rural Retreat. Cette petite ville pittoresque, située en bordure du centre technologique et toujours animée ville de Silicon Valley, chérit son atmosphère rurale et s'efforce de préserver sa beauté naturelle et son espace ouvert. La conception simple de la maison et du site est une référence directe à ce patrimoine. La refonte de la propriété, qui à l'origine était un terrain équestre, offrait la possibilité de restaurer le terrain tout en créant une maison pour une famille de cinq personnes. La cour d'arrivée soigneusement composée crée une sensation d'entrée et accueille un terrain de jeu pour les enfants ainsi que l'accès et le revirement requis pour les camions de pompiers. Les zones d'activités comprennent des gazons, de vastes patios, une piscine tranquille, un potager et un verger et des sentiers de découverte à travers la propriété. Les problèmes de nivellement, de drainage et de gestion des eaux de surface ont été atténués par des terrasses de gazon calibrées pour fournir une capacité de rétention des eaux souterraines. Un bosquet de Lilas d'Inde ajoute de la couleur et de l'intérêt au fil des saisons.

Das Verständnis der Portola Valley Community war der Schlüssel zur Gestaltung des Rural Retreat-Projekts. Diese malerische kleine Stadt, etwas außerhalb des geschäftigen Technologiezentrums von Silicon Valley, schätzt die ländliche Atmosphäre und ist bestrebt, ihre natürliche Schönheit und Freiflächen zu bewahren. Das einfache Design des Hauses und des Ortes ist ein direkter Hinweis auf dieses Erbe. Die Neugestaltung des Grundstücks, ursprünglich ein Reitanwesen, bot die Möglichkeit, das Gelände wiederherzustellen und gleichzeitig ein Zuhause für eine fünfköpfige Familie zu schaffen. Der sorgfältig gestaltete Eingangshof beherbergt einen Spielbereich für Kinder und den notwendigen Zugang für Feuerwehrfahrzeuge. Zu den verschiedenen Aktivitätsbereichen gehören elegante Gärten, weitläufige, unterhaltsame Innenhöfe, ein ruhiger Pool, ein Obstgarten und verschiedene Wanderwege auf dem gesamten Grundstück. Nivellierungs-, Entwässerungs- und Oberflächenwassermanagementprobleme wurden mit ebenen Rasenterrassen gemildert, um die Grundwasserretention zu fördern. Ein Myrtenwald bringt Farbe und Interesse während der Jahreszeiten.

Entender la comunidad de Portola Valley fue clave para diseñar el proyecto Rural Retreat. Esta pequeña y pintoresca ciudad, a las afueras del centro tecnológico y siempre animada ciudad de Silicon Valley, valora su ambiente rural y se esfuerza por preservar su belleza natural y espacios abiertos. El diseño sencillo de la casa y del lugar es una referencia directa a este patrimonio. El rediseño de la propiedad, originalmente una finca ecuestre, ofreció la oportunidad de restaurar el terreno mientras se creaba un hogar para una familia de cinco miembros. El patio de entrada, cuidadosamente diseñado, alberga una zona de juegos para niños y el acceso necesarios para los vehículos del parque de bomberos. Varias áreas de actividad incluyen elegantes jardines, amplios patios de entretenimiento, una tranquila piscina, un huerto y varios senderos por toda la propiedad. Los problemas de nivelación, drenaje y gestión de aguas superficiales se mitigaron con terrazas con césped niveladas para favorecer la retención de aguas subterráneas. Un bosque de mirtos añade color e interés a lo largo de las estaciones.

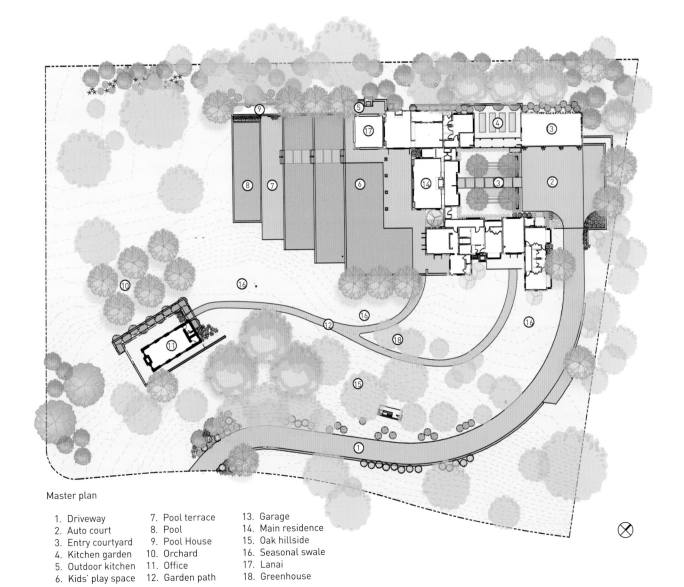

Master plan

1. Driveway	7. Pool terrace	13. Garage
2. Auto court	8. Pool	14. Main residence
3. Entry courtyard	9. Pool House	15. Oak hillside
4. Kitchen garden	10. Orchard	16. Seasonal swale
5. Outdoor kitchen	11. Office	17. Lanai
6. Kids' play space	12. Garden path	18. Greenhouse

SLOT HOUSE

LOS ALTOS HILLS, CALIFORNIA   Project size: 4.8 acres

Located amid oak woodlands in the Los Altos Hills, the striking modernism of Slot House called for a decisive but restrained approach to its landscape plan, with colors and textures that stand up to the home's bold forms yet soften its angularity. A minimal palette of warm tones on the house and paving with pops of red in plants and an architectural fountain, and a living roof with succulent garden add interest and invite exploration while deftly integrating the home into its hillside site. The integrated design of the architecture and landscape was shaped by the client's appreciation for modern design and keen attention to its oak woodlands context. A minimalist landscape palette complements the strong lines of the house while linking it to the surrounding forested hills. Sustainability drove the approach to water management through the use of drought-tolerant plants, hydrozoned irrigation, the introduction of fruit trees for shade, and the installation of dissipation basins, which slow runoff and return water to the ground.

Située au milieu des forêts de chênes des collines de Los Altos, le modernisme frappant de la Slot House exigeait une approche décisive mais sobre de son plan paysager, avec des couleurs et des textures qui résistent aux formes audacieuses de la maison tout en adoucissant son angularité. Une palette minimale de tons chauds sur la maison et le pavage avec des touches de rouge dans les plantes et une fontaine architecturale, ainsi qu'un toit vivant avec un jardin succulent ajoutent de l'intérêt et invitent à l'exploration, tout en intégrant habilement la maison dans son site à flanc de colline. La conception intégrée de l'architecture et du paysage a été façonnée par l'appréciation du client pour le design moderne et l'attention particulière portée à son contexte de bois de chêne. Une palette paysagère minimaliste complète les lignes fortes de la maison tout en la reliant aux collines boisées environnantes. La durabilité a guidé l'approche de la gestion de l'eau par l'utilisation de plantes tolérantes à la sécheresse, l'irrigation hydrozonée, l'introduction d'arbres fruitiers pour l'ombre et l'installation de bassins de distribution, qui ralentissent le ruissellement et renvoient l'eau au sol.

Inmitten der Eichenwälder der Hügel von Los Altos verlangte die markante Moderne von Slot House eine entschlossene, aber zurückhaltende Herangehensweise an die Landschaftsgestaltung mit Farben und Texturen, die den kühnen Formen des Hauses standhalten und gleichzeitig seine Winkligkeit mildern. Eine minimale Palette von warmen Farbtönen auf dem Haus und Pflaster mit Rottönen in den Pflanzen und einem architektonischen Brunnen sowie ein lebendes Dach mit einem saftigen Garten sorgen für Interesse und laden zur Erkundung ein, während sie gleichzeitig einbeziehen gekonnt das Haus in Hanglage. Das integrierte Design von Architektur und Landschaft wurde durch die Wertschätzung des Kunden für modernes Design und die besondere Aufmerksamkeit für den Kontext von Eichenholz geprägt. Eine minimalistische Landschaftspalette ergänzt die starken Linien des Hauses und verbindet es mit den umliegenden bewaldeten Hügeln. Nachhaltigkeit hat den Ansatz des Wassermanagements durch den Einsatz dürretoleranter Pflanzen, die Bewässerung in Hydrozonen, die Einführung von Obstbäumen für Schatten und die Installation von Verteilungsbecken geleitet. die den Abfluss verlangsamen und Wasser in den Boden zurückführen.

Situada en medio de los bosques de robles en las colinas de Los Altos, el llamativo modernismo de la Slot House exigía un enfoque decisivo pero sobrio del diseño paisajista, con colores y texturas que resistieran las formas atrevidas de la casa y a la vez suavizaran su angulosidad. Una paleta mínima de tonos cálidos en la casa y el pavimento con estallidos de rojo en las plantas y una cubierta verde con un suculento jardín añaden interés e invitan a la exploración mientras integran hábilmente la casa en la ladera. El aprecio del cliente por el diseño moderno y la gran atención al paisaje circundante moldearon la arquitectura y el paisaje. Una estilo minimalista también en el exterior complementa las fuertes líneas de la casa uniéndola a las colinas boscosas de alrededor. La sostenibilidad impulsó el enfoque de la gestión del agua mediante el uso de plantas tolerantes a la sequía; el riego por hidrozonificación, la introducción de árboles frutales para dar sombra y la instalación de cuencas de disipación para devolver el agua al terreno.

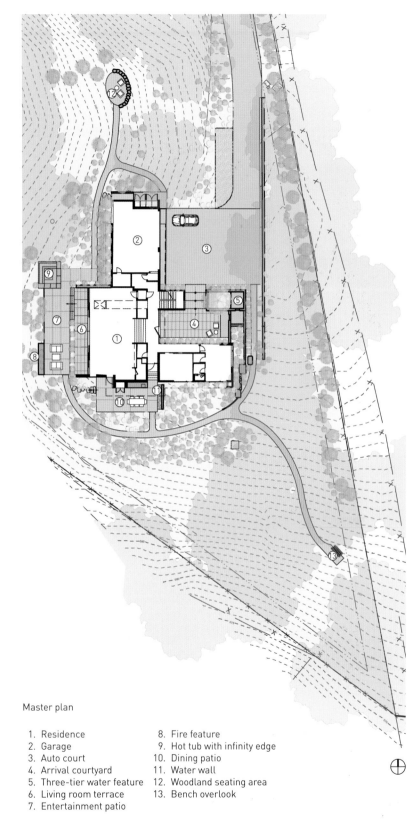

Master plan

1. Residence
2. Garage
3. Auto court
4. Arrival courtyard
5. Three-tier water feature
6. Living room terrace
7. Entertainment patio
8. Fire feature
9. Hot tub with infinity edge
10. Dining patio
11. Water wall
12. Woodland seating area
13. Bench overlook

TARONGA

SANTA LUCIA PRESERVE, CALIFORNIA

Everything about Taronga is driven by context. Nestled into an oak woodland on a ridgeline within the Santa Lucia Preserve, the project's dramatic views and challenging topography required a thoughtful approach. The result is an intriguing composition of the house, guest quarters, pool, and cabana that complements the land without altering it. The proximity of fire-prone wildlands drove the materials palette of Cor-ten steel, stucco, and limestone enhanced by low-fuel plantings. The main house and guest quarters lie parallel to each other along the contours of the hillside, while the vanishing-edge pool, spa, and detached office are juxtaposed in orientation, creating distinctly different experiences. Linking these volumes is a diagonal limestone wall that interrupts the geometry to direct views to the ridge across the valley. This axis runs through the house and extends into the site, while the Cor-ten fire pit and outdoor kitchen further complement these lines. The green roof atop the garage gives the breezeway sitting area the feel of a treetop perch as one gazes into the oak canopy with glimpses across the valley.

Tout dans Taronga est dicté par le contexte. Niché dans une forêt de chênes sur une crête dans la réserve de Santa Lucia, les vues spectaculaires et la topographie difficile du projet ont nécessité une approche réfléchie. Le résultat est une composition intrigante de la maison, des quartiers des invités, de la piscine et de la cabane qui complète le terrain sans le modifier. La proximité de terrains sujets aux incendies a conduit à la palette de matériaux tels que l'acier Cor-ten, du stuc et du calcaire, ainsi qu'un pavage et des plantations pare feu. La maison principale et les quartiers des invités sont parallèles le long des contours de la colline, tandis que la piscine, le jacuzzi et le bureau détaché sont juxtaposés en orientation, créant des expériences distinctes. Reliant ces volumes est un mur de calcaire diagonal qui interrompt la géométrie pour diriger les vues vers la crête à travers la vallée. Cet axe traverse la maison et se prolonge dans le site, tandis que le foyer Cor-ten et la cuisine extérieure complètent ces lignes. Le toit vert au-dessus du garage donne au salon de passage couvert la sensation d'un perchoir à la cime des arbres alors que l'on regarde dans la canope de chêne avec des aperçus à travers la vallée.

Alles an Taronga wird vom Kontext bestimmt. Eingebettet in den Eichenkamm des kalifornischen Santa Lucia Preserve, der eine spektakuläre Aussicht und eine herausfordernde Topographie bietet, war ein sorgfältiger Ansatz erforderlich. Das Ergebnis ist eine faszinierende Komposition aus Haus, Gästeflügel, Pool und Cabana, die das Gelände vervollständigt, ohne es so zu verändern, dass es nicht mehr wiederzuerkennen ist. Der Bau in feuergefährdeten Wildnisgebieten ermöglichte die Verwendung aller Materialien: Cortenstahl, Stuck, Metalldach, Kalksteinmauern, Pflaster und kaum brennende Pflanzungen. Das Haupthaus und die Gästezimmer haben parallele und relative Konturen, während sich der Pool und die Cabana entsprechend ihrer Ausrichtung drehen, wodurch ein deutlich anderes Erlebnis entsteht. All dies ist durch eine diagonale Kalksteinwand verbunden, die die Geometrie unterbricht, um den Blick auf den Kamm über das Tal zu lenken. Diese Achse kreuzt das Haus und erstreckt sich in die Baustelle. Der Corten-Kamin und die Außenküche vervollständigen diese Linien. Ein Gründach, das die Garage bedeckt, lässt den Loungebereich des überdachten Durchgangs wie eine Sitzstange in den Baumwipfeln aussehen.

Todo sobre Taronga está determinado por el contexto. La propiedad, ubicada en la cresta de robles de la Reserva Santa Lucía en California, con vistas espectaculares y una topografía desafiante, requería un enfoque reflexivo. El resultado es una intrigante composición, con un ala de invitados separada y una piscina y una cabaña que complementan el terreno sin alterarlo. La construcción en tierras silvestres propensas al fuego impulsó la selección de materiales: acero corten, estuco, techo metálico, paredes de piedra caliza y pavimento y plantaciones cortafuegos. La casa principal y las habitaciones para invitados tienen contornos paralelos, mientras que la piscina y la cabaña giran de acuerdo con su orientación, creando una experiencia claramente diferente. Una pared diagonal de piedra caliza interrumpe la geometría para dirigir las vistas hacia la cresta a traves del valle. Este eje atraviesa la casa extendiéndose hacia el terreno. Un brasero de acero corten y una cocina exterior completan el conjunto. Una cubierta verde sobre el garaje hace que el área de descanso del pasaje cubierto se parezca a una percha en las copas de los árboles.

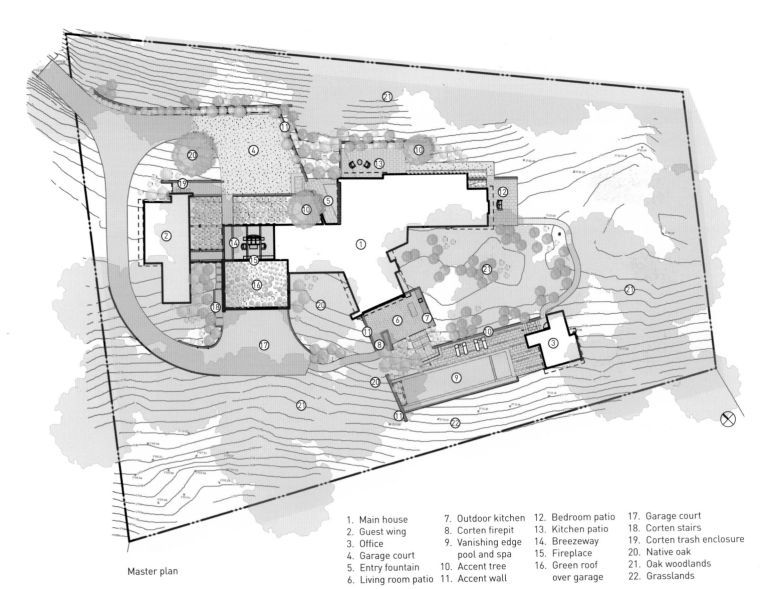

Master plan

1. Main house	7. Outdoor kitchen	12. Bedroom patio	17. Garage court
2. Guest wing	8. Corten firepit	13. Kitchen patio	18. Corten stairs
3. Office	9. Vanishing edge	14. Breezeway	19. Corten trash enclosure
4. Garage court	pool and spa	15. Fireplace	20. Native oak
5. Entry fountain	10. Accent tree	16. Green roof	21. Oak woodlands
6. Living room patio	11. Accent wall	over garage	22. Grasslands

ANGUS | McCAFFREY
INTERIOR DESIGN INC.

angusmccaffrey.com

ATHERTON RESIDENCE

Interior Design: ANGUS | MCCAFFREY
INTERIOR DESIGN

Architect: Arcanum Architecture

Photographer: Brad Knipstein

SONOMA RESIDENCE

Interior Design: ANGUS | MCCAFFREY
INTERIOR DESIGN

Architect: George Bevan, Bevan & Associates

Landscape Architect: Paul Rozanski

General Contractor: Landers Curry, Inc.

Photographer: James Carriere

WOODSIDE RESIDENCE

Interior Design: ANGUS | MCCAFFREY
INTERIOR DESIGN

Architect: Killian O'Sullivan

Photographer: Mariko Reed

ANGUS | McCAFFREY INTERIOR DESIGN is a full-service interior design company with over 20 years of experience creating luxurious spaces that reflect our clients' individual lifestyles, tastes, and aspirations.

Whether it's a bold pied-à-terre filled with color or a stunning wine country estate in calm agrarian hues, we create designs that transcend eras and trends to deliver inspiring spaces that are timeless, tailored, artful, unique, and functional for each and every client. Bringing a keen curatorial eye to each project, we offer a depth of knowledge in architecture and building, color theory, contemporary art, furnishings, craftsmanship, and materials. Our focus is on enduring designs while steering away from ephemeral trends to ensure that we provide the best impact on our clients' investment.

ANGUS | McCAFFREY INTERIOR DESIGN est un cabinet de design d'intérieur à service complet avec plus de 20 ans d'expérience dans la création d'espaces luxueux qui reflètent les styles de vie, les goûts et les aspirations individuelles de nos clients.

Qu'il s'agisse d'un pied-à-terre audacieux rempli de couleurs ou d'un magnifique domaine viticole aux teintes agraires calmes, nous créons des designs qui transcendent les époques et les tendances pour offrir des espaces inspirants, intemporels, sur mesure, astucieux, uniques et fonctionnels pour chacun et chaque client. En apportant une grande expérience et un œil vif à chaque projet, nous offrons une connaissance approfondie de l'architecture et du bâtiment, de la théorie des couleurs, de l'art contemporain, du mobilier, de l'artisanat et des matériaux. Nous nous concentrons sur les conceptions durables tout en nous éloignant des tendances éphémères pour nous assurer que nous fournissons le meilleur impact sur l'investissement de nos clients.

ANGUS | McCAFFREY INTERIOR DESIGN ist ein Innenarchitekturstudio mit mehr als 20 Jahren Erfahrung in der Schaffung luxuriöser Räume, die den individuellen Lebensstil, Geschmack und die Wünsche unserer Kunden widerspiegeln. Egal, ob es sich um ein gewagtes zweites Zuhause voller Farben oder um ein großartiges Weingut mit ruhigen landwirtschaftlichen Nuancen handelt, wir kreieren Designs, die Epochen und Trends überschreiten und inspirierende und zeitlose Räume in Maß bieten, intelligent, einzigartig und funktional für jeden unserer Kunden. Wir bieten ein tiefes Wissen über Architektur und Bauwesen, Farbtheorie, zeitgenössische Kunst, Möbel, Handwerk und Materialien und bieten Erfahrung und ein gutes Auge für jedes Projekt. Wir konzentrieren uns auf nachhaltiges Design und entfernen uns von flüchtigen Trends, um den besten Einfluss auf die Investition unserer Kunden zu erzielen.

ANGUS | McCAFFREY INTERIOR DESIGN es un estudio de diseño de interiores con más de 20 años de experiencia en la creación de espacios lujosos que reflejan los estilos de vida, los gustos y las aspiraciones individuales de nuestros clientes.

Ya sea una atrevida segunda vivienda llena de color o una magnífica bodega con tranquilos matices agrarios, creamos diseños que trascienden eras y tendencias para ofrecer espacios inspiradores y atemporales en medida, inteligentes, únicos y funcionales para todos y cada uno de los clientes. Ofrecemos un conocimiento profundo de la arquitectura y la construcción, teoría del color, arte contemporáneo, muebles, artesanías y materiales aportando experiencia y buen ojo para cada proyecto. Nos centramos en diseños sostenibles mientras nos alejamos de las tendencias efímeras para generar el mejor impacto en la inversión de nuestros clientes.

ATHERTON RESIDENCE

ATHERTON, CALIFORNIA

ANGUS | McCAFFREY delivered the interior design of this custom-built home in Silicon Valley for a fashion-forward couple with three children and a knock-out contemporary art collection. The brief was to create a stylish (the wife is a fashion executive) yet comfortable kid-friendly home to showcase the owners' art collection and flair for design and style. The result is a highly livable space with a clean elevated style.

The traditional Mediterranean style of the house exterior purposefully contrasts with the detail-lean interior architecture. Large windows and full-height French doors create light-infused spaces that inspired many of the interior design decisions and offered the ideal environment to showcase the interplay of art, form, and function.

ANGUS | McCAFFREY a livré le design intérieur de cette maison construite sur mesure dans la Silicon Valley pour un couple avant-gardiste avec trois enfants et une collection d'art contemporain à couper le souffle. Le dossier était de créer une maison élégante (la femme est une dirigeante de la mode) mais confortable pour les enfants tout en mettant en valeur la collection d'art des propriétaires et leurs sens du design et du style. Le résultat est un espace très habitable avec un style épuré et élevé.

Le style méditerranéen traditionnel de l'extérieur de la maison contraste volontairement avec l'architecture intérieure simple. Les grandes fenêtres et les portes-fenêtres créent des espaces imprégnés de lumière qui ont inspiré de nombreuses décisions de design d'intérieur et ont offert l'environnement idéal pour mettre en valeur l'interaction entre l'art, la forme et la fonction.

ANGUS | McCAFFREY lieferte das Innendesign für dieses maßgeschneiderte Silicon Valley-Haus für ein avantgardistisches Paar mit drei Kindern und einer beeindruckenden Sammlung zeitgenössischer Kunst. Ziel war es, ein elegantes Zuhause zu schaffen (die Frau ist eine Führungskraft in der Modewelt), das sich jedoch für Kinder wohlfühlt, und gleichzeitig die Kunstsammlung der Eigentümer mit einem großen Sinn für Design und Stil zu präsentieren. Das Ergebnis ist ein sehr lebenswerter Raum mit einem sauberen und eleganten Stil.

Der traditionelle mediterrane Stil des Äußeren des Hauses kontrastiert bewusst mit der einfachen Architektur des Inneren. Große Fenster und Terrassentüren schaffen lichtdurchflutete Räume, die viele Designentscheidungen inspiriert haben und den perfekten Rahmen bieten, um das Zusammenspiel von Kunst, Form und Funktion zu demonstrieren.

ANGUS | McCAFFREY entregó el diseño interior de esta casa hecha a medida en Silicon Valley para una pareja vanguardista con tres hijos y una impresionante colección de arte contemporáneo. El objetivo era crear un hogar elegante (la mujer es una ejecutiva en el mundo de la moda) pero cómodo para los niños, y a la vez, exhibir la colección de arte de los propietarios con un gran sentido del diseño y estilo. El resultado es un espacio muy habitable con un estilo limpio y elegante.

El estilo tradicional mediterráneo del exterior de la casa contrasta deliberadamente con la sencilla arquitectura del interior. Las grandes ventanas y puertas de patio crean espacios llenos de luz que han inspirado muchas decisiones de diseño y han proporcionado el entorno perfecto para demostrar la interacción entre el arte, la forma y la función.

SONOMA RESIDENCE

SONOMA, CALIFORNIA

A newly retired couple's custom-built home in the heart of Sonoma's wine country is a collaboration between ANGUS | McCAFFREY, George Bevan, and Landers Curry Construction. Despite being nearly lost before completion in the devastating Sonoma wildfires of 2017, this home celebrates the Sonoma wine country lifestyle of bringing the outdoors in and the exceptional indoor/outdoor living. The owner is fond of color, and the brief was to incorporate fun notes and still nod to the landscape while not letting the country vibes rule the design decisions. There is an emphasis on reflecting the new Sonoma wine country while embracing the clients' love of color and fun-loving personalities. Arched windows and doors shelter timeless furnishings and contemporary art. The owners took a unique approach to this home and worked with ANGUS | McCAFFREY to curate an almost entirely new art collection just for this residence. The husband, in his spare time, is a competitive Ping-Pong player, so a space that could be dedicated to this activity was a must. The "barn" holds a guest suite, a kitchen for entertainment, and of course, a space for Ping Pong practice.

La maison d'un couple récemment retraité au cœur du pays viticole de Sonoma est la collaboration entre Angus | McCAFFREY, George Bevan et Landers Curry Construction. Bien que presque perdue lors des incendies dévastateurs de Sonoma en 2017, cette maison célèbre le style de vie de la région dans un cadre intérieur / extérieur. Les propriétaires adorent la couleur et une des exigences de conception était d'incorporer des notes ludiques tout en faisant référence au paysage sans laisser le cadre rural dominer les décisions de conception. L'accent était mis sur le nouveau pays viticole de Sonoma et sur l'amour des clients pour la couleur et les personnalités amusantes. De grandes fenêtres et des portes cintrées donnent à des espaces avec des meubles intemporels et de l'art contemporain. Les propriétaires ont adopté une approche unique de cette maison et ont travaillé avec ANGUS | McCAFFREY pour organiser une collection d'art presque entièrement nouvelle pour cette résidence. Le mari, dans son temps libre, est un joueur de tennis de table compétitif, donc un espace qui pourrait être dédié à cette activité était essentiel. L '« étable » contient une chambre d'amis, une cuisine et, bien sûr, un espace pour pratiquer le tennis de table.

Das Haus eines frisch pensionierten Paares im Herzen von Sonomas Weinland ist die Zusammenarbeit zwischen Angus | McCAFFREY, George Bevan und Landers Curry Construction. Obwohl dieses Haus während der verheerenden Sonoma-Brände von 2017 fast verloren gegangen ist, feiert es dank einer Innen- / Außenumgebung den Lebensstil der Region. Die Eigentümer lieben die Farbe und baten um spielerische Noten, während sie sich auf die Landschaft beziehen, ohne dass die ländliche Umgebung die Designentscheidungen dominiert. Der Fokus lag auf dem neuen Sonoma-Weinland und der Liebe der Kunden zu Farben und lebenslustigen Persönlichkeiten. Große Fenster und gewölbte Türen öffnen sich zu Räumen mit zeitlosen Möbeln und zeitgenössischer Kunst. Die Eigentümer verfolgten einen einzigartigen Ansatz für dieses Haus und arbeiteten mit ANGUS | McCAFFREY zusammen, um eine fast völlig neue Kunstsammlung nur für diese Residenz zu kuratieren. Der Ehemann ist in seiner Freizeit ein konkurrenzfähiger Tischtennisspieler, daher war ein Raum, der dieser Aktivität gewidmet war, unerlässlich. Der „Stall" enthält ein Gästezimmer, eine Küche und natürlich einen Bereich zum Tischtennisspielen.

La casa de una pareja recién jubilada en el corazón de la región vinícola de Sonoma es la colaboración entre Angus | McCAFFREY, George Bevan y Landers Curry Construction. Aunque casi se perdió durante los devastadores incendios de Sonoma de 2017, esta casa celebra el estilo de vida de la región gracias a una configuración interior/exterior. A los propietarios les encanta el color y pidieron que se incorporaran notas divertidas a la vez que se hacía referencia al paisaje sin dejar que el entorno rural dominara las decisiones de diseño. La atención se centró en la nueva región vinícola de Sonoma y en ese amor de los clientes por el color y las personalidades divertidas. Grandes ventanales y puertas arqueadas dan a espacios con muebles atemporales y arte contemporáneo. Los propietarios adoptaron un enfoque único para esta casa y trabajaron con ANGUS | McCAFFREY para crear una colección de arte casi completamente nueva para esta residencia. El marido, en su tiempo libre, es un jugador de tenis de mesa competitivo, por lo que era fundamental un espacio dedicado a esta actividad. El «establo» contiene una habitación de invitados, una cocina y, por supuesto, un área para la práctica del tenis de mesa.

WOODSIDE RESIDENCE

WOODSIDE, CALIFORNIA

A mother of three set out to build her dream home. Collaborating with architect Killian O'Sullivan, Angus | McCaffrey fulfilled her desire, a house that reflects the client's love for Santa Barbara's Spanish Mediterranean style. The home also responds to its beautiful natural setting in Woodside and accommodates the quintessential California indoor-outdoor lifestyle. The tiled swimming pool and guest house are surrounded by a David Austin Rose garden. Beyond the pool, the landscaping blends into the woodlands offering a perfect private setting for the enjoyment of this elegant yet relaxed home. The interior, filled with light thanks to the generous windows, was designed to accentuate the client's beautifully curated art collection, including works from Nathan Olivera, Wayne Thiebaud, and Richard Diebenkorn, and her magnificent collection of antiques. To elaborate on that theme, Katie McCaffrey and Martha Angus purchased new items to blend seamlessly with the old. Furnishings in all rooms and outdoors were designed and selected around comfort and family, supporting laid back gatherings large and small.

Une mère de trois enfants a entrepris de construire la maison de ses rêves. Angus | McCaffrey a collabore avec l'architecte Killian O'Sullivan pour exaucer son désir, une maison qui reflète l'amour du client pour le style méditerranéen espagnol de Santa Barbara. La maison répond également à son magnifique cadre naturel à Woodside et s'adapte au style de vie intérieur-extérieur par excellence de la Californie. La piscine carrelée et la maison d'hôtes sont entourées d'une roseraie David Austin. Au-delà de la piscine, l'aménagement paysager se fond dans les bois offrant un cadre privé parfait pour le plaisir de cette maison élégante et décontractée. L'intérieur, rempli de lumière grâce aux fenêtres généreuses, a été conçu pour mettre en valeur la collection d'art magnifiquement organisée du client, y compris des œuvres de Nathan Olivera, Wayne Thiebaud et Richard Diebenkorn, et sa magnifique collection d'antiquités. Pour élaborer sur ce thème, Katie McCaffrey et Martha Angus ont acheté de nouveaux articles pour se fondre parfaitement avec l'ancien. L'ameublement dans toutes les pièces et à l'extérieur a été conçu et sélectionné autour du confort et de la famille, favorisant les rassemblements décontractés, petits et grands.

Eine Mutter von drei Kindern machte sich daran, das Haus ihrer Träume zu bauen. Zusammenarbeit mit dem Architekten Killian O'Sullivan, Angus | McCaffrey erfüllte seinen Wunsch, ein Zuhause, das die Liebe des Kunden zu Santa Barbaras spanischem mediterranen Flair widerspiegelt. Das Haus reagiert auch auf seine wunderschöne natürliche Umgebung in Woodside und beherbergt den Inbegriff des kalifornischen Lebensstils im Innen- und Außenbereich. Der gefliese Pool und das Gästehaus sind von einem Rosengarten von David Austin umgeben. Jenseits des Pools fügt sich die Landschaft in den Wald ein und bietet eine private Umgebung, die sich ideal für den Genuss dieses eleganten und entspannten Hauses eignet. Der dank der großzügigen Fenster lichtdurchflutete Innenraum wurde gestaltet, um die Sammlung von Antiquitäten und Kunst mit Werken von Nathan Olivera, Wayne Thiebaud und Richard Diebenkorn hervorzuheben. Katie McCaffrey und Martha Angus kauften auch moderne Möbel, die zur Antiquität passten. Die Möbel in allen Zimmern und im Freien wurden mit Blick auf Komfort und Familiengeist ausgewählt, um einen entspannten Rahmen für große und kleine Versammlungen zu schaffen.

Una madre de tres hijos se propuso construir la casa de sus sueños. Colaborando con el arquitecto Killian O'Sullivan, Angus | McCaffrey cumplió su deseo, una casa que refleja el amor del cliente por el estilo mediterráneo español de Santa Bárbara. La casa también responde a su hermoso entorno natural en Woodside y se adapta al estilo de vida interior y exterior por excelencia de California. La piscina de azulejos y la casa de huéspedes están rodeadas por un jardín de rosas David Austin. Más allá de la piscina, el paisaje se funde con los bosques y ofrece un entorno privado ideal para el disfrute de esta casa elegante y relajada. El interior, lleno de luz gracias a las generosas ventanas, fue diseñado para poner en valor la colección de antigüedades y de arte con obras de Nathan Olivera, Wayne Thiebaud y Richard Diebenkorn. Katie McCaffrey y Martha Angus también compraron muebles modernos para combinarlos con los antiguos. Los muebles en todas las habitaciones y al aire libre se seleccionaron teniendo en cuenta la comodidad y el espíritu familiar, creando entornos relajados para reuniones grandes y pequeñas.

Assembledge+

assembledge.com

LAUREL HILLS RESIDENCE

Design Team: David Thompson (Principal-in-Charge), Greg Marin (Project Manager), and Raul Aguilera (Project Architect)

Interior Design: Susan Mitnick Design Studio

Landscape Architect: Fiore Landscape Design

Structural Engineer: Peck

General Contractor: Assembledge+

Photographer: Matthew Millman

PHELPS RESIDENCE

Design Team: Assembledge+: David Thompson (Principal-in-Charge) Mitchell Streichhirsch

Landscape Architect: Armstrong Design

Structural Engineer: Peck

Photographer: Paul Vu

OAKDELL RESIDENCE

Design Team: David Thompson (Principal-in-Charge), and Gregory Marin

Landscape Architect: Fiore Landscape Design

Photographer: Michael Weschler

Since its founding in 1997, Assembledge+ has been pursuing an architecture that is driven by a commitment to collaboration and craftsmanship with the goal of creating enduring environments that are user-focused, innovative, and sustainable. The firm is led by David Thompson, Design Principal and Founder, who was joined by his father in 2013, Richard Thompson, FAIA, as Principal of Urban Design. The name Assembledge+ was deliberately chosen to convey the firm's passion for "assembling" all the often-complex elements of the design process to produce an architecture that is precise, considered, and placed firmly on the leading edge of contemporary discourse. The + signifies an approach that looks at the whole as an inextricable combination of interrelated parts.

As an award-winning firm, Assembledge+ shares a deep passion for contemporary world architecture and its execution in the temperate Southern California climate. Following in the tradition of the region's modernist design and guided by a desire to design responsibly and sustainably, Assembledge+ strives to create architecture that exemplifies a harmony between nature and the built environment, but perhaps most importantly, creates human environments that support and nourish the people who occupy their buildings.

Depuis sa fondation en 1997, Assembledge+ est dirigé par David Thompson, directeur et fondateur du design, qui a été rejoint par son père en 2013, Richard Thompson, FAIA, en tant que directeur du design urbain. Le nom Assembledge+ a été délibérément choisi pour exprimer la passion de la firme pour « l'assemblage » de tous les éléments souvent complexes du processus de conception afin de produire une architecture qui soit précise, réfléchie, et placée fermement à la pointe du discours contemporain. Le + signifie une approche qui considère l'ensemble comme une combinaison inextricable de parties interdépendantes.

En tant que firme primée, Assembledge+ partage une profonde passion pour l'architecture mondiale contemporaine et son exécution dans le climat tempéré du sud de la Californie. S'inscrivant dans la tradition du design moderniste de la région et guidée par le désir de concevoir de manière responsable et durable, Assembledge+ s'efforce de créer une architecture qui illustre l'harmonie entre la nature et l'environnement bâti, mais surtout, qui crée des environnements humains qui soutiennent et nourrissent les personnes qui occupent leurs bâtiments.

Seit der Gründung im Jahr 1997 wird Assembledge+ von David Thompson, dem Design Principal und Gründer, geleitet. 2013 trat sein Vater Richard Thompson, FAIA, als Principal of Urban Design bei. Der Name Assembledge+ wurde bewusst gewählt, um die Leidenschaft des Unternehmens für das „Zusammenfügen" all der oft komplexen Elemente des Designprozesses zu einer Architektur zu vermitteln, die präzise und überlegt ist und sich an der Spitze des zeitgenössischen Diskurses befindet. Das + steht für einen Ansatz, der das Ganze als eine untrennbare Kombination von miteinander verbundenen Teilen betrachtet.

Als preisgekröntes Unternehmen teilt Assembledge+ eine tiefe Leidenschaft für die zeitgenössische Weltarchitektur und ihre Ausführung im gemäßigten Klima Südkaliforniens. In der Tradition des modernistischen Designs der Region und geleitet von dem Wunsch, verantwortungsbewusst und nachhaltig zu entwerfen, ist Assembledge+ bestrebt, Architektur zu schaffen, die eine Harmonie zwischen Natur und gebauter Umwelt veranschaulicht, aber der es dabei vielleicht am wichtigsten ist, förderliche Umgebungen zu schaffen, welche die Menschen, die ihre Gebäude bewohnen, unterstützen und nähren.

Desde su fundación en 1997, Assembledge+ está dirigida por David Thompson, Director de Diseño y Fundador, a quien se unió su padre en 2013, Richard Thompson, FAIA, como Director de Diseño Urbano. El nombre Assembledge+ fue elegido deliberadamente para transmitir la pasión de la empresa por «ensamblar» todos los elementos, a menudo complejos, del proceso de diseño para producir una arquitectura precisa, considerada y situada firmemente en la vanguardia del discurso contemporáneo. El + significa un enfoque que considera el conjunto como una combinación inextricable de partes interrelacionadas.

Como empresa galardonada, Assembledge+ comparte una profunda pasión por la arquitectura contemporánea y su ejecución en el clima templado del sur de California. Siguiendo la tradición del diseño modernista de la región y guiada por el deseo de diseñar de forma responsable y sostenible, Assembledge+ se esfuerza por crear una arquitectura que ejemplifique la armonía entre la naturaleza y el entorno construido. Quizás lo más importante para ellos sea crear entornos humanos que apoyen y alimenten a las personas que ocupan sus edificios.

LAUREL HILLS RESIDENCE

LOS ANGELES, CALIFORNIA

Lot size: 17,930 sq ft
Project size: 4,900 sq ft

The single-story residence is composed of three pavilions connected by a series of glass hallways, creating a residential oasis in the heart of Los Angeles. Unlike many iconic Los Angeles homes that orient themselves around panoramic city views, the Laurel Hills Residence is in the foothills of the Laurel Canyon, where the property offers a secluded and inwardly focused experience with a majestic backdrop of lush and mature trees. The surrounding landscape is taken to be the building envelope, and the exterior walls of the house are reconceived as partition walls. The grounds are interlocked with the interior space, and the entire ensemble is activated by the purposeful arrangement of deeply layered sightlines, vignettes, and circulation connections. A minimalist palette of charcoal-colored panels and Western red cedar serves as a neutral canvas complementing the home's landscape featuring California native species. The large living volume provides enough surface for over fifty solar panels that allow the residence to be sustainable and remove itself from the city power grid.

La résidence de plein-pied est composée de trois pavillons reliés par une série de couloirs en verre, créant ainsi une oasis résidentielle au cœur de Los Angeles. Contrairement à de nombreuses maisons emblématiques de Los Angeles qui s'orientent autour de vues panoramiques de la ville, la Laurel Hills Residence se trouve au pied du Laurel Canyon, où la propriété offre une expérience retirée et centrée sur l'intérieur avec un majestueux décor d'arbres luxuriants . Le paysage environnant est considéré comme l'enveloppe du bâtiment, et les murs extérieurs de la maison sont reconçus comme des cloisons. Le terrain est imbriqué dans l'espace intérieur et l'ensemble est activé par l'agencement délibéré de lignes de vue, de vignettes et de connexions de circulation en couches profondes. Une palette minimaliste de panneaux de couleur charbon et de cèdre rouge de l'Ouest sert de toile neutre complétant le paysage de la maison qui met en valeur les espèces indigènes de Californie. Le volume habitable offre suffisamment de surface pour plus de cinquante panneaux solaires qui permettent à la résidence d'être durable et de se soustraire au réseau électrique de la ville.

Das einstöckige Wohnhaus besteht aus drei Pavillons, die durch eine Reihe von Glasfluren miteinander verbunden sind und eine Wohnoase im Herzen von Los Angeles bilden. Im Gegensatz zu vielen ikonischen Häusern in Los Angeles, die sich an Panoramablicken auf die Stadt orientieren, befindet sich die Laurel Hills Residence in den Ausläufern des Laurel Canyon, wo das Anwesen ein abgeschiedenes und nach innen gerichtetes Erlebnis mit einer majestätischen Kulisse aus üppigen und ehrwürdigen Bäumen bietet. Die umgebende Landschaft wird als Gebäudehülle verstanden, und die Außenwände des Hauses sind als Trennwände neu konzipiert. Die Außenanlagen sind mit dem Innenraum verzahnt, und das gesamte Ensemble wird durch die gezielte Anordnung von tief geschichteten Sichtachsen, Vignettierungen und Erschließungsverbindungen aktiviert. Eine minimalistische Palette aus anthrazitfarbenen Paneelen und westlichem Rotzedernholz dient als neutrale Leinwand, die die Landschaft des Hauses mit einheimischen kalifornischen Arten ergänzt. Das große Wohnvolumens bietet genügend Fläche für über fünfzig Solarpaneele, die es ermöglichen, das Haus nachhaltig zu gestalten und sich vom städtischen Stromnetz zu trennen.

La vivienda se compone de tres pabellones conectados por una serie de pasillos acristalados, creando un oasis residencial en el corazón de Los Ángeles. A diferencia de muchas casas icónicas de Los Ángeles que se orientan en torno a vistas panorámicas de la ciudad, la Residencia Laurel Hills está en las faldas de la colina Laurel, donde ofrece una experiencia aislada y centrada en el interior con un majestuoso telón de fondo de árboles exuberantes. El paisaje circundante conforma la envoltura del edificio, y los muros exteriores de la casa se reconciben como paredes divisorias. El terreno está entrelazado con el espacio interior y todo el conjunto se activa por la disposición intencionada de líneas de visión, viñetas y conexiones de circulación. Una paleta minimalista de paneles de color carbón y cedro rojo sirve como un lienzo neutro que complementa el paisaje de especies autóctonas de California. El volumen habitable proporciona suficiente superficie para más de cincuenta paneles solares que permiten que la residencia sea sostenible y no dependa de la red eléctrica de la ciudad.

Section perspective view

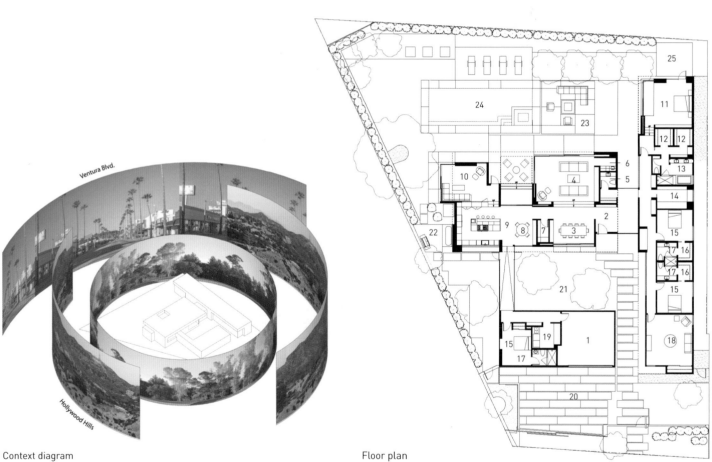

Context diagram

Ventura Blvd.

Hollywood Hills

Floor plan

1. Garage
2. Entry
3. Dining room
4. Living room
5. Powder room
6. Bar
7. Pantry
8. Breakfast room
9. Kitchen
10. Family room
11. Master bedroom
12. Master closet
13. Master bathroom
14. Office
15. Bedroom
16. Closet
17. Bathroom
18. Play room
19. Laundry room
20. Driveway
21. Entry courtyard
22. BBQ area
23. Fire pit
24. Pool
25. Meditation garden

PHELPS RESIDENCE

HUNTINGTON BEACH, CALIFORNIA

Lot size: 7,901 sq ft
Project size: 3,537 sq ft

Located steps from the waterways of Huntington Harbor, Phelps Residence is a remodel of a regional mid-century house, developed in the 1960s. The goal of the renovation was to honor the mid-century bones of the existing structure featuring full-height windows and open-beam ceilings while infusing new life and detail via a ground-up renovation. The volume of the house is a two-story stucco façade structure with vertical cedar and black metal accents. Stack bond CMU garden walls in the front yard define the entry sequence, honoring the mid-century history of the residence. The wall-to-wall, full-height sliding doors create an indoor-outdoor experience by extending the front yard fire pit and seating area through the living room to the backyard swimming pool and cabana beyond. The climate of the Harbor provides an ideal environment to open the space up to the yards year-round, thereby expanding the footprint of the house and allowing for an uninterrupted flow between rooms and indoor and outdoor areas.

Située à quelques pas des voies navigables de Huntington Harbor, la résidence Phelps est une rénovation d'une maison régionale du milieu du siècle, développée dans les années 1960. L'objectif de la rénovation était d'honorer les structures existantes du milieu du siècle, avec des fenêtres sur toute la hauteur et des plafonds à poutres apparentes, tout en insufflant une nouvelle vie et de nouveaux détails grâce à une rénovation de fond. Le volume de la maison est une structure de façade de deux étages en stuc avec des accents verticaux en cèdre et en métal noir. Les murs du jardin de la CMU dans la cour avant définissent l'entrée, honorant l'histoire du milieu du siècle de la résidence. Les portes coulissantes pleine hauteur, mur à mur, créent une expérience intérieur-extérieur en prolongeant le brasero de jardin de la cour avant et l'emplacement des sièges à travers le salon jusqu'à la piscine et la cabane de la cour arrière. Le climat offre un environnement idéal pour ouvrir l'espace toute l'année, ce qui élargit l'empreinte de la maison et permet une circulation ininterrompue entre les pièces et les zones intérieures et extérieures.

Die Phelps Residence liegt nur wenige Schritte von den Wasserwegen des Huntington Harbor entfernt und ist eine Neugestaltung eines regionalen Hauses, das in den 1960er Jahren erbaut wurde. Ziel der Renovierung war es, die bestehende Struktur aus der Mitte des Jahrhunderts durch die Eröffnung zu würdigen von großen Fenstern und freiliegenden Holzbalkendecken, die durch eine Renovierung des Geländes neues Leben einhauchen. Das Volumen des Hauses besteht aus einer zweistöckigen Stuckfassadenstruktur mit vertikalen Elementen aus Zeder und Schwarzmetall. Stapelverklebte CMU-Gartenmauern im Vorhof definieren die Eingangsreihenfolge und ehren die Geschichte des Hauses aus der Mitte des Jahrhunderts. Die von Wand zu Wand verlaufenden Schiebetüren in voller Höhe schaffen ein Innen-Außen-Erlebnis, indem sie die Feuerstelle und den Sitzbereich im Vorgarten durch das Wohnzimmer bis zum Swimmingpool und der Cabana im Hinterhof verlängern. Das Klima des Hafens bietet eine ideale Umgebung, um den Raum das ganze Jahr über zu den Höfen hin zu öffnen und so die Grundfläche des Hauses zu erweitern und einen ununterbrochenen Fluss zwischen den Räumen und den Innen- und Außenbereichen zu ermöglichen.

Ubicada a pocos pasos de las vías fluviales del puerto de Huntington, la Residencia Phelps es una remodelación de una casa regional construida durante la década de 1960. El objetivo de la renovación era honrar la estructura existente de mediados de siglo pasado a través de la apertura de grandes ventanales y techos de vigas a la vista, infundiendo una nueva vida a través de una renovación del terreno. El volumen de la casa consiste en una estructura de fachada de estuco de dos pisos con elementos verticales de cedro y metal negro. Los muros del jardín en el patio delantero definen la secuencia de la entrada. Las puertas corredizas de altura completa, de pared a pared, crean una experiencia interior-exterior al expandir el patio delantero y el área de asientos a través de la sala de estar hasta la piscina del patio trasero y la cabaña situada más allá. El clima del puerto proporciona un entorno ideal para abrir el espacio hacia los patios durante todo el año, permitiendo un paso ininterrumpido entre las habitaciones y las zonas interiores y exteriores.

Second floor plan

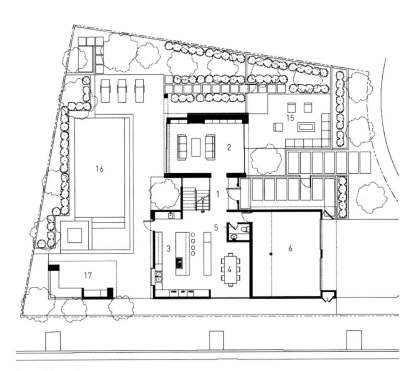

Ground floor plan

1. Entry
2. Living room
3. Kitchen
4. Dining room
5. Powder room
6. Garage
7. Bedroom
8. Bathroom
9. Master bedroom
10. Master bathroom
11. Master closet
12. Family room
13. Balcony
14. Driveway
15. Fire pit
16. Pool
17. Cabana grill

OAKDELL RESIDENCE

STUDIO CITY, CALIFORNIA

Lot size: 26,045 sq ft
Project size: 5,755 sq ft

Nestled in the hills of the Fryman Canyon Estates area in Studio City, the Oakdell Residence is a remodel and an addition to an existing 1960s mid-century home. The clients asked for an open-floor experience to maximize views of the surrounding landscape. A meandering path of concrete panels, set amidst the landscaping and decomposed granite, leads to the glassed-in entry foyer of the house. Together with the floor-to-ceiling windows and sliding glass doors on the other side of the house, the residence gives a sense of transparency, bringing in ample light and extending the living area outside the house and into the landscape.

The two-story addition consists of a master bedroom on the upper level and an office on the lower level, integrated into the hillside and taking advantage of the home's canyon site. A minimalist palette of stone, hardwood floor, and white plaster echoes the qualities of the existing home and preserves its original spirit and character.

Nichée dans les collines de la région de Fryman Canyon Estates à Studio City, la résidence Oakdell est une rénovation et un ajout à une maison existante des années 1960. Les clients ont demandé un espace ouvert afin de maximiser la vue sur le paysage environnant. Un chemin sinueux de panneaux de béton, placé au milieu de l'aménagement paysager et du granit décomposé, mène au foyer d'entrée vitrée de la maison. Avec les fenêtres du sol au plafond et les portes coulissantes en verre de l'autre côté de la maison, la résidence donne une impression de transparence, apportant une lumière abondante et prolongeant la zone de vie à l'extérieur de la maison et dans le paysage.

L'ajout de deux étages comprend une chambre principale au niveau supérieur et un bureau au niveau inférieur, intégré dans le flanc de la colline et profitant du site du canyon de la maison. Une palette minimaliste de pierre, de plancher en bois dur et de plâtre fait écho aux qualités de la maison existante et préserve son esprit et son caractère d'origine.

Die in den Hügeln des Fryman Canyon Estates in Studio City gelegene Oakdell Residence ist eine Umgestaltung und Ergänzung eines bestehenden Hauses aus der Mitte der 1960er Jahre. Die Bauherren wünschten sich eine offene Bauweise, um die Aussicht auf die umliegende Landschaft zu maximieren. Ein mäandrierender Weg aus Betonplatten, der inmitten der Landschaftsgestaltung und des zersetzten Granits liegt, führt zum verglasten Eingangsfoyer des Hauses. Durch die vom Boden bis zur Decke reichenden Fenster und Glasschiebetüren auf der anderen Seite des Hauses erhält dieses ein Gefühl von Transparenz, lässt viel Licht herein und erweitert den Wohnbereich nach außen und in die Landschaft hinein.

Der zweistöckige Anbau besteht aus einem Hauptschlafzimmer auf der oberen Ebene und einem Büro auf der unteren Ebene, das in den Hang integriert ist und die Schluchtlage des Hauses nutzt. Eine minimalistische Palette aus Stein, Hartholzboden und Putz erinnert an die Qualitäten des bestehenden Hauses und bewahrt dessen ursprünglichen Geist und Charakter.

Ubicada en las colinas del área de Fryman Canyon Estates en Studio City, la Residencia Oakdell es una remodelación y extensión a una casa existente de 1960. Los clientes pidieron una planta abierta para maximizar las vistas del paisaje circundante. Un camino serpenteante de paneles de hormigón y granito, situado en medio del paisaje, conduce al vestíbulo de entrada acristalado de la casa. Gracias a las ventanas de suelo a techo y a las puertas corredizas de vidrio del otro lado, la vivienda da una sensación de transparencia, atrayendo luz natural y extendiendo los interiores hace el exterior y al paisaje.

El anexo de dos pisos consiste en un dormitorio principal en el nivel superior y una oficina en el nivel inferior que ha quedado integrada en la ladera. Se ha utilizado una gama minimalista de colores. El uso de la piedra, de los suelos de madera y del yeso resaltan las cualidades de la casa existente conservando el espíritu y carácter original.

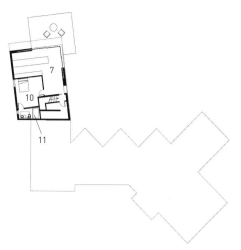

Second floor plan

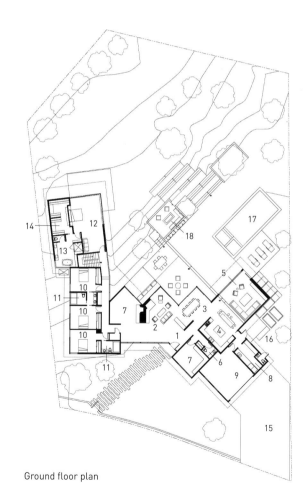

Ground floor plan

1. Entry
2. Living room
3. Dining room
4. Kitchen
5. Family room
6. Powder room
7. Den
8. Laundry room
9. Garage
10. Bedroom
11. Bathroom
12. Master bedroom
13. Master bathroom
14. Master closet
15. Driveway
16. Outdoor kitchen
17. Pool
18. Fire pit

Baumgartner + Uriu

bplusu.com

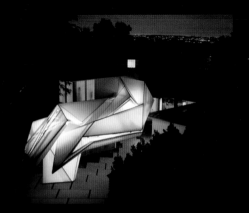

FRANK/KIM RESIDENCE

Design Team: Herwig Baumgartner, Principal; Scott Uriu, Principal; Slavko Vukic; Daniel Saltee; Philip Ramirez; and Sven Neumann

Interior Designer: Rozalynn Woods

Structural Engineer: GMS

Climate Engineer: Transsolar

Landscape Architect: EPT Design

General Contractor: HWI Construction

Canopy Contractor: Tomas Osinski

Photographer: Joshua White

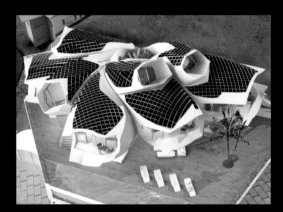

LOS ANGELES RESIDENCE

Design Team: Herwig Baumgartner, Principal; Scott Uriu, Principal; Garrett Sutherlin Santo; Shahe Gregorian; and Hseng Tai Lintner

Structural Engineer: Nous Engineering

MEP Engineer: TK1SC

Civil Engineer: Kimley Horn

Climate Engineer: Transsolar

Landscape Architect: Place

3D visualizations: B+U

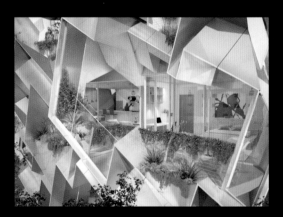

BEVERLYWOOD DEVELOPMENT

Design Team: Herwig Baumgartner, principal; Scott Uriu, Principal; Garrett Sutherlin Santo; Ke Li; Yi Ning Lui; Yiting Hsieh; Yifan Zhang; and Saragan Sinnarajahgorian

Structural Engineer: Nous Engineering

3D visualizations: B+U

Headquartered in Los Angeles, California, and established in 2000 by architects Herwig Baumgartner and Scott Uriu, Baumgartner + Uriu (B+U) are an internationally recognized and award-winning design duo operating at the forefront of contemporary design. Their design process is driven by digital techniques and advanced computation that utilizes new technologies and material resources. Baumgartner+Uriu's work consistently pushes the boundaries of architecture and urban design by experimenting with new spatial concepts, intensifying existing urban landscapes in pursuit of a visionary aesthetic that encompasses all fields of design. The architects' work has comprised cultural locations (including museums, concert halls, and exhibition spaces), educational and transportation facilities, master planning and urban design, offices and mixed-use developments, restaurants, and residential work. Baumgartner+Uriu's work has been widely published and discussed in books, magazines, and newspapers, and exhibited at leading galleries and museums worldwide.

Basé à Los Angeles, en Californie, et créé en 2000 par les architectes Herwig Baumgartner et Scott Uriu, Baumgartner + Uriu (B+U) est un duo de designers internationalement reconnu et primé qui opère à l'avant-garde du design contemporain. Leur processus de conception s'appuie sur des techniques numériques et des calculs avancés qui utilisent les nouvelles technologies et les ressources matérielles. Le travail de Baumgartner+Uriu repousse constamment les limites de l'architecture et du design urbain en expérimentant de nouveaux concepts spatiaux, en intensifiant les paysages urbains existants à la recherche d'une esthétique visionnaire qui englobe tous les domaines du design. Le travail des architectes a porté sur des lieux culturels (y compris des musées, des salles de concert et des espaces d'exposition), des établissements d'enseignement et de transport, des plans directeurs et des projets d'urbanisme, des bureaux et des aménagements à usage mixte, des restaurants et des travaux résidentiels. Le travail de Baumgartner+Uriu a été largement publié et discuté dans des livres, des magazines et des journaux, et a été exposé dans les principales galeries et musées du monde entier.

Baumgartner+Uriu (B+U) mit Sitz in Los Angeles, Kalifornien, wurde im Jahr 2000 von den Architekten Herwig Baumgartner und Scott Uriu gegründet. Baumgartner + Uriu (B+U) ist ein international anerkanntes und preisgekröntes Design-Duo, das an der Spitze des zeitgenössischen Designs steht. Ihr Designprozess wird durch digitale Techniken und fortschrittliche Berechnungen vorangetrieben, die neue Technologien und Materialressourcen nutzen. Die Arbeit von Baumgartner+Uriu überschreitet konsequent die Grenzen von Architektur und Städtebau, indem sie mit neuen Raumkonzepten experimentiert und bestehende Stadtlandschaften im Streben nach einer visionären Ästhetik, die alle Bereiche des Designs umfasst, intensiviert. Die Arbeit der Architekten umfasste kulturelle Orte (einschließlich Museen, Konzert- und Ausstellungsräume), Bildungs- und Verkehrseinrichtungen, Masterplanung und Städtebau, Büros und Mischnutzungen, Restaurants und Wohnbauten. Die Arbeit von Baumgartner+Uriu wurde in Büchern, Zeitschriften und Zeitungen veröffentlicht und diskutiert und in führenden Galerien und Museen weltweit ausgestellt.

Con sede en Los Ángeles, California desde el año 2000 y formado por los arquitectos Herwig Baumgartner y Scott Uriu, Baumgartner + Uriu (B+U) son un dúo de diseño internacionalmente reconocido y premiado que opera a la vanguardia del diseño contemporáneo. Su proceso está impulsado por técnicas digitales y computación avanzada que utiliza nuevas tecnologías y recursos materiales. El trabajo de Baumgartner+Uriu empuja consistentemente los límites de la arquitectura y el diseño urbano experimentando con nuevos conceptos espaciales, intensificando los paisajes urbanos existentes en busca de una estética visionaria que cubre todos los campos del diseño. La labor de los arquitectos ha abarcado lugares culturales (incluidos museos, salas de concierto y espacios de exposición), instalaciones educativas y de transporte, planificación general y diseño urbano, oficinas y urbanizaciones de uso mixto, restaurantes y obras residenciales. La obra de Baumgartner+Uriu se ha publicado y debatido ampliamente en libros, revistas y periódicos y se ha expuesto en las principales galerías y museos de todo el mundo.

FRANK/KIM RESIDENCE

PASADENA, CALIFORNIA

Lot size: 22,000 sq ft
Project size: 4,300 sq ft

Approaching the elongated north-oriented front of the property on the edge of a hillside, one passes by oak trees and a lush landscape. The existing two-story, single-family home reveals itself to the south-facing hillside with a large terrace and a pool overlooking San Marino.
Innovative design combined with sustainability redefines the front yard as a new space to accommodate large gatherings and form a new dynamic entrance to the house. A gazebo and a canopy, two cantilevering steel structures clad with white translucent fabric lit from the inside illuminate the garden with a soft glow during the evening. Inside the house, semi-transparent light elements connect the various rooms of the house and soften the transition between the interior and the exterior. Faithful to B+U's design philosophy to create sustainable environments, the property's redesign includes a photovoltaic roof, natural ventilation, low-VOC materials, and radiant cooling and heating.

En s'approchant de la façade nord allongée de la propriété, au bord d'une colline, on passe à côté de chênes et d'un paysage luxuriant. La maison unifamiliale de deux étages existants se révèle sur le versant sud de la colline, avec une grande terrasse et une piscine donnant sur San Marino.
Un design innovant combiné à la durabilité redéfinit la cour avant comme un nouvel espace pour accueillir de grands rassemblements et former une nouvelle entrée dynamique à la maison. Un gazebo et un auvent, deux structures en acier en porte-à-faux revêtues de tissu blanc translucide, éclairées de l'intérieur illuminent le jardin d'une douce lueur le soir. À l'intérieur de la maison, des éléments lumineux semi-transparents relient les différentes pièces de la maison et adoucissent la transition entre l'intérieur et l'extérieur. Fidèle à la philosophie de conception de B+U visant à créer des environnements durables, le réaménagement de la propriété comprend, un toit photovoltaïque, une ventilation naturelle, des matériaux à faible teneur en COV et un système de refroidissement et de chauffage par rayonnement.

Nähert man sich der langgestreckten, nach Norden ausgerichteten Front des Grundstücks am Rande eines Hügels, kommt man an Eichen und einer üppigen Landschaft vorbei. Das bestehende zweistöckige Einfamilienhaus öffnet sich zum Südhang hin mit einer großen Terrasse und einem Pool mit Blick auf San Marino.
Innovatives Design kombiniert mit Nachhaltigkeit erfindet den Vorgarten als einen neuen Raum, der große Versammlungen ermöglicht und einen neuen dynamischen Eingang zum Haus bildet. Ein Pavillon und ein Vordach, zwei freitragende Stahlkonstruktionen, die mit weißem, lichtdurchlässigem Stoff verkleidet und von innen beleuchtet sind, erhellen den Garten abends mit sanftem Licht. Im Inneren des Hauses verbinden semitransparente Lichtelemente die verschiedenen Räume und mildern den Übergang zwischen Innen und Außen. Getreu der Designphilosophie von B+U, nachhaltige Umgebungen zu schaffen, umfasst die Neugestaltung der Immobilie ein Photovoltaikdach, natürliche Belüftung, VOC-arme Materialien sowie Strahlungskühlung und -heizung.

Al acercarse al frente alargado de la propiedad orientado al norte en el borde de una ladera, uno pasa por robles y un paisaje exuberante. La casa unifamiliar de dos pisos existente aaprece en la ladera orientada al sur con una gran terraza y una piscina con vistas a San Marino.
El diseño innovador combinado con la sostenibilidad redefine el patio delantero como un nuevo espacio para acomodar grandes reuniones y configurar una nueva y dinámica entrada a la casa. Un cenador y un dosel, dos estructuras de acero en voladizo y tela blanca translúcida iluminada desde el interior iluminan el jardín con un suave resplandor durante la noche. Dentro de la casa, elementos de luz semitransparentes conectan las diferentes habitaciones, suavizando la transición entre el interior y el exterior. Fiel a la filosofía de diseño de B+U de crear ambientes sostenibles, el rediseño de la propiedad incluye un techo fotovoltaico, ventilación natural, materiales de bajo COV y refrigeración y calefacción radiante.

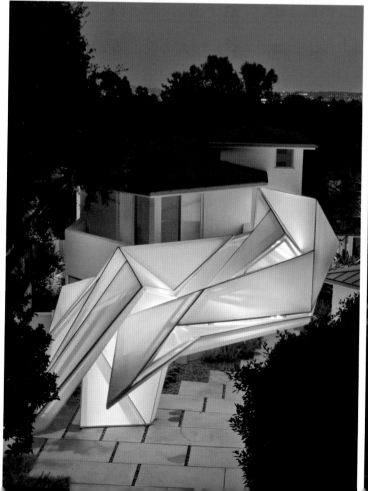
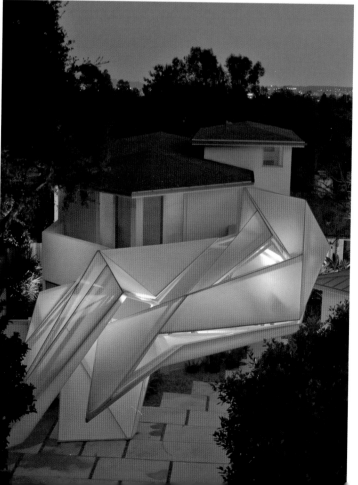

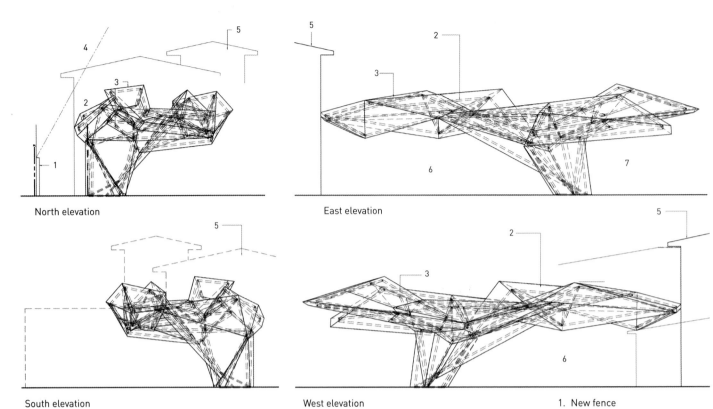

North elevation

East elevation

South elevation

West elevation

1. New fence
2. Painted new 5" steel structure
3. Translucent cladding
4. Encroachment plane
5. Outline of existing house
6. Renovated courtyard
7. Front courtyard

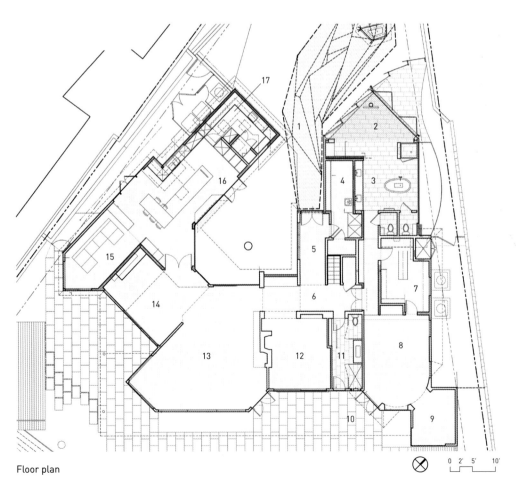

Floor plan

1. New canopy above
2. Solarium
3. New master bathroom
4. Remodeled laundry
5. Existing foyer
6. Lower hall
7. New master closet
8. Master bedroom
9. Sitting area
10. Deck
11. Remodeled bathroom
12. Existing den
13. Existing living room
14. Dining room
15. Existing family room
16. Remodeled kitchen
17. New pantry

0 2' 5' 10'

LOS ANGELES RESIDENCE

LOS ANGELES, CALIFORNIA

Lot size: 34,888 sq ft
Project size: 9,800 sq ft

The project is an iconic single-family residence located on a steep hillside property overlooking downtown Los Angeles to the Santa Monica Bay with unobstructed views. The design engages this unique site with a large plinth, grounding the house as a sculptural object. The ambition of client and architect alike was to design a California lifestyle house of the twenty-first century that would push the limits of design, materiality, structure, and sustainability. The structure builds on the design tradition of mid-century modernism with an open ground floor plan and large shaded outdoor spaces that are an extension of the living areas. Besides its formal exuberance and its cutting-edge technology, the house is also designed as a net-zero energy house, meaning all energy used by the house is produced through an integrated photovoltaic envelope that stretches across the roof. The Los Angeles Residence can be totally off the grid yet it maintains its open feel and connection to the surrounding landscape that is so pivotal for the Southern California lifestyle and climate.

Le projet est une résidence unifamiliale emblématique située sur une propriété à flanc de colline abrupte qui surplombe le centre-ville de Los Angeles jusqu'à la baie de Santa Monica, avec une vue imprenable. La conception engage ce site unique avec un grand socle, mettant la maison au sol comme un objet sculptural. L'ambition du client et de l'architecte était de concevoir une maison californienne du XXIe siècle qui repousserait les limites de la conception, de la matérialité, de la structure et de la durabilité. La structure s'appuie sur la tradition de conception du modernisme du milieu du siècle avec un plan de rez-de-chaussée ouvert et de grands espaces extérieurs ombragés qui sont une extension des espaces de vie. Outre son exubérance formelle et sa technologie de pointe, la maison est également conçue comme une maison à énergie nette zéro, ce qui signifie que toute l'énergie utilisée par la maison est produite par une enveloppe photovoltaïque intégrée qui s'étend sur le toit. La maison de Los Angeles peut être totalement hors réseau tout en conservant son aspect ouvert et son lien avec le paysage environnant qui est si important pour le mode de vie et le climat de la Californie du Sud.

Das Projekt ist eine ikonische Einfamilienresidenz auf einem Hügel mit Blick auf die Innenstadt von Los Angeles und die Santa Monica Bay. Der Entwurf greift diesen einzigartigen Ort mit einem großen Sockel auf, der das Haus als skulpturales Objekt erdet. Der Ehrgeiz von Bauherr und Architekt gleichermaßen war es, ein kalifornisches Lifestyle-Haus des 21. Jahrhunderts zu entwerfen, das die Grenzen von Design, Materialität, Struktur und Nachhaltigkeit sprengt. Die Struktur baut auf der Designtradition des Modernismus aus der Mitte des Jahrhunderts auf, mit einem offenen Grundriss im Erdgeschoss und großen schattigen Außenräumen, die eine Erweiterung der Wohnbereiche darstellen. Neben seinem formalen Überschwang und seiner Spitzentechnologie ist das Haus auch als Netto-Nullenergiehaus konzipiert, d. h. die gesamte vom Haus verbrauchte Energie wird durch eine integrierte photovoltaische Hülle erzeugt, die sich über das Dach erstreckt. Das Haus in Los Angeles kann vollständig vom Stromnetz abgeschaltet werden, behält aber dennoch seine offene Atmosphäre und Verbindung zur umgebenden Landschaft, die für den Lebensstil und das Klima in Südkalifornien so entscheidend ist.

El proyecto es una emblemática residencia unifamiliar situada en la ladera de una colina con vistas al centro de Los Ángeles y a la bahía de Santa Mónica. Este lugar único es incorporado en el diseño con un gran pedestal, que convierte la casa en un objeto escultórico. La ambición del cliente y del arquitecto era diseñar una casa de estilo de vida californiana del siglo XXI que superara los límites del diseño, la materialidad, la estructura y la sostenibilidad. La estructura se basa en la tradición de diseño del modernismo de mediados de siglo XX con una planta baja abierta y grandes espacios exteriores sombreados que son una extensión de las áreas de vivienda. Además de su exuberancia formal y su tecnología de vanguardia, la casa también está diseñada como una casa de energía neta cero, donde toda la energía utilizada por la casa se produce a través de una envoltura fotovoltaica que se extiende por todo el tejado. La casa puede estar totalmente desconectada de la red, pero mantiene su sensación de apertura y conexión con el paisaje circundante que es tan fundamental para el estilo de vida y el clima del sur de California.

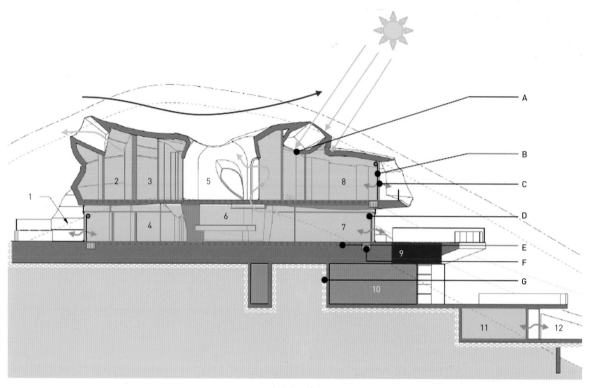

High comfort space
Unconditioned space

Comfort and energy scheme

A. Shading required for roof opening for natural ventilation at top of roof
B. Selective double glazing 50/25 front shaded/side fritted all with black-out shades
C. Motorized ventilation openings for natural ventilation
D. Internal sun and glare protection
E. Floor heating/cooling
F. Convector heating
G. Insulation

1. Natural grade
2. Guest bathroom
3. Laundry room
4. Dining area
5. Garden
6. Kitchen
7. Living area
8. Master bedroom
9. Pool
10. Garage
11. Guest house
12. Deck

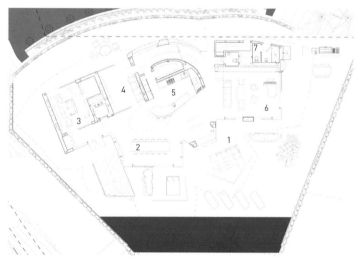

Level 1 floor plan

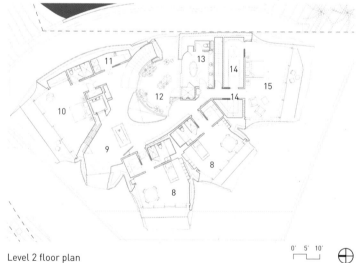

Level 2 floor plan

0' 5' 10'

1. Outdoor sitting area
2. Dining area
3. Study
4. AV room
5. Kitchen
6. Living area
7. Pool Bathroom
8. Bedroom
9. Family room
10. Guest bedroom
11. Laundry room/storage
12. Courtyard
13. Master bathroom
14. Master closet
15. Master bedroom

BEVERLYWOOD DEVELOPMENT

LOS ANGELES, CALIFORNIA

Lot size: 5,025 sq ft
Project size: 12,700 sq ft

For over a century, the model for Los Angeles housing has been one based on the California lifestyle; individual single-family residences, indoor-outdoor living, material innovations, and contemporary architecture. As the city densifies and its public transportation network expands, the lifestyle in Los Angeles has been changing. The demand for housing—especially affordable housing—has exploded as part of this densification and poses the challenge of adapting the Southern California indoor-outdoor living model from a horizontal into a vertical one. Beverlywood development is a ten-unit apartment complex that delivers a high-quality architecture with generous shared and individual outdoor spaces and a net-zero footprint. The project deploys modular manufacturing techniques that pre-fabricate and assemble parts more like a car in a factory than traditional wood/stick construction on-site. The units are assembled in the factory and trucked to the site where they are stacked and secured, ready to receive a permanent exterior enclosure.

Depuis plus d'un siècle, le modèle de logement de Los Angeles est basé sur le mode de vie californien : résidences individuelles, vie à l'intérieur et à l'extérieur, innovations matérielles et architecture contemporaine. À mesure que la ville se densifie et que son réseau de transports publics s'étend, le mode de vie à Los Angeles a changé. La demande de logements - en particulier de logements abordables - a explosé dans le cadre de cette densification et pose le défi d'adapter le modèle de vie intérieur-extérieur de la Californie du Sud, d'une configuration horizontale à une verticale. Le développement de Beverlywood est un complexe de dix appartements qui offre une architecture de haute qualité avec de généreux espaces extérieurs partagés et individuels et sans empreinte. Le projet déploie des techniques de fabrication modulaire qui préfabriquent et assemblent les pièces comme une voiture dans une usine, plutôt que de recourir à la construction traditionnelle sur place. Les unités sont assemblées dans l'usine et transportées par camion jusqu'au site où elles sont empilées et sécurisées, prêtes à recevoir une enceinte extérieure permanente.

Seit über einem Jahrhundert ist das Vorbild für den Wohnungsbau in Los Angeles ein Modell, das auf dem kalifornischen Lebensstil basiert: individuelle Einfamilienhäuser, Wohnen drinnen und draußen, Materialinnovationen und zeitgenössische Architektur. Mit der Verdichtung der Stadt und dem Ausbau des öffentlichen Verkehrsnetzes hat sich der Lebensstil in Los Angeles verändert. Die Nachfrage nach Wohnraum - vor allem bezahlbaren Wohnraum - explodierte innerhalb dieser Verdichtung und stellt sich die Herausforderung, die Indoor-Outdoor-Wohnmodell von Südkalifornien Anpassung einer horizontalen Konfiguration in eine vertikale. Bei der Beverlywood-Siedlung handelt es sich um einen Wohnkomplex mit 10 Wohneinheiten, der eine qualitativ hochwertige Architektur mit großzügigen gemeinsamen und individuellen Außenräumen und einem Netto-Fußabdruck von Null aufweist. Das Projekt entwirft Techniken der modularen Fertigung, bei denen die Stücke vorgefertigt und zusammengebaut werden, und zwar unter Verwendung des üblichen Konstruktionsbereichs. Die Einheiten werden in der Fabrik produziert und mit Lastwagen zum Standort transportiert, wo sie montiert und gesichert werden und bereit sind, eine dauerhafte Außenhülle zu werden.

Durante más de un siglo, el modelo de vivienda de Los Ángeles se ha basado en el estilo de vida californiano: residencias unifamiliares individuales, vida interior-exterior, innovaciones materiales y arquitectura contemporánea. A medida que la ciudad se densifica y su red de transporte público se expande, el estilo de vida en Los Ángeles ha ido cambiando. La demanda de viviendas, especialmente de viviendas asequibles, se ha disparado como parte de esta densificación y plantea el reto de adaptar el modelo de vida interior-exterior del sur de California, de horizontal a vertical. El desarrollo de Beverlywood es un complejo de diez apartamentos que ofrece una arquitectura de alta calidad con generosos espacios exteriores compartidos e individuales y una huella ecológica cero. El proyecto implementa técnicas de fabricación realizadas en una fábrica en vez de recurrir a una construcción tradicional. Las unidades se ensamblan en la fábrica y se transportan en camión al lugar donde se apilan y se aseguran, listas para ser acogidas por un espacio exterior permanente.

Section A

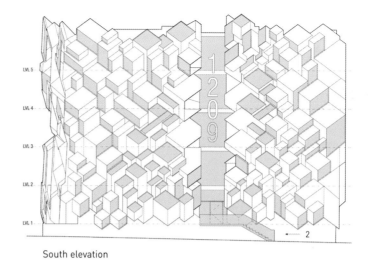

South elevation

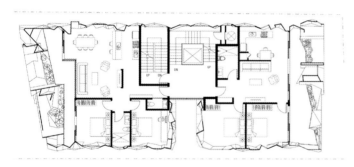

Fourth level floor plan

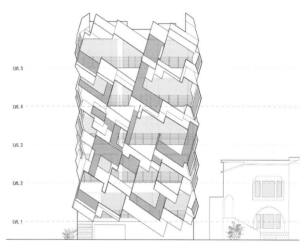

West elevation

Ground floor plan

0   5'   20'

Brookside Landscape Design

designbybrookside.com

AZURE

Design Team: Landscape Design and Decor by Brookside Landscape Design; 3D Renderings by Juan Dorta-Duque; and Graphic Design by Annie Potter

Custom Steel Work: Poc Studio

Hand Painted Concrete Pots: Momma Pots

Fire bowl: Paloform

Photographer: Emma Almendarez

HIGHLAND

Design Team: Landscape Design and Decor by Brookside Landscape Design; 3D Renderings by Juan Dorta-Duque; and Graphic Design by Annie Potter

Photographer: Emma Almendarez

PERCH PLACE

Design Team: Landscape Design and Decor by Brookside Landscape Design; 3D Renderings by Juan Dorta-Duque; and Graphic Design by Annie Potter

Custom TV Lift Console: Cabinet Tronix

Hand Painted Concrete Pots: Momma Pots

Hanging Mobile: Circle & Line Design

Photographer: Emma Almendarez

Award-winning design company, Brookside Landscape Design is based out of Carlsbad, California by Brooks and Jenny Crawford. They transform exterior spaces to be both functional and aesthetically beautiful by designing and integrating hardscape with custom-built elements, plants, and decor. Brooks is adept at designing, managing, and overseeing the whole vision to ensure it is well-executed. Jenny specializes in plant selections and décor decisions for the finishing touches to each project. A husband and wife team with complete synergy and dedication, their landscape designs transform exterior environments with the goal of encouraging homeowners to spend more time outdoors. Brookside maintains a small client workload with two to three construction projects at a time for dedication and attention to detail. They collaborate with a build team, who are licensed and experienced in the trade. Their design aesthetic is contemporary and organic with hints of culture, warmth, and coastal vibes.

Brookside Landscape Design, une société de design primée, est basée à Carlsbad, en Californie à l'initiative de Brooks et Jenny Crawford. Ils transforment les espaces extérieurs pour qu'ils soient à la fois fonctionnels et esthétiquement beaux en concevant et en intégrant un paysage avec des éléments, des plantes et un décor personnalisés. Brooks conçoit, gère et supervise l'ensemble de la vision pour s'assurer qu'elle est bien exécutée. Jenny se spécialise dans la sélection des plantes et les décisions de décoration pour la finition de chaque projet. Une équipe de mari et femme avec une synergie et un dévouement complets, leurs conceptions de paysage transforment les environnements extérieurs dans le but d'encourager les propriétaires à passer plus de temps à l'extérieur. Brookside maintient une petite charge de travail client avec deux à trois projets de construction à la fois pour le dévouement et l'attention aux détails. Ils collaborent avec une équipe de construction, agréée et expérimentée dans le métier. Leur esthétique de conception est contemporaine et organique avec des notes de culture, de chaleur et d'ambiance côtière.

Das preisgekrönte Designunternehmen Brookside Landscape Design mit Sitz in Carlsbad, Kalifornien, wird von Brooks und Jenny Crawford gegründet. Sie verwandeln Außenräume in funktionale und ästhetische Schönheit, indem sie Hardscape mit maßgeschneiderten Elementen, Pflanzen und Dekorationen entwerfen und integrieren. Brooks ist geschickt darin, die gesamte Vision zu entwerfen, zu verwalten und zu überwachen, um sicherzustellen, dass sie gut umgesetzt wird. Jenny ist spezialisiert auf Pflanzenauswahl und Dekorentscheidungen für den letzten Schliff jedes Projekts. Als Land-und-Frau-Team mit voller Synergie und Engagement verändern ihre Landschaftsdesigns die Außenumgebung mit dem Ziel, Hausbesitzer zu ermutigen, mehr Zeit im Freien zu verbringen. Brookside unterhält eine kleine Kundenbelastung mit zwei bis drei Bauprojekten gleichzeitig, um Engagement und Liebe zum Detail zu gewährleisten. Sie arbeiten mit einem Build-Team zusammen, das lizenziert und erfahren im Handel ist. Ihre Designästhetik ist zeitgemäß und organisch mit einem Hauch von Kultur, Wärme und Küstenstimmung.

Brookside Landscape Design es un galardonado estudio de diseño con sede en Carlsbad, California, dirigido por Brooks y Jenny Crawford. Transforman los espacios exteriores para que sean funcionales y estéticamente bellos, diseñando e integrando el paisaje con elementos construidos a medida, plantas y decoración. Brooks es experto en el diseño, la gestión y la supervisión general. Jenny cree plenamente en el poder del diseño exterior para elevar y transformar un espacio y un hogar. Ella se especializa en la selección de plantas y decisiones de decoración para el toque final perfecto de cada proyecto. Como equipo de marido y mujer con una completa sinergia y dedicación, sus diseños de paisajes dan a los ambientes exteriores un aspecto de acabado. Brookside mantiene una pequeña carga de trabajo de clientes con dos o tres proyectos de construcción a la vez que permite la dedicación y atención a los detalles. Colaboran con un equipo de construcción homologado, con experiencia y cumplidor. La estética de su diseño es contemporánea y moderna con toques de cultura, calidez y buen ambiente costero.

AZURE

ENCINITAS, CALIFORNIA

At Azure clients purchased a newly constructed home and had a blank pie shaped backyard and a front yard on a busy street. The front yard is enclosed with a redwood fence to keep a child and dog safely inside while offering privacy for a downstairs street-facing bedroom. The coastal property has artificial turf for low maintenance and a sunken fire bowl with concrete built-in benches outside the back patio. A thermally treated wood deck extends the usable space outside, where a teak dining table, multiple lounge areas, and a corten steel-wrapped hot tub near a wall shower create the ultimate space for entertaining and relaxing. Along one side of the property, a raised bocce ball court creates functional space out of a slope. This slope is planted with *Leucodendron* "Safari Sunset", which will grow to fence height while preserving ocean views for homeowners and neighbors. A combination of drought-tolerant succulents and grasses with a *Beaucarnea* "Gold Star" beautify the space. Three *Metrosideros excelsa* trees provide a shade canopy for the turf to enable barefoot walking on a sunny day.

Chez Azure, les clients ont acheté une maison nouvellement construite et avaient une cour arrière en forme de tarte vierge et une cour avant dans une rue animée. La cour avant est entourée d'une clôture en séquoia pour garder un enfant et un chien en sécurité tout en offrant une intimité pour une chambre à coucher située au rez-de-chaussée. La propriété dispose d'un gazon artificiel pour un entretien réduit et d'un brasero de jardin encastrée avec des bancs en béton intégrés dans le patio arrière. Une terrasse en bois traité thermiquement prolonge l'espace utilisable à l'extérieur, où une table à manger en teck, de multiples espaces de détente et un jacuzzi recouvert en acier corten près d'une douche créent l'espace ultime pour se divertir et se détendre. Le long d'un côté de la propriété, un terrain de pétanque surélevé crée un espace fonctionnel à partir d'une pente. Cette pente est plantée de *Leucodendron* « Safari Sunset », qui poussera à hauteur de clôture tout en préservant la vue sur l'océan pour les propriétaires et les voisins. Une combinaison de plantes grasses et de graminées tolérantes à la sécheresse, avec une *Beaucarnea* « Gold Star », embellissent l'espace. Trois arbres *Metrosideros excelsa* fournissent un ombrage pour le gazon afin de permettre de marcher pieds nus lors d'une journée ensoleillée.

Bei Azure kauften Kunden ein neu gebautes Haus und hatten einen leeren, kuchenförmigen Hinterhof und einen Vorgarten in einer belebten Straße. Der Vorgarten ist von einem Redwood-Zaun umgeben, um ein Kind und einen Hund auf dem Grundstück zu schützen. Der Zaun bietet auch Privatsphäre für ein Schlafzimmer im Erdgeschoss. Der Hinterhof verfügt über pflegeleichtes Kunstrasen, eine Feuerstelle und eingebaute Betonbänke. Eine wärmebehandelte Holzterrasse erweitert den nutzbaren Raum im Freien, wo ein Esstisch aus Teakholz, mehrere Sitzbereiche und ein Whirlpool aus Cortenstahl den idealen Raum für Unterhaltung und Entspannung schaffen. Entlang einer abfallenden Seite des Grundstücks schafft ein Petanque-Bereich zusätzlichen Funktionsraum. An diesem Hang wächst die *Leucodendron* „Safari Sunset" bis zur Höhe des Zauns, ohne den Blick auf den Ozean zu behindern. Eine Kombination aus dürreresistenten Gräsern und einem Exemplar von *Beaucarnea* „Gold Star" verschönert den Raum, während drei *Metrosideros excelsa* einen schattigen Baldachin für den Rasen bieten, der sich ideal zum Barfußlaufen an einem sonnigen Tag eignet.

En el proyecto Azure, los clientes compraron una casa recién construida con un patio trasero y otro en la parte delantera junto a una calle muy transitada. El patio delantero está cerrado con una valla de madera de secoya para mantener seguros a un niño y un perro en la propiedad. La valla ofrece, además, privacidad para un dormitorio en la planta baja. El patio trasero tiene césped artificial de bajo mantenimiento, un brasero y bancos empotrados de hormigón. Una tarima de madera tratada térmicamente amplía el espacio utilizable en el exterior, donde una mesa de comedor de teca, múltiples áreas de descanso y una bañera de hidromasaje acabada en acero corten crean el espacio ideal para el entretenimiento y la relajación. A lo largo de un lado inclinado de la propiedad, una zona de petanca crea un espacio funcional adicional. En esta pendiente, *Leucodendron* «Safari Sunset» crecerá hasta alcanzar la altura de la valla sin obstruir las vistas hacia el océano. Una combinación de hierbas resistentes a la sequía, combinadas con un ejemplar de *Beaucarnea* «Gold Star», embellecen el espacio, mientras tres *Metrosideros excelsa* proporcionan un dosel de sombra para el césped, ideal para caminar descalzo en un día soleado.

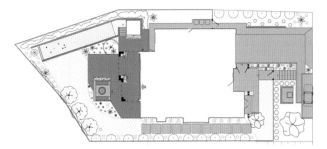

Hardscape plan

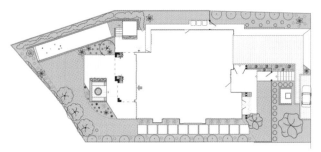

Vegetation plan

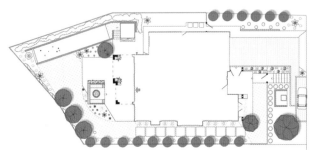

Trees plan

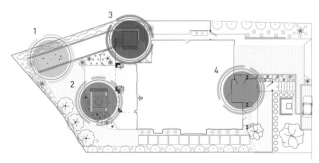

Program elements plan

1. Outdoor yard games
2. Built-in fire pit and bench
3. Above ground spa
4. Accentuated entrance

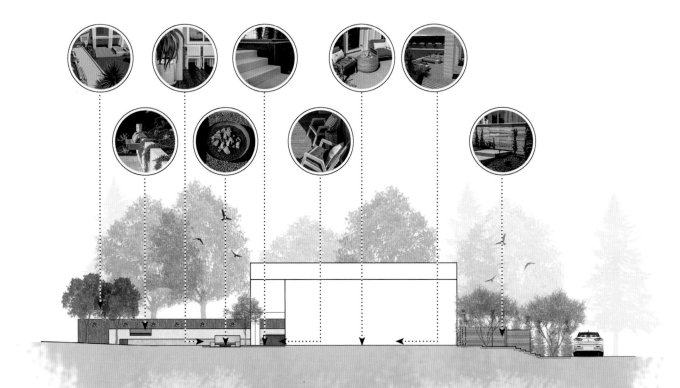

Section

HIGHLAND

CARLSBAD, CALIFORNIA

Lot size: 10,019 sq ft
Project size: 7,500 sq ft

The Highland project began when the owners wanted to create usable out-door space despite a challenging existing backyard slope with a change in elevation of over twenty feet. The primary objective was to make the bottom part of the property accessible to family members and visitors. The owners desired plenty of areas to lounge and needed a location to place an all-natural cedar tub for evening soaks. An outdoor shower, heating sources to extend the enjoyment of the spaces into brisk evenings, and a sports court for family games were included in the design. The home-owners insisted on a low maintenance plant scheme. The property had existing *Nasella tenuissima* grass, Agave *attenuata*, and a Jacaranda *mimo-sifolia* tree, which were left in place to keep the budget in check. *Pandorea jasminiodes* "Alba" was added to the bottom Cedar posts and cables to create a flowering shade canopy. Ipe decking, soldier fencing, and a patio out of Porphyry flagstone were used to tie everything together.

Le projet Highland a débuté lorsque les propriétaires ont voulu créer un espace extérieur utilisable malgré une pente de cour existante difficile avec un changement d'élévation de plus de vingt pieds. L'objectif premier était de rendre la partie inférieure de la propriété accessible aux membres de la famille et aux visiteurs. Les propriétaires souhaitaient disposer de nombreux espaces pour se détendre et avaient besoin d'un endroit où placer une baignoire en cèdre entièrement naturelle pour les bains du soir. Une douche extérieure, des sources de chauffage pour prolonger le plaisir des espaces dans les soirées animées, et un terrain de sport pour les jeux familiaux ont été inclus dans la conception. Les propriétaires ont insisté pour que les installations ne nécessitent que peu d'entretien. La propriété possédait de l'herbe *Nasella tenuissima*, de l'agave *attenuata* et un arbre Jacaranda *mimosifolia*, qui ont été laissés en place pour contrôler le budget. *Pandorea jasminiodes* « Alba » a été ajouté aux poteaux et câbles de cèdre inférieurs pour créer un auvent fleuri. Une terrasse en Ipe, une clôture de soldat et un patio en dalle de porphyre ont été utilisés pour tout lier.

Das Highland-Projekt begann, als die Eigentümer trotz eines herausfor-dernden bestehenden Hinterhofhangs mit einem Niveauunterschied von über sechs Metern einen nutzbaren Außenraum schaffen wollten. Das pri-märe Ziel war es, den unteren Teil des Grundstücks für Familienmitglieder und Besucher zugänglich zu machen. Die Eigentümer wünschten sich viele Aufenthaltsbereiche und brauchten einen Ort, an dem sie eine ganz natür-liche Zedernwanne für abendliche Erfrischungen platzieren konnten. Eine Außendusche, Heizquellen, um die Freude an den Räumen auf rege Abende auszudehnen, und ein Sportplatz für Familienspiele wurden in den Entwurf einbezogen. Die Hausbesitzer bestanden auf einem wartungsarmen Anla-genkonzept. Das Anwesen hatte *Nasella tenuissima*-Gras, Agave *attenuata* und einen Jacaranda *mimosifolia*-Baum, die zur Kontrolle des Budgets an Ort und Stelle belassen wurden. *Pandorea jasminiodes* „Alba" wurde an den unteren Zedernpfosten und Kabeln angebracht, um einen blumigen Balda-chin zu schaffen. Eine Ipe-Terrasse, ein Soldatenzaun und eine Porphyr-platte wurden verwendet, um alles zusammenzubinden.

El proyecto Highland comenzó cuando los propietarios pretendían crear un espacio exterior utilizable a pesar de una desafiante pendiente en el patio trasero con un cambio en la elevación de más de 6 m. El objetivo principal era conseguir que la parte inferior de la propiedad fuera acce-sible a los miembros de la familia y a los visitantes. Los dueños deseaban tener varias áreas para descansar y necesitaban un lugar para colocar una bañera de cedro natural con hidromasaje para los baños nocturnos. Se incluyeron en el proyecto una ducha exterior, fuentes de calefacción para extender el disfrute de los espacios durante las tardes y una pis-ta de deportes para juegos familiares. Los propietarios insistieron en un esquema de plantas de bajo mantenimiento. La propiedad original tenía césped *Nasella tenuissima* y un árbol de Jacarandá *mimosifolia*, que se mantuvieron para controlar el presupuesto. Se añadió una *Pandorea jas-miniodes* «Alba» a los postes y cables de cedro de la parte inferior para crear un dosel de sombra en forma de flor. El entarimado de madera Ipé, la valla y un patio se usaron para conectar todo el conjunto.

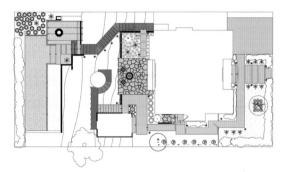

Hardscape

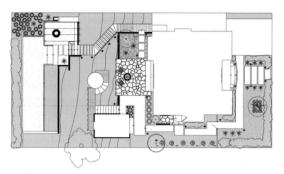

Vegetation

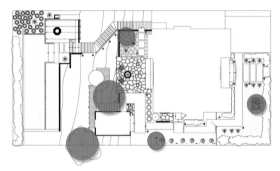

Trees

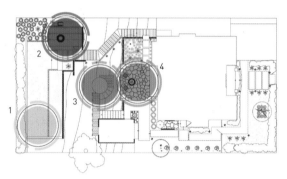

Elements

1. Outdoor yard games
2. Built-in fire pit and bar
3. Above ground spa
4. Built-in fire pit adjacent to interior

Section

PERCH PLACE

ENCINITAS, CALIFORNIA

Lot size: 24,393 sq ft
Project size: 3,500 sq ft

At Perch Place, clients wanted to maximize outdoor canyon views while providing family members of different ages a variety of outdoor recreational activities. A ping pong table, miniature golf, and outdoor shower were added to the expansive terrace. An elevated hot tub provides natural views and is within viewing range of an outdoor television enclosed in an automated and fully rotating lift cabinet system. Thermally treated decking surrounds the hot tub to allow the family to sit or lay in the sun. Comfortable sofa and swivel chairs surround a board-formed concrete fire pit that keeps the family warm while enjoying evening televised sports. Custom hand-painted concrete pots were added throughout and planted with Dracaena *reflexa* for visual interest. A statement Dracaena *marginata* was added near the hot tub and underplanted with Liriope *spicata* "Silver Dragon". Podocarpus *henkelii* provides a privacy screen and the fire pit area has low maintenance succulents combined with Festuca *glauca*. Belgard non-slip porcelain tile flooring was chosen to reduce annual maintenance and provide an easy to clean surface.

Chez Perch Place, les clients voulaient maximiser les vues extérieures tout en offrant aux membres de la famille de différents âges une variété d'activités de loisirs en plein air. Une table de ping-pong, un golf miniature et une douche extérieure ont été ajoutés à la grande terrasse. Un bain à remous surélevé offre une vue sur le paysage et se trouve à portée de vue d'un téléviseur. Une terrasse en bois entoure la baignoire pour permettre à la famille de s'asseoir ou de s'allonger au soleil. Des canapés confortables et des chaises pivotantes entourent un foyer qui réchauffe la famille tout en profitant des sports télévisés. Des pots peints à la main et des plantes Pléomele ont été ajoutés pour les rendre plus attractifs. Un Dracaena *marginata* a été ajouté près du bain à remous et planté à côté d'un Liriope *spicata* Silver. Podocarpus *henkelii*, combiné avec Festuca *glauca*, fournit un écran de confidentialité dans une zone qui nécessite peu d'entretien. Un sol en porcelaine antidérapant Belgard a été choisi pour réduire l'entretien annuel et fournir une surface facile à nettoyer.

Am Perch Place wollten die Kunden den Blick ins Freie maximieren und gleichzeitig Familienmitgliedern unterschiedlichen Alters eine Vielzahl von Freizeitaktivitäten im Freien anbieten. Eine Tischtennisplatte, Minigolf und eine Außendusche wurden auf der geräumigen Terrasse hinzugefügt. Ein erhöhter Whirlpool bietet Blick auf die Landschaft und befindet sich im Sichtbereich eines Fernsehers, der in einem automatisierten Aufzugsschrank untergebracht ist. Eine wärmebehandelte Abdeckung umgibt den Whirlpool, damit die Familie in der Sonne sitzen oder liegen kann. Bequeme Sofas und Drehstühle umgeben eine Feuerstelle aus Beton, die die Familie wärmt, während sie im Fernsehen Sport treiben. Handbemalte Töpfe und Pléomele-Pflanzen wurden hinzugefügt, um sie attraktiver zu machen. Eine Dracaena *marginata* wurde in der Nähe des Whirlpools hinzugefügt und neben einem Liriope *spicata* „Silver Dragon" gepflanzt. Podocarpus *henkelii* bietet in Kombination mit Festuca *glauca* einen Sichtschutz in einem wartungsarmen Bereich. Ein rutschfester Belgard-Porzellanboden wurde ausgewählt, um die jährliche Wartung zu reduzieren und eine leicht zu reinigende Oberfläche bereitzustellen.

En Perch Place, los clientes querían maximizar las vistas al exterior y al mismo tiempo ofrecer a los miembros de una familia de diferentes edades una variedad de actividades recreativas al aire libre. Una mesa de ping pong, un minigolf y una ducha exterior se añadieron a la amplia terraza. Una bañera de hidromasaje elevada proporciona vistas al paisaje y se encuentra dentro del rango de visión de un televisor. Una tarima de madera envuelve la bañera para permitir a la familia sentarse o tumbarse al sol. Cómodos sofás y sillas giratorias rodean un brasero que calienta a la familia mientras disfruta de los deportes televisados. Se añadieron macetas pintadas a mano y plantas *Pléomele* para que resultaran más atractivas. Una *Dracaena marginata* fue añadida cerca de la bañera de hidromasaje y plantada junto a un Liriope *spicata* Silver. El *Podocarpus henkelii*, combinado con *Blue Festuca* proporcionan una pantalla de privacidad en una zona que requiere poco mantenimiento. Se eligió un suelo de porcelana antideslizante Belgard para reducir el mantenimiento anual y proporcionar una superficie fácil de limpiar.

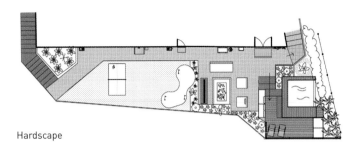

Hardscape

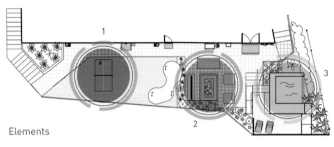

Elements

1. Outdoor yard games
2. Built-in fire pit
3. Above ground spa

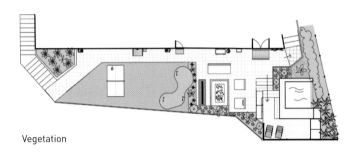

Vegetation

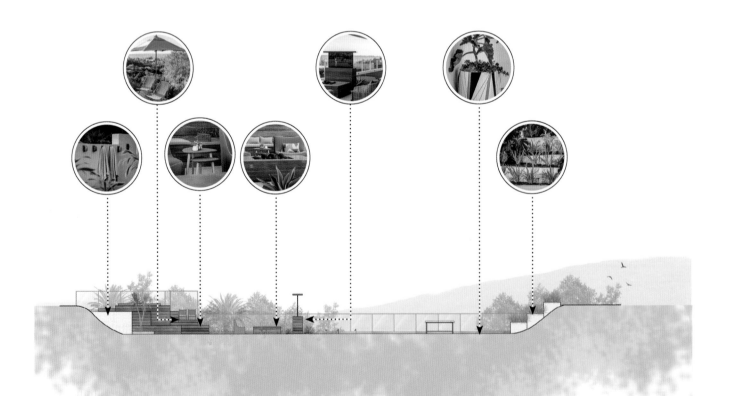

Section

HEALDSBURG COMPOUND

Landscape Architect: Lucas+Lucas
Landscape Architecture

General Contractor: Robinwood Construction

Photographer: Cesar Rubio

HILLTOP ESTATE

Landscape Architect: Roche + Roche
Landscape Architecture

General Contractor: Landers Curry, Inc.

Photographer: Bart Edson and Marion Brenner

MODERN FARMHOUSE

Design Team: CahillStudio with John David Rulon

Interior Design: Fairacres Studio

General Contractor: Landers Curry, Inc.

Photographer: Cesar Rubio

Principal Chris Cahill

Modern in concept and detail, CahillStudio's work is known for its fresh interpretations of vernacular traditions in Northern California wine country. With 30 years of professional practice in the San Francisco Bay Area, the firm specializes in custom-designed, multi-building residences rooted in authenticity. CahillStudio's work is enduringly appropriate for the natural environment and site. Each project presents a singular opportunity for innovative design that is site-responsive and derived from a highly collaborative process. The essential character of a specific place—defined by its natural habitat, topography, light exposure, and views—is the inspiration for every CahillStudio project.

Moderne dans le concept et les détails, le travail de CahillStudio est connu pour ses interprétations fraîches des traditions vernaculaires dans la région viticole du nord de la Californie. Avec 30 ans de pratique professionnelle dans la région de la baie de San Francisco, le cabinet se spécialise dans les résidences multi-bâtiments conçues sur mesure et ancrées dans l'authenticité. Le travail de CahillStudio est toujours approprié pour l'environnement naturel et le site. Chaque projet présente une occasion unique pour une conception innovante, adaptée au site et issue d'un processus hautement collaboratif. Le caractère essentiel d'un lieu spécifique - défini par son habitat naturel, sa topographie, son exposition à la lumière et ses vues - est l'inspiration de chaque projet CahillStudio.

CahillStudios Werk ist in Konzept und Detail modern und bekannt für seine frischen Interpretationen der einheimischen Traditionen im nordkalifornischen Weinland. Mit 30 Jahren Berufserfahrung in der San Francisco Bay Area ist das Unternehmen auf maßgeschneiderte Mehrfamilienhäuser spezialisiert, die auf Authentizität basieren. Die Arbeit von CahillStudio ist dauerhaft für die natürliche Umgebung und den Standort geeignet. Jedes Projekt bietet eine einzigartige Gelegenheit für innovatives Design, das auf den Standort reagiert und aus einem äußerst kollaborativen Prozess abgeleitet wird. Der wesentliche Charakter eines bestimmten Ortes - definiert durch seinen natürlichen Lebensraum, seine Topographie, seine Belichtung und seine Aussicht - ist die Inspiration für jedes CahillStudio-Projekt.

Moderno en concepto y detalle, el trabajo de CahillStudio es conocido por sus nuevas interpretaciones de las tradiciones vernáculas de la región vinícola del norte de California. Con 30 años de práctica profesional en el área de la bahía de San Francisco, el estudio se especializa en residencias de edificios múltiples diseñadas a medida y arraigadas en la autenticidad. El trabajo de CahillStudio es duraderamente apropiado para el entorno natural y el lugar. Cada proyecto presenta una oportunidad única para un diseño innovador que responde al lugar y se deriva de un proceso altamente colaborativo. El carácter esencial de un lugar específico —definido por su hábitat natural, topografía, exposición a la luz y vistas— es la inspiración para cada proyecto de CahillStudio.

HEALDSBURG COMPOUND

HEALDSBURG, CALIFORNIA

Lot size: 10 acres
Project size: 11,700 sq ft

This expansive hillside property includes two single-story residences, a studio tower with formal wine cellar, and multiple outdoor living areas, forming a unified compound for one family's three generations. The owners' initial vision for the property was a traditional farmhouse design. However, the site's steep slope required a non-traditional approach that considered grade, sun, wind patterns, and views. Considerable level ground was needed to site the buildings and pool to the best advantage, which was achieved through terracing. CahillStudio's design solution employed simplified, linear forms and generously proportioned volumes. Cross-views connect to year-round patios, comingling interior/exterior space. The design firm collaborated closely with Lucas & Lucas Landscape Architecture from the outset, ensuring a thoroughly integrated approach to the master planning process.

Cette vaste propriété à flanc de colline comprend deux résidences de plein-pied, une tour de studios avec une cave à vin formelle, et de multiples espaces de vie extérieurs, formant un ensemble unifié pour les trois générations d'une même famille. La vision initiale des propriétaires pour la propriété était une conception traditionnelle de ferme. Cependant, la pente abrupte du site nécessitait une approche non traditionnelle qui tenait compte de la pente, du soleil, des vents et des vues. Un terrain considérablement plat était nécessaire pour placer les bâtiments et la piscine de façon optimale, ce qui a été réalisé grâce à des terrasses. La solution de conception de CahillStudio a utilisé des formes linéaires simplifiées et des volumes généreusement proportionnés. Les vues croisées sont reliées à des patios ouverts toute l'année, mêlant l'espace intérieur et extérieur. Le cabinet de design a collaboré étroitement avec Lucas & Lucas Landscape Architecture dès le début, garantissant une approche totalement intégrée du processus de planification générale.

Dieses ausgedehnte Anwesen in Hanglage umfasst zwei einstöckige Wohnhäuser, einen Atelierturm mit formellem Weinkeller und mehrere Wohnbereiche im Freien, die einen einheitlichen Komplex für die drei Generationen einer Familie bilden. Die ursprüngliche Vision der Eigentümer für das Anwesen war ein traditionelles Bauernhausdesign. Der steile Hang des Grundstücks erforderte jedoch einen nicht traditionellen Ansatz, der Neigung, Sonne, Windverhältnisse und Ausblicke berücksichtigte. Um die Gebäude und den Pool bestmöglich zu lokalisieren, war ein sehr flaches Gelände erforderlich, was durch Terrassen erreicht wurde. Die Designlösung von CahillStudio verwendete vereinfachte, lineare Formen und großzügig proportionierte Volumen. Queransichten verbinden sich mit ganzjährig nutzbaren Innenhöfen, die Innen- und Außenräume miteinander vernetzen. Das Designbüro arbeitete von Anfang an eng mit Lucas & Lucas Landscape Architecture zusammen, wodurch ein gründlich integrierter Ansatz für den Masterplanungsprozess gewährleistet wurde.

Esta amplia propiedad situada en la ladera de un monte, incluye dos viviendas de un solo piso, un estudio ubicado en una torre, una bodega y varias zonas al aire libre, formando un conjunto unificado para las tres generaciones de una familia. La visión inicial de los propietarios consistió en un diseño basado en la idea de granja tradicional. Sin embargo, la fuerte pendiente del terreno requería de un enfoque no tradicional que considerara dicha pendiente, el sol, los patrones de viento y las vistas. Se necesitaba un terreno considerablemente llano para ubicar los edificios y la piscina de la mejor manera, lo que se logró mediante terrazas. La solución de diseño de CahillStudio empleó formas lineales simplificadas y volúmenes generosamente proporcionados. Las vistas cruzadas se conectan a los patios durante todo el año, mezclando el espacio interior y exterior. La empresa de diseño colaboró estrechamente con Lucas & Lucas Landscape Architecture desde el principio, asegurando un enfoque completamente integrado en el proceso de planificación.

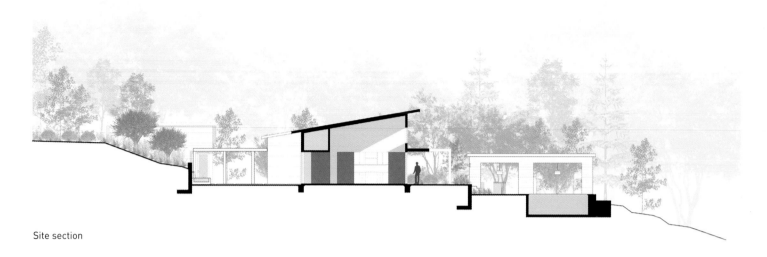

Site section

Site plan

1. Entry	5. Pantry	9. Breezeway	13. Second dwelling
2. Living area	6. Exercise room	10. Pavilion	14. Guest house
3. Dining area	7. Study/office	11. Pool	15. Tower
4. Kitchen	8. Bedroom	12. Terrace/patio	16. Bocce ball

HILLTOP ESTATE

SONOMA, CALIFORNIA

Project size: 19 acres
Project size: 8,000 sq ft

From a steep perch on wooded acreage, this 8,000 square-foot compound is energy self-sufficient and sited to maximize its 360-degree views of Sonoma Valley and the San Francisco skyline. Site challenges included limited access to level ground and a priority to preserve the oak woodlands. To achieve the single-level main house the owners desired, including year-round outdoor living rooms, CahillStudio worked closely with the landscape architect from the outset to tuck the buildings into the rugged, vertical site. The aesthetic feel is rural-contemporary, expressed through spare geometry and a material palette including stone, cedar, concrete, and glass expanses. Our design strategy for the primary residence varied spatial volumes and ceiling height to visually distinguish larger communal spaces from secondary ones throughout the house.

D'un perchoir escarpé sur un terrain boisé, ce complexe d'environ 745 mètres carrés est autosuffisant sur le plan énergétique et situé de manière à maximiser sa vue à 360 degrés de la vallée de Sonoma et de la ligne d'horizon de San Francisco. Les défis du site comprennent un accès limité à un terrain plat et la priorité de préserver les bois de chênes. Pour réaliser la maison principale à un seul niveau que les propriétaires souhaitaient, y compris des salons extérieurs toute l'année, CahillStudio a travaillé en étroite collaboration avec l'architecte paysagiste dès le début pour intégrer les bâtiments dans le site vertical et accidenté. L'aspect esthétique est rural-contemporain, exprimé par une géométrie libre et une palette de matériaux comprenant des étendues de pierre, de cèdre, de béton et de verre. Notre stratégie de conception pour la résidence principale a varié les volumes spatiaux et la hauteur des plafonds afin de distinguer visuellement les grands espaces communs des espaces secondaires dans toute la maison.

Von einem schroffen Barsch auf einem bewaldeten Grundstück aus ist dieses ca. 745 Quadratmeter große Resort energieautark und befindet sich so, dass der 360-Grad-Blick auf das Sonoma Valley und die Skyline von San Francisco maximiert wird. Zu den Herausforderungen des Standorts zählen der eingeschränkte Zugang zu flachem Land und die Priorität der Erhaltung von Eichenwäldern. Um das einstöckige Haupthaus zu erreichen, das die Eigentümer wollten, einschließlich ganzjähriger Wohnzimmer im Freien, arbeitete CahillStudio von Anfang an eng mit dem Landschaftsarchitekten zusammen, um die Gebäude in das vertikale und raue Gelände zu integrieren. Der ästhetische Reiz ist ländlich-zeitgemäß, ausgedrückt durch freie Geometrie und eine Palette von Materialien, einschließlich Flächen aus Stein, Zeder, Beton und Glas. Unsere Entwurfsstrategie für den Hauptwohnsitz variierte das räumliche Volumen und die Höhe der Decken, um die großen Gemeinschaftsräume visuell von den Nebenräumen im gesamten Haus zu unterscheiden.

Situada en una superficie boscosa en altura, este complejo de 750 m², con vistas de 360 grados al Valle de Sonoma y el horizonte de San Francisco, es energéticamente autosuficiente. Los desafíos del proyecto incluían el acceso limitado a un terreno plano y la prioridad de preservar los bosques de robles. Para lograr la casa de un solo nivel que deseaban los propietarios, incluyendo salas de estar al aire libre durante todo el año, CahillStudio trabajó estrechamente con el arquitecto paisajista desde el principio para arraigar los edificios en el terreno escarpado y vertical. La sensación estética es de estilo rural-contemporáneo, expresada a través de una geometría sobria y una paleta de materiales que incluye piedra, cedro, hormigón y cristal. Nuestra estrategia de diseño para la vivienda principal hizo que variaran los volúmenes espaciales y la altura del techo para distinguir visualmente los espacios comunes más grandes de los secundarios.

Site section

Site plan

1. Entry	6. Family room	11. Auto court
2. Living area	7. Study/office	12. Game room
3. Dining area	8. Bedroom	13. Guest house
4. Kitchen	9. Car barn	14. Pool
5. Pantry	10. Exercise room	15. Terrace/patio

Situated between Sonoma and Napa Valleys, this residence sits quietly within its natural surroundings. Our design strategy, rooted in traditional farmhouse design, considered an existing barn and rustic cottage the owners wished to retain. However, CahillStudio reinterpreted tradition, most notably with a plan comprising three distinct wings unified under a single gabled roofline. Recurring throughout the house, clerestory windows, which mirror the gable roof form, and large glass cupolas cut into the ceilings to amplify natural light. Oversized windows and expansive door openings dissolve spatial boundaries. Terraces connect the buildings to the site, and a refined car barn breezeway connects the main home to the guesthouse and pool area under a single roof-scape.

Située entre les vallées de Sonoma et de Napa, cette résidence se trouve au calme dans son environnement naturel. Notre stratégie de conception, ancrée dans la conception des fermes traditionnelles, a pris en compte une grange existante et un cottage rustique que les propriétaires souhaitaient conserver. Cependant, CahillStudio a réinterprété la tradition, notamment avec un plan comprenant trois ailes distinctes réunies sous une seule ligne de toit à pignon. Récurrentes dans toute la maison, les fenêtres à claire-voie, qui reflètent la forme du toit à pignon, et les grandes coupoles en verre découpent les plafonds pour amplifier la lumière naturelle. Des fenêtres surdimensionnées et de larges ouvertures de portes dissolvent les limites spatiales. Des terrasses relient les bâtiments au site et un passage couvert bien raffiné pour les voitures relient la maison principale à la maison d'hôtes et à la piscine sous un seul toit.

Zwischen den Tälern von Sonoma und Napa gelegen, liegt diese Residenz ruhig in ihrer natürlichen Umgebung. Unsere Entwurfsstrategie, die im traditionellen Bauernhausdesign verwurzelt ist, berücksichtigte eine bestehende Scheune und ein rustikales Häuschen, die die Eigentümer beibehalten wollten. CahillStudio interpretierte die Tradition jedoch mit einem Plan neu, der drei verschiedene Flügel umfasst, die unter einem einzigen Satteldach vereint sind. Im ganzen Haus wiederkehrende Fenster, die die Form des Satteldachs widerspiegeln, und große Glaskuppeln zieren die Decken, um das natürliche Licht zu verstärken. Große Fenster und breite Türöffnungen lösen die räumlichen Grenzen auf. Terrassen verbinden die Gebäude mit dem Gelände, und ein raffinierter Fahrzeugschuppen verbindet das Haupthaus mit dem Gästehaus und dem Poolbereich unter einem Dach.

Situada entre los valles de Sonoma y Napa, esta residencia se adapta tranquilamente a su entorno natural. Nuestro concepto, enraizado en el diseño tradicional de casa de campo, consideraba un granero existente y una casa de campo rústica que los propietarios deseaban conservar. Sin embargo, CahillStudio reinterpretó la tradición con un plan que comprende tres alas distintas unificadas bajo un solo techo a dos aguas. Recurrentes en toda la casa, ventanas de triforio, que reflejan la forma del techo a dos aguas, y grandes cúpulas de vidrio recortan los techos para amplificar la luz natural. Grandes ventanales y amplias aperturas de puerta disuelven los límites espaciales. Las terrazas conectan los edificios con el sitio, y un refinado cobertizo para vehículos conecta la casa principal con la casa de huéspedes y el área de la piscina bajo un solo tejado.

Site plan

1. Entry
2. Great room
3. Kitchen
4. Dining area
5. Pantry
6. Living area
7. Bedroom
8. Carport
9. Guest house
10. Pool
11. Terrace
12. Barn/loft

Conner + Perry Architects

conner-perry.com

RUSTIC CANYON RESIDENCE

Executive Architect: Conner + Perry
Architects

Concept Architect: Nicholson Architects

Interior Designer: Merrell Design Co
and Olivia Williams Interior Design

Structural Engineer: Peter T. Erdelyi
& Associates,

Landscape Design:
Landscape Workspace

General Contractor: RAM Development
& Construction Company, and
Dick Minium Construction

Photographer: Taiyo Watanabe

Conner + Perry Architects specialize in modern, organic architecture: modern in the context of a design that is timeless, enduring, and unique while avoiding historic reference or stylistic trends; organic, in the philosophy described by Louis Sullivan, Frank Lloyd Wright, and John Lautner rather than in the aesthetic associated with digital form-making. It is a way of practicing that relies heavily on the power of the individual imagination to coalesce a singular structural and spatial solution to the complex calculus of the program and uses of buildings, the constraints and opportunities that sites present, and the unique desires of clients and/or end-users. In its purest form, organic architecture is natural in all that word connotes. Conner + Perry Architects look at human beings as an integral part of architecture's ecology, not separate from it, and as such, buildings are conceived as a means to connect us to our natural surroundings. Form and structure grow instinctively outward from a core concept, details and assemblies reflect the essence of their physical materiality, and boundaries between interior and exterior become blurred.

Conner + Perry Architects sont spécialisés dans l'architecture moderne et organique : moderne dans le contexte d'un design intemporel, durable et unique tout en évitant les références historiques ou les tendances stylistiques ; organique, dans la philosophie décrite par Louis Sullivan, Frank Lloyd Wright et John Lautner plutôt que dans l'esthétique associée à la création de formes numériques. C'est une façon de pratiquer qui s'appuie fortement sur le pouvoir de l'imagination individuelle pour fusionner une solution structurelle et spatiale singulière au calcul complexe du programme et des utilisations des bâtiments, aux contraintes et aux opportunités que les sites présentent, et aux désirs uniques des clients et/ou des utilisateurs finaux. Dans sa forme la plus pure, l'architecture organique est naturelle dans tout ce que le mot évoque. Les architectes Conner + Perry considèrent les êtres humains comme faisant partie intégrante de l'écologie de l'architecture, et non pas comme en étant séparés, et à ce titre, les bâtiments sont conçus comme un moyen de nous relier à notre environnement naturel. La forme et la structure se développent instinctivement vers l'extérieur à partir d'un concept central, les détails et les assemblages reflètent l'essence de leur matérialité physique, et les frontières entre l'intérieur et l'extérieur deviennent floues.

Conner + Perry Architects haben sich auf moderne, organische Architektur spezialisiert: modern im Kontext eines zeitlosen, beständigen und einzigartigen Designs unter Vermeidung historischer Referenzen oder stilistischer Trends; organisch in der von Louis Sullivan, Frank Lloyd Wright und John Lautner beschriebenen Philosophie und nicht in der Ästhetik, die mit der digitalen Formgebung assoziiert wird. Es handelt sich um eine Art der Praxis, die sich stark auf die individuelle Vorstellungskraft stützt, um eine einzigartige strukturelle und räumliche Lösung für das komplexe Kalkül des Programms und die Nutzung von Gebäuden zu schaffen und die Zwänge und Möglichkeiten, die die Standorte kennzeichnen, und die individuellen Wünsche der Kunden und/oder Endnutzer zusammenzuführen. In ihrer reinsten Form ist organische Architektur in allem, was das Wort bedeutet, natürlich. Conner + Perry Architects betrachten den Menschen als integralen Bestandteil der Ökologie der Architektur und nicht getrennt von ihr, und als solcher sind Gebäude als Mittel konzipiert, um uns mit unserer natürlichen Umgebung zu verbinden. Form und Struktur wachsen instinktiv von einem Kernkonzept nach außen, Details und Baugruppen spiegeln die Essenz ihrer physischen Materialität wider, und die Grenzen zwischen Innen und Außen verschwimmen.

Conner + Perry Architects se especializan en arquitectura moderna y orgánica: moderna en el contexto de un diseño que es intemporal, duradero y único, evitando las referencias históricas o las tendencias estilísticas; orgánica, en la filosofía descrita por Louis Sullivan, Frank Lloyd Wright y John Lautner más que en la estética asociada con la creación de formas digitales. Es una forma de practicar que se basa en gran medida en el poder de la imaginación individual para unir una solución estructural y espacial singular al complejo cálculo del programa y los usos de los edificios, las limitaciones y oportunidades que presentan los lugares y los deseos únicos de los clientes y/o usuarios finales. En su forma más pura, la arquitectura orgánica es natural en todo lo que esa palabra conlleva. Los arquitectos de Conner + Perry miran a los seres humanos como una parte integral de la ecología de la arquitectura, no separada de ella, y como tal, los edificios se conciben como un medio para conectarnos con nuestro entorno natural. La forma y la estructura crecen instintivamente hacia el exterior a partir de un concepto central. Los detalles y los ensamblajes reflejan la esencia de su materialidad física, y los límites entre el interior y el exterior se vuelven borrosos.

RUSTIC CANYON RESIDENCE

PACIFIC PALISADES, CALIFORNIA

The Rustic Canyon Residence strives to honor its site's history and natural splendor, to maintain a connection to the outdoors, and to feature the client's extensive art collection while providing an elegant yet informal space for a growing family to thrive. The plan is organized around three gardens: an atrium garden featuring two protected California live oaks, around which smaller private rooms are arranged and a double-height glazed stairwell rises; a pool courtyard that parallels the circulation of the house; and the rear garden that connects a deck and outdoor dining area to the canyon views beyond.

The natural copper and other materials, such as concrete, corten steel, limestone, charred Douglas fir, oiled oak, and weathered brass were chosen for their compatibility with the local environment and their ability to age in place, harmonizing with the surroundings over time. Site-specific landscape comprised of existing mature specimens, and primarily California native and drought-tolerant plantings.

La Rustic Canyon Residence s'efforce d'honorer l'histoire et la splendeur naturelle de son site, de maintenir un lien avec l'extérieur et de mettre en valeur la vaste collection d'art du client, tout en offrant un espace élégant mais informel, pour permettre à une famille grandissante de s'épanouir. Le plan s'articule autour de trois jardins : un jardin en atrium avec deux chênes de Californie protégés, autour duquel sont disposées des pièces privées plus petites et s'élève un escalier à garde-corps en verre ; une cour de piscine parallèle à la circulation de la maison ; et le jardin arrière qui relie une terrasse et une salle à manger extérieure avec vues sur le canyon.

Le cuivre naturel et d'autres matériaux, tels que le béton, l'acier corten, la pierre calcaire, le sapin Douglas carbonisé, le chêne huilé et le laiton patiné, ont été choisis pour leur compatibilité avec les alentours et leur capacité à vieillir sur place, s'harmonisant ainsi avec l'environnement au fil du temps. Le paysage spécifique au site comprend des spécimens matures existants, et principalement des plantations indigènes de Californie et tolérantes à la sécheresse.

Die Rustic Canyon Residence würdigt die Geschichte und die natürliche Pracht des Ortes, an dem sie sich befindet, verbessert die Verbindung mit der Außenwelt und zeigt eine umfangreiche Kunstsammlung in einem eleganten, aber informellen Raum, in dem eine Familie gedeihen kann. Der Plan gliedert sich in drei Gärten: einen Atriumgarten mit zwei geschützten kalifornischen Eichen, um den private und gemütliche Räume angeordnet sind und eine Treppe mit einem Glasgeländer steigt; eine Terrasse mit einem Swimmingpool, der parallel zur Zirkulation des Hauses liegt; und einen hinteren Garten, der eine Terrasse und ein Esszimmer im Freien mit Blick auf den Canyon im Hintergrund verbindet.

Natürliches Kupfer, Beton, Cortenstahl, Kalkstein, verkohlte Douglasie, geölte Eiche und gealtertes Messing wurden aufgrund ihrer Kompatibilität mit der örtlichen Umwelt und ihrer Fähigkeit, vor Ort zu altern und mit der Umgebung in Einklang zu kommen, ausgewählt. die lange der Zeit. Die geländespezifische Landschaft bestand aus erhaltenen reifen Exemplaren und einheimischen Pflanzen aus Kalifornien, die sehr dürretolerant sind.

La Residencia Rustic Canyon honra la historia y el esplendor natural del lugar en el que se encuentra, potenciando la conexión con el exterior y expone una extensa colección de arte en un espacio elegante pero informal para que una familia prospere. El plan se organiza en torno a tres jardines: un atrio-jardín con dos robles de California protegidos, alrededor del cual se disponen habitaciones privadas y acogedoras y se alza una escalera con barandilla de cristal; un patio con piscina situado en paralelo a la circulación de la casa; y un jardín trasero que conecta una terraza y un comedor exterior con vistas del cañón en el fondo.

El cobre natural, el hormigón, el acero corten, la piedra caliza, el abeto Douglas carbonizado, el roble aceitado y el latón envejecido se eligieron por su compatibilidad con el entorno local y su capacidad de envejecer en el lugar, armonizándose con el entorno a lo largo del tiempo. El paisaje específico del terreno comprendía especímenes maduros existentes y plantas nativas de California, muy tolerantes a la sequía.

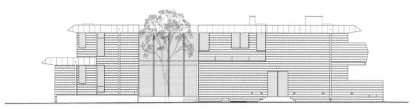

North elevation

East elevation

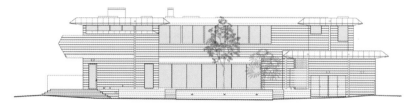

South elevation

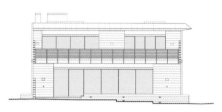

West elevation

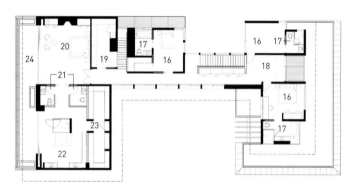

Second floor plan

1. Garage	13. Pool/spa
2. Laundry room	14. Outdoor shower/
3. Powder room	powder
4. Office	15. Mechanical
5. Atrium garden	16. Bedroom
6. Library/media	17. Bathroom
room	18. Hallway lounge
7. Living room	19. Storage
8. Outdoor dining	20. Master bedroom
9. Deck	21. Water closet (his/hers)
10. Kitchen/dining	22. Master bathroom
11. Pantry	23. Walk-in closet
12. Patio	24. Master suite deck

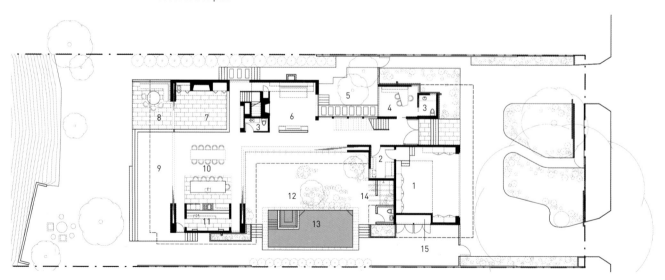

Ground floor plan

0 2' 6'   12'   20'   30'

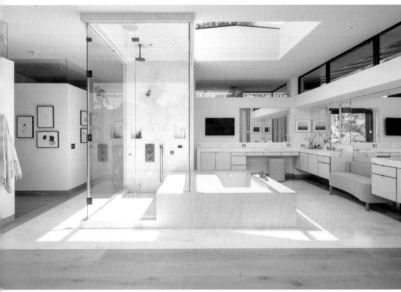

Architecture

craigsteely.com

ROOFLESS HOUSE

Design Team: Craig Steely (Lead), Luigi Silverman, Ryan Leidner, Tune Kantharoup, and Anastasia Victor

Structural Engineer: Strandberg Engineering

General Contractor: Drew Maran Construction

Photographer: Darren Bradley

PAM AND PAUL'S HOUSE

Design Team: Craig Steely (Lead), Luigi Silverman, Ryan Leidner, and Chris Talbott

Structural Engineer: Val Rabichev

General Contractor: Forsythe General Contractors

Photographer: Darren Bradley

PETER AND JAN'S HOUSE

Design Team: Craig Steely (Lead), Luigi Silverman, and Mary Barensfeld

Structural Engineer: Val Rabichev

General Contractor: Structura Builders

Photographer: Bruce Damonte

Craig Steely is a California and Hawaii based architect. His buildings have been described as true and unique hybrids of these two environments. They embrace the realities of the environment and our separation/connection to it over the subjugation of it, all the while focusing on developing a singular architecture rooted in its context. Active projects include work in Hawaii, Mexico, as well as several along the coast of California—from Sea Ranch to San Francisco to Big Sur.
He received his architecture degree from Cal Poly, San Luis Obispo. He has lectured at the University of Hawaii, the University of California at Berkeley, Cal Poly and at many conferences including the Monterey Design Conference. His work has been awarded recognition by the American Institute of Architects and published widely in books and periodicals. In 2009 he was selected as an "Emerging Talent" by the AIA California Council. His office was chosen the top firm in the 2013 Residential Architect Magazine leadership awards.

Craig Steely est un architecte basé en Californie et à Hawaii. Ses bâtiments ont été décrits comme de véritables et uniques hybrides de ces deux environnements. Ils embrassent les réalités du cadre et notre séparation/connexion à celui-ci par rapport à son assujettissement, tout en se concentrant sur le développement d'une architecture singulière enracinée dans son contexte. Parmi les projets en cours, on compte des travaux à Hawaï, au Mexique, ainsi que plusieurs sur la côte californienne, de Sea Ranch à Big Sur en passant par San Francisco.
Il a obtenu son diplôme d'architecture à Cal Poly, San Luis Obispo. Il a donné des conférences à l'université d'Hawaï, à l'université de Californie à Berkeley, à Cal Poly et à de nombreuses conférences dont la Monterey Design Conference. Son travail a été reconnu par l'American Institute of Architects et largement publié dans des livres et des périodiques. En 2009, il a été sélectionné comme «Talent émergent» par le Conseil californien de l'AIA. Son bureau a été choisi comme le meilleur cabinet lors des prix de leadership du magazine Residential Architect en 2013.

Craig Steely ist ein in Kalifornien und Hawaii ansässiger Architekt. Seine Gebäude wurden als wahre und einzigartige Hybride dieser beiden Umgebungen beschrieben. Sie nehmen die Realitäten der Umwelt und unsere Trennung/Verbindung zu ihr über die Unterwerfung der Umwelt auf und konzentrieren sich gleichzeitig auf die Entwicklung einer einzigartigen, in ihrem Kontext verwurzelten Architektur. Zu den aktiven Projekten gehören Arbeiten in Hawaii und Mexiko sowie mehrere entlang der Küste Kaliforniens – von Sea Ranch über San Francisco bis Big Sur.
Seinen Abschluss in Architektur erhielt er an der Cal Poly in San Luis Obispo. Er hielt Vorträge an der Universität von Hawaii, der Universität von Kalifornien in Berkeley, Cal Poly, und auf vielen Konferenzen, darunter die Monterey Design Conference. Seine Arbeit wurde vom American Institute of Architects anerkannt und in zahlreichen Büchern und Zeitschriften veröffentlicht. Im Jahr 2009 wurde er vom AIA California Council als „Emerging Talent" ausgewählt. Sein Büro wurde bei der Verleihung der Führungsauszeichnungen des Residential Architect Magazine 2013 zum besten Büro gewählt.

Craig Steely es un arquitecto con base en California y Hawái. Sus edificios han sido descritos como verdaderos y únicos, híbridos de estos dos ambientes. Abarcan las realidades del medio ambiente y la separación/conexión con él, al tiempo que se centran en el desarrollo de una arquitectura singular enraizada en su contexto. Los proyectos incluyen trabajos en Hawái, México, así como varios a lo largo de la costa de California, desde Sea Ranch a San Francisco y Big Sur.
Recibió su título de arquitecto en Cal Poly, San Luis Obispo. Ha dado conferencias en la Universidad de Hawái, en la Universidad de California en Berkeley, en Cal Poly y en muchos otros lugares, incluida la Conferencia de Diseño de Monterrey. Su trabajo ha sido reconocido por el Instituto Americano de Arquitectos y publicado ampliamente en libros y revistas. En 2009 fue seleccionado como «Talento emergente» por el Consejo de California del AIA. Su oficina fue elegida como el mejor estudio en los premios de liderazgo de 2013 de la revista Residential Architect Magazine.

ROOFLESS HOUSE

ATHERTON, CALIFORNIA

Lot size: 20,000 sq ft
Project size: 2,900 sq ft interior and 3,000 sq ft exterior

The owner of this project wanted a house where she could live outdoors as much as possible, making the most of the temperate climate. This desire was challenged by the site's long and narrow proportions and views of the neighboring houses. But above these neighboring houses, the mature tree canopy and sky were alive, constantly changing. Focusing on this view "up" rather than horizontally "out", Craig Steely Architecture created a seemingly roofless house that directs the view up. The living spaces, surrounded by outdoor courtyards, are open planned and blur the connection between indoor/outdoor with retractable sliding doors and continuous materials like travertine on the floors and cedar on the walls. But what sets this building apart is the continuous curving wall that surrounds it. The wall blocks out the less desirable views while focusing on the more meaningful ones and creates interest as the sunlight and shadows move through the day along its surfaces. A meadow of native grasses flows from the sidewalk with existing oaks, redwoods, and newly planted birch trees flowing inside and outside of the curving wooden wall.

La propriétaire de ce projet voulait une maison où elle pourrait vivre à l'extérieur autant que possiblepour profiter du climat tempéré. Ce désir a été remis en question par les proportions longues et étroites du site et les vues des maisons voisines. Mais au-dessus de ces maisons proches, la voûte des arbres matures et le ciel étaient en constante évolution. En se concentrant sur cette vue "vers le haut" plutôt que « vers l'extérieur », Craig Steely Architecture a créé une maison apparemment sans toit qui dirige la vue vers le haut. Les espaces de vie, entourés de cours extérieures, sont planifiés de manière ouverte et brouillent le lien entre l'intérieur et l'extérieur, grâce à des portes coulissantes et des matériaux continus comme le travertin au sol et le cèdre sur les murs. Mais ce qui distingue ce bâtiment, c'est le mur courbe continu qui l'entoure. Le mur bloque les vues moins souhaitables en se concentrant sur les plus significatives au fur et à mesure que la journée passe et que la lumière du soleil et les ombres glissent sur sa surface. Des herbes indigènes coulent du trottoir, avec des chênes, des séquoias et des bouleaux nouvellement plantés qui s'écoulent à l'intérieur et à l'extérieur du mur de bois incurvé.

Die Eigentümerin dieses Projekts wollte ein Haus, in dem sie so viel wie möglich draußen leben konnte, um das gemäßigte Klima zu nutzen. Dieser Wunsch wurde durch die langen, engen Proportionen des Geländes und die Aussicht auf benachbarte Häuser in Frage gestellt. Aber über diesen nahe gelegenen Häusern veränderten sich ständig die Baumkronen und der Himmel. Craig Steely Architecture konzentrierte sich auf diese Ansicht „nach oben" und nicht nach „außen" und schuf ein scheinbar dachloses Haus, das den Blick nach oben lenkt. Die von Außenhöfen umgebenen Wohnräume sind offen gestaltet und verwischen dank Schiebetüren und durchgehenden Materialien wie Travertin auf dem Boden und Zeder an den Wänden die Verbindung zwischen Innen und Außen. Aber was dieses Gebäude auszeichnet, ist die durchgehende gekrümmte Wand, die es umgibt. Die Wand blockiert weniger wünschenswerte Ansichten, indem sie sich im Laufe des Tages auf die aussagekräftigeren konzentriert und Sonnenlicht und Schatten über ihre Oberfläche gleiten. Einheimische Gräser fließen vom Bürgersteig, und neu gepflanzte Eichen, Redwoods und Birken fließen in die gebogene Holzwand hinein und aus ihr heraus.

La dueña de este proyecto deseaba una casa donde pudiera vivir al aire libre tanto como fuera posible, aprovechando el clima templado de la zona. Este deseo se encontró con el desafío consecuencia de las largas y estrechas proporciones del terreno y las vistas a las casas vecinas. Pero por encima de estas casas vecinas, se contemplaba el cambiante dosel de los árboles maduros y el cielo. Centrándose en esta vista «hacia arriba» en lugar de «hacia fuera», Craig Steely Architecture creó una casa aparentemente sin tejado que dirige la vista hacia arriba. Los espacios interiores, rodeados de patios exteriores, son diáfanos y desdibujan la conexión entre el interior y el exterior con puertas correderas y materiales como el travertino en los suelos y el cedro en las paredes. Pero lo más destacable de esta construcción es el muro curvo que la rodea. La pared bloquea las vistas menos deseables centrándose en las más significativas a medida que pasa el día y la luz del sol y las sombras se deslizan por su superficie. Gramíneas nativas fluyen de la acera, mientras robles, secoyas y abedules recién plantados fluyen tanto dentro como fuera del muro curvo de madera.

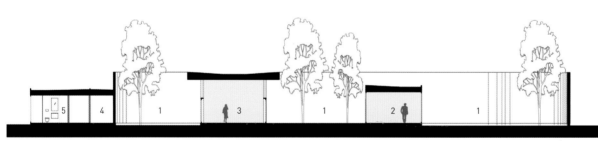

Section A

1. Courtyard
2. Master bedroom
3. Living room
4. Breezeway
5. Guest bedroom

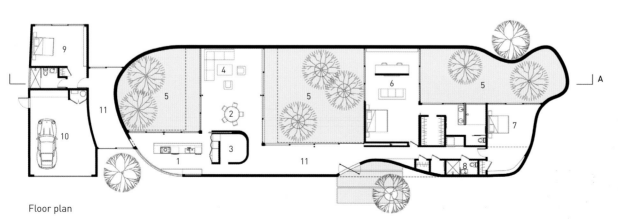

Floor plan

1. Kitchen
2. Dining area
3. Pantry
4. Living room
5. Courtyard
6. Master bedroom
7. Bedroom
8. Bathroom
9. Guest suite
10. Garage
11. Breezeway

PAM AND PAUL'S HOUSE

CUPERTINO, CALIFORNIA

Lot size: 1 acre
Project size: 3,000 sq ft

The house floats in the canopy of a dense oak grove in the foothills of the Santa Cruz Mountains just west of Silicon Valley. The conceptual idea came clearly and quickly—float a glass box in the leaves of the trees on two trunk-like columns, disrupting as few oaks as possible. The dense tree canopy offers the opportunity to build a glass-walled house, protected from the direct rays of the sun yet filled with dappled sunlight. Strong geometric lines of light in the ceiling, reminiscent of a Dan Flavin sculpture, are visible from outside looking up through the leaves. The steepness of the site directs the entry to the living level from above through a grass-covered roof. The house sits at the boundary between the suburb and wilderness, straddling the two as it sits on the site. Just as they did before construction, Mule deer rest in the shade of the cantilever, which is now a continuation of the oak canopy. Gray squirrels run along the branches, and wild turkeys roost in the treetops. The expanse of glass feels permeable and disappears only to leave nature as it always has been in the grove.

La maison flotte dans la canopée d'une dense chênaie située au pied des montagnes de Santa Cruz, juste à l'ouest de la Silicon Valley. L'idée conceptuelle est venue rapidement et clairement: faire flotter une boîte en verre dans la cime des arbres et sur deux colonnes en forme de tronc, en abattant le moins de chênes possible. Le bosquet dense offre la possibilité de construire une maison avec des clôtures en verre, protégées des rayons directs du soleil mais remplies de lumière à l'intérieur. De fortes lignes géométriques de lumière dans le plafond, rappelant une sculpture de Dan Flavin, sont visibles de l'extérieur en regardant à travers les feuilles. La pente du terrain permet à l'entrée de la maison de se situer en partie haute, à travers une toiture paysagée. La maison est située à la frontière entre la banlieue et le désert. Les cerfs se reposent à l'ombre du surplomb, qui est maintenant une continuation de la chênaie. Les écureuils gris se baladent le long des branches et les dindes sauvages se perchent à la cime des arbres. La structure en verre est perméable et ne disparaît que pour laisser place à la nature.

Das Haus schwebt im Vordach eines dichten Eichenhains in den Ausläufern der Santa Cruz Mountains westlich des Silicon Valley. Die konzeptionelle Idee kam klar und schnell: Ein Glaskasten schwebt im Laub der Bäume auf zwei stammartigen Säulen und stört so wenige Eichen wie möglich. Das dichte Baumkronendach bot die Möglichkeit, ein Haus mit Glaswänden zu bauen, das vor den direkten Sonnenstrahlen geschützt und dennoch mit gesprenkeltem Sonnenlicht gefüllt ist. Starke geometrische Lichtlinien in der Decke, die an eine Skulptur von Dan Flavin erinnern, sind von außen sichtbar, wenn man durch die Blätter nach oben schaut. Die Steilheit des Grundstücks lenkt den Zugang zur Wohnebene von oben durch ein mit Gras gedecktes Dach. Das Haus befindet sich an der Grenze zwischen Vorstadt und Wildnis und überspannt beide, während es auf dem Grundstück steht. Wie vor dem Bau ruhen die Maultierhirsche im Schatten des Auslegers, der nun eine Fortsetzung des Eichenvordachs ist. Graue Eichhörnchen laufen entlang der Äste, und wilde Truthähne rasten in den Baumkronen. Die Glasfläche fühlt sich durchlässig an und belässt die Natur im Hain so wie sie immer war.

La casa flota en el dosel de un denso robledal al pie de las montañas de Santa Cruz, al oeste de Silicon Valley. La idea conceptual llegó clara y rápidamente: conseguir hacer flotar una caja de cristal en las copas de los árboles y sobre dos columnas en forma de tronco, talando el menor número posible de robles. La densa arboleda ofrece la oportunidad de construir una casa con cerramientos acristalados, protegida de los rayos directos del sol pero llena de luz en el interior. Fuertes líneas geométricas de luz en el techo, que recuerdan a una escultura de Dan Flavin, son visibles desde el exterior mirando a través de las hojas. La inclinación del terreno permite ubicar la entrada de la vivienda en la parte superior, a través de un techo ajardinado. La casa se encuentra en el límite entre el suburbio y el desierto. Los ciervos descansan a la sombra del voladizo, que es ahora una continuación del robledal. Ardillas grises corretean a lo largo de las ramas, y los pavos salvajes se posan en las copas de los árboles. La estructura de vidrio se siente permeable y desaparece sólo para dejar paso a la naturaleza.

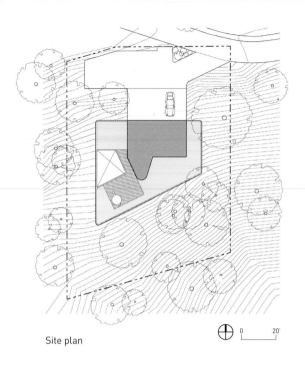

Site plan

0 20'

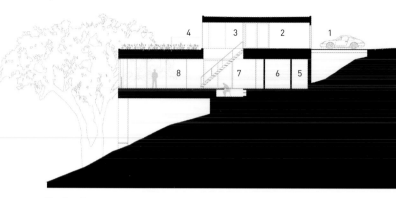

Section A

1. Bridge
2. Garage
3. Foyer
4. Deck
5. Mechanical
6. Laundry
7. Office
8. Living room

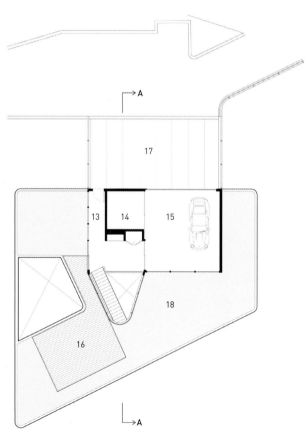

Entry level plan

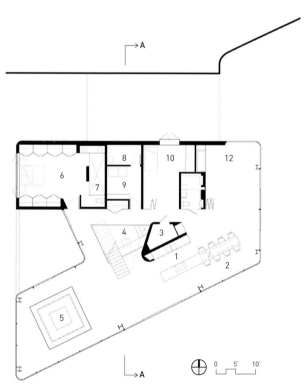

Main level plan

0 5' 10'

1. Kitchen
2. Dining area
3. Pantry
4. Sunken office
5. Sunken living room
6. Master bedroom
7. Master bathroom
8. Mechanical
9. Laundry
10. Bedroom
11. Bathroom
12. Guest room
13. Entry
14. Storage
15. Garage
16. Deck
17. Bridge
18. Planted roof

PETER AND JAN'S HOUSE

SAN FRANCISCO, CALIFORNIA

Located above San Francisco's Dolores Park on a steep site bordering a public garden, the small house locates a 24-foot square cast-in-place concrete garage at the lowest level and builds a three-story glass tower above it, minimizing the impact on the land and the native hillside drainage. The top living floor then spans from a flat plateau at the top of the lot to the tower like a bridge, essentially reducing the amount of excavation typically involved in this type of construction by two thirds. Beyond the structural challenges, the biggest issue in designing the house was opening the building to the expansive view while maintaining a level of privacy. During the design phase of the house, the new on-ramp to the Golden Gate Bridge was under construction, which necessitated clearing a grove of Monterey Cypress trees in its path from the Presidio. Craig Steely Architecture secured some of these trees and, working with a local milling shop, turned them into ninety solid wood louvers that regulate openness and privacy.

Située au-dessus du Dolores Park de San Francisco, sur un site escarpé en bordure d'un jardin public, la petite maison abrite un garage en béton coulé sur place formant un carré d'environ 7 metres au niveau le plus bas et construit une tour de verre de trois étages au-dessus, minimisant l'impact sur le terrain et le drainage indigène de la colline. Le dernier étage d'habitation s'étend ensuite d'un plateau plat au sommet du terrain jusqu'à la tour comme un pont, ce qui réduit essentiellement de deux tiers la quantité d'excavation généralement nécessaire à ce type de construction. Au-delà des défis structurels, le plus grand problème dans la conception de la maison a été d'ouvrir le bâtiment à la vue étendue tout en maintenant un niveau d'intimité. Pendant la phase de conception de la maison, la nouvelle bretelle d'accès au Golden Gate Bridge était en cours de construction, ce qui a nécessité le déboisement d'un bosquet de cyprès de Monterey sur son chemin depuis le Presidio. Craig Steely Architecture a sécurisé certains de ces arbres et, en collaboration avec une meunerie locale, les a transformés en quatre-vingt-dix persiennes en bois massif qui régulent l'ouverture et l'intimité.

Das kleine Haus befindet sich oberhalb des Dolores-Parks von San Francisco an einem steilen, an einen öffentlichen Garten angrenzenden Ort. Es befindet sich auf der untersten Ebene in einer 24-Fuß-Garage aus Ortbeton und baut darüber einen dreistöckigen Glasturm, der die Auswirkungen minimiert das Land und die einheimische Hangentwässerung. Das oberste Wohngeschoss spannt sich dann wie eine Brücke von einem flachen Plateau an der Spitze des Grundstücks bis zum Turm, wodurch der für diese Art von Bauwerk typische Aushub um zwei Drittel reduziert wird. Abgesehen von den strukturellen Herausforderungen bestand das größte Problem beim Entwurf des Hauses darin, das Gebäude für die weite Aussicht zu öffnen und gleichzeitig ein Maß an Privatsphäre zu wahren. Während der Entwurfsphase des Hauses befand sich die neue Auffahrt zur Golden Gate Bridge im Bau, was die Rodung eines Hains von Monterey-Zypressen auf dem Weg vom Presidio erforderlich machte. Craig Steely Architecture sicherte sich einige dieser Bäume und verwandelte sie in Zusammenarbeit mit einer örtlichen Fräserei in neunzig Massivholzjalousien, die Offenheit und Privatsphäre regulieren.

Situada sobre el Dolores Park de San Francisco, en un terreno empinado que bordea un jardín público, la pequeña casa ubica un garaje cuadrado de 7 por 7 metros hormigonado in situ en el nivel más bajo y construye una torre de vidrio de tres pisos sobre él, minimizando el impacto en el terreno y en el drenaje de la ladera. El piso superior de la vivienda se extiende desde una meseta plana en la parte superior del terreno hasta la torre, como un puente, reduciendo esencialmente en dos tercios la cantidad de excavación que normalmente se realiza en este tipo de construcción. Más allá de los desafíos estructurales, el mayor problema en el diseño de la casa fue abrir el edificio lo suficiente mientras se mantenía la privacidad. Durante la fase de diseño se estaba construyendo la nueva rampa de acceso al mítico puente Golden Gate, lo que obligó a despejar de la zona de Presidio una arboleda de cipreses de Monterrey. Craig Steely Architecture consiguió algunos de estos árboles y, trabajando con un taller de fresado local, los convirtió en noventa persianas de madera maciza para la casa.

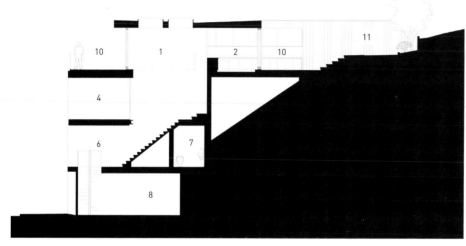

Section A

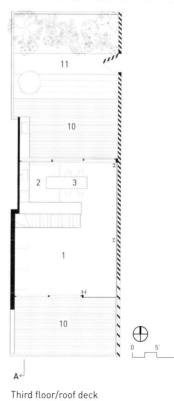

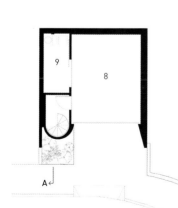

Garage/basement floor plan

First floor plan

Second floor plan

Third floor/roof deck

0 5' 10'

1. Living room
2. Kitchen
3. Dining room
4. Master bedroom
5. Master bathroom
6. Office
7. Bathroom
8. Garage
9. Mechanical
10. Deck
11. Garden

Dennis E. Zirbel
Architect

zirbelarchitect.com

MC 53

Architect: Dennis E. Zirbel, Architect

Interior Designer: Natalie Zirbel |
Dennis E. Zirbel, Architect

Landscape Architect: Ed Hagg

Photographer: Martis Camp Realty

MC 15

Project Team: Dennis E. Zirbel, Architect

Interior Designer: Natalie Zirbel |
Dennis E. Zirbel, Architect

Landscape Architect: Ed Hagg

Photographer: Vance Fox Photography

WAWONA CABIN

Architect: Dennis E. Zirbel, Architect

Interior Designer: Natalie Zirbel |
Dennis E. Zirbel, Architect

Builder: Heslin Construction

Photography: Chris Murray Productions

Dennis E. Zirbel, Architect approaches architectural design with a creative blending of form and function, viewing architecture as art with a structure. Each building becomes an expression of the client's vision and an extension of its natural setting, a timeless art form that functions well with regards to its use, environment, and sustainability. Not only are the lives of the people who use the building enriched, but the natural beauty of the site is enhanced by the structure as well. A sustainable building philosophy ensures the enjoyment of these places for generations to come.

Dennis E. Zirbel is licensed to practice architecture in both California and Nevada. As a registered Architect in both states and an accredited LEED professional, he gives his clients the ability to "green" certify their project if they so desire. He is also NCARB certified by the National State Board of Architects, which allows the firm to seek architectural licensure in all 50 States. Dennis E. Zirbel, Architect has designed or worked on over eighteen resort/recreation facilities in the Lake Tahoe/Truckee area and over 250 residences in both Nevada and California. The firm has also been involved in ten Master Planning projects in the Lake Tahoe/Truckee area.

Dennis E. Zirbel, Architect, aborde la conception architecturale par un mélange créatif de forme et de fonction, en considérant l'architecture comme un art avec une structure. Chaque bâtiment devient une expression de la vision du client et une extension de son cadre naturel, une forme d'art intemporelle qui fonctionne bien en ce qui concerne son utilisation, l'environnement et la durabilité. Non seulement la vie des personnes qui utilisent le bâtiment est enrichie, mais la beauté naturelle du site est également mise en valeur par la structure. Une philosophie de construction durable garantit la jouissance de ces lieux pour les générations à venir.

Dennis E. Zirbel est autorisé à pratiquer l'architecture en Californie et au Nevada. En tant qu'architecte agréé dans ces deux États et professionnel LEED accrédité, il donne à ses clients la possibilité de certifier leur projet «vert» s'ils le souhaitent. Il est également certifié NCARB par le National State Board of Architects, ce qui lui permet de demander une licence d'architecte dans les 50 États. Dennis E. Zirbel, architecte a conçu ou travaillé sur plus de dix-huit installations de villégiature / de loisirs dans la région de Lake Tahoe / Truckee et plus de 250 résidences au Nevada et en Californie. L'entreprise a également été impliquée dans dix projets de Master Planning dans la région de Lake Tahoe / Truckee.

Dennis E. Zirbel Architect nähert sich dem architektonischen Design mit einer kreativen Mischung aus Form und Funktion und betrachtet Architektur als Kunst. Jedes Gebäude ist Ausdruck der Vision des Kunden und eine Erweiterung der natürlichen Umwelt, eine zeitlose und funktionale Kunstform in Bezug auf Nutzung, Umwelt und Nachhaltigkeit. Das Leben der Menschen, die sich mit der Architektur beschäftigen, wird nicht nur bereichert, sondern die natürliche Schönheit des Ortes wird auch dadurch bereichert. Eine nachhaltige Bauphilosophie sichert den Genuss dieser Orte für kommende Generationen.

Dennis E. Zirbel ist sowohl in Kalifornien als auch in Nevada als Architekt zugelassen. Als in beiden Bundesstaaten registrierter Architekt und akkreditierter LEED-Fachmann gibt er seinen Kunden die Möglichkeit, ihr Projekt „grün" zu zertifizieren, wenn sie dies wünschen. Er ist außerdem vom National State Board of Architects NCARB zertifiziert, was es dem Büro ermöglicht, in allen 50 Bundesstaaten eine Architektenlizenz zu beantragen. Dennis E. Zirbel, Architect hat über 18 Resort- / Freizeiteinrichtungen in der Region Lake Tahoe / Truckee und über 250 Residenzen in Nevada und Kalifornien entworfen oder daran gearbeitet. Das Unternehmen war auch an zehn Masterplanungsprojekten in der Region Lake Tahoe / Truckee beteiligt.

Dennis E. Zirbel, Architect se acerca al diseño arquitectónico con una creativa mezcla de forma y función, contemplando la arquitectura como un arte. Cada edificio es la expresión de la visión del cliente y una extensión del entorno natural, una forma de arte atemporal y funcional en cuanto a su uso, el medio ambiente y la sostenibilidad. No sólo se enriquecen las vidas de las personas que ocupan la arquitectura, sino que la belleza natural del lugar también se ve realzada por ésta. Una filosofía de construcción sostenible asegura el disfrute de estos lugares para las generaciones venideras.

Dennis E. Zirbel tiene licencia para practicar la arquitectura en California y en Nevada. Como arquitecto registrado en ambos estados y profesional acreditado con la homologación LEED, ofrece a sus clientes la certificación de sostenibilidad para sus proyecto si así lo desean. También dispone de la certificación NCARB del National State Board of Architects, lo que le permite trabajar en los 50 estados de Norteamérica. Dennis E. Zirbel, Architect ha diseñado o trabajado en más de dieciocho centros turísticos/instalaciones recreativas en el área de Lake Tahoe/Truckee y más de 250 residencias en Nevada y California. El estudio también ha estado involucrado en diez proyectos de Planificación Maestra en el área de Lake Tahoe/Truckee.

MC 53

MARTIS CAMP, TRUCKEE, CALIFORNIA

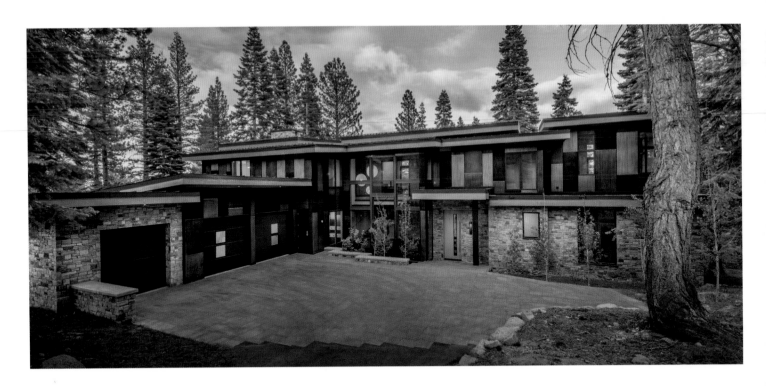

Homesite 53 is a downslope site, sitting proud of its adjacent neighbors, in relationship and proximity to a golf course. This proximity to the golf course positioned the residence in the flattest area in the whole homesite, the views and privacy increased dramatically. Creative solutions, combined with the topography and the features described above, enabled the design to capture 180 degrees of unobstructed views of the golf course, along with some mountain corridor views from virtually any room in the house. The residence embraces the outdoor living experience. Every single space has access to the extensive outdoor patios and the three balconies at the upper level. These outdoor patios were intelligently designed, allowing some privacy from neighbors and within more social areas of the residence.

The unique beauty of this home lies in its commanding yet serene presence achieved by a seamless expression of contemporary architectural concepts at a mountainous scale.

Homesite 53 est un site en pente, fier de ses voisins adjacents, en relation et à proximité d'un terrain de golf. Cette proximité avec le terrain de golf a placé la résidence dans la zone la plus plate de tout le site, la vue et l'intimité ont augmenté de façon spectaculaire. Des solutions créatives, combinées à la topographie et aux caractéristiques décrites ci-dessus, ont permis une vision complète de 180 degrés sur le du terrain de golf, ainsi que quelques vues sectorielles de montagne depuis pratiquement n'importe quelle pièce de la maison. La résidence offre une expérience de vie en plein air. Chaque espace a accès aux vastes patios extérieurs et aux trois balcons du niveau supérieur. Ces patios extérieurs ont été intelligemment conçus, permettant une certaine intimité avec les voisins et dans les zones plus sociales de la résidence.

La beauté unique de cette maison réside dans sa présence imposante mais sereine, obtenue par l'expression sans faille de concepts architecturaux contemporains à l'échelle de la montagne.

Homesite 53 ist ein heruntergekommener Standort, der stolz auf seine angrenzenden Nachbarn blickt, in Beziehung und in der Nähe eines Golfplatzes. Diese Nähe zum Golfplatz positionierte die Residenz in der flachsten Gegend der gesamten Wohnanlage, die Aussicht und die Privatsphäre nahmen dramatisch zu. Kreative Lösungen, kombiniert mit der Topographie und den oben beschriebenen Merkmalen, ermöglichten es dem Entwurf, 180 Grad freie Sicht auf den Golfplatz sowie einige Bergkorridoransichten von praktisch jedem Raum im Haus einzufangen. Die Residenz schließt das Wohnerlebnis im Freien mit ein. Jeder einzelne Raum hat Zugang zu den weitläufigen Außenterrassen oder den drei Balkonen auf der oberen Ebene. Diese Außenterrassen wurden auf intelligente Weise gestaltet, so dass eine gewisse Privatsphäre gegenüber den Nachbarn und innerhalb der sozialen Bereiche der Residenz gewährleistet ist.

Die einzigartige Schönheit dieses Hauses liegt in seiner souveränen und doch ruhigen Präsenz, die durch einen nahtlosen Ausdruck zeitgenössischer architektonischer Konzepte in gebirgiger Größe erreicht wird.

El proyecto MC53 está ubicado en un terreno en bajada junto a un campo de golf. La vivienda se sitúa en el área más plana de todo el terreno, lo que permitió aumentar las vistas y la privacidad. Las soluciones creativas, combinadas con la topografía y las características descritas anteriormente, permitieron vistas de 180 grados sobre el campo de golf y hacia la montaña desde prácticamente cualquier habitación de la casa. La vivienda es un exponente de la experiencia de la vida al aire libre. Cada espacio tiene acceso a los extensos patios exteriores y a los tres balcones del nivel superior. Estos patios exteriores fueron diseñados inteligentemente, permitiendo cierta privacidad en las áreas más habitadas de la residencia.

La belleza única de esta casa radica en su presencia dominante y serena lograda por una expresión perfecta de los conceptos arquitectónicos contemporáneos.

MC 15

MARTIS CAMP, TRUCKEE, CALIFORNIA

Homesite 15 is a unique site with good sun exposure, golf course views, distant mountain corridor views, and a stunning two-story-high rock outcropping on the property. Its impressive size and majestic height provide the homesite with a rare and distinctive experience within the Martis Camp community. The design of the home celebrates and incorporates this natural marvel by meandering around its peaks and projections. The residence weaves around and embraces the two-story-high rock outcropping, allowing all of its bedrooms and the most important spaces to take advantage of this natural sculpture. While many modern homes can conceivably be picked up and placed anywhere, this home distinctly belongs to the mountains and its sloping, bouldered site. This exceptional residence is a unique example of mountain modern style, incorporating counter match sloped roofs and large glazed panels with both contemporary and rustic detailing. The creative architectural solutions, along with its unique setting, make this custom residence special among other residences in the Martis Camp community.

Homesite 15 est un site unique avec une bonne exposition au soleil, des vues sur le terrain de golf, des visions lointaines sur le couloir de montagne et un superbe affleurement rocheux de deux étages sur la propriété. Sa taille impressionnante et sa hauteur majestueuse offrent au site une expérience rare et distinctive au sein de la communauté de Martis Camp. La conception de la maison célèbre et intègre cette merveille naturelle en serpentant autour de ses sommets et de ses saillies. La résidence se faufile et embrasse les affleurements rocheux de deux étages, permettant à toutes ses chambres et aux espaces les plus importants de profiter de cette sculpture naturelle. Alors que de nombreuses maisons modernes peuvent être placées n'importe où, cette maison appartient distinctement à la montagne et à son site incliné et rocailleux. Cette résidence exceptionnelle est un exemple unique de style moderne montagnard, intégrant des toits en pente assortis aux paysages et de grands panneaux vitrés avec des détails à la fois contemporains et rustiques. Les solutions architecturales créatives, ainsi que son cadre unique, font de cette résidence une exception parmi les autres résidences de la communauté de Martis Camp.

Homesite 15 ist ein einzigartiger Standort mit guter Sonneneinstrahlung, Blick auf den Golfplatz, weitem Blick auf den Bergkorridor und einem atemberaubenden zweistöckigen Felsen, der auf dem Grundstück zu Tage tritt. Seine beeindruckende Größe und majestätische Höhe bieten dem Homesite ein seltenes und unverwechselbares Erlebnis innerhalb der Martis-Camp-Gemeinschaft. Das Design des Hauses zelebriert und integriert dieses Naturwunder, indem es sich um seine Gipfel und Vorsprünge schlängelt. Die Residenz schlängelt sich um den zweistöckigen Felsvorsprung herum und umarmt ihn, so dass alle seine Schlafzimmer und die wichtigsten Räume von dieser natürlichen Skulptur profitieren können. Während viele moderne Häuser überall aufgestellt werden können, gehört dieses Haus eindeutig zum Berg und seiner abfallenden, felsigen Lage. Diese außergewöhnliche Residenz ist ein einzigartiges Beispiel für modernen Bergstil. Sie verfügt über geneigte Dächer, die zu den Landschaften passen, und große Glasscheiben mit zeitgenössischen und rustikalen Details. Die kreativen architektonischen Lösungen sowie die einzigartige Umgebung machen diese Residenz zu einer Ausnahme unter anderen Residenzen in der Gemeinde Martis Camp.

El Homesite 15 es un sitio único con buena exposición al sol, vistas al campo de golf y a las montañas y rodeado de un impresionante conjunto de rocas de dos pisos de altura que aflora en la propiedad. Su impresionante tamaño y majestuosa altura proporcionan al terreno una experiencia rara y distintiva dentro de la comunidad de Martis Camp. El diseño de la casa celebra esta maravilla natural que serpentea alrededor de las rocas permitiendo que todos sus dormitorios y los espacios más importantes de la vivienda se aprovechen de esta escultura natural. Si bien muchas casas modernas se pueden ubicar en cualquier lugar, esta casa pertenece claramente a la montaña y a su sitio rocoso e inclinado. Esta excepcional residencia es un ejemplo único de estilo moderno de montaña, que incorpora tejados inclinados y grandes paneles acristalados con detalles tanto contemporáneos como rústicos. Las creativas soluciones arquitectónicas, junto con su entorno único, hacen que esta residencia sea especial entre otras residencias de la comunidad de Martis Camp.

WAWONA CABIN

MARTIS CAMP, TRUCKEE, CALIFORNIA

The boulders, the steep slope, the views, the glamour, the love of the outdoors, all these elements present in the first meeting with the clients, came together in what is now their Martis Camp family home.

A cantilevered lower level, clad in large format corrugated steel, drove the design of the home, as a portion of the site was determined unbuildable due to its pronounced slope. The entry-level above, covered in a reclaimed wood mosaic, captures the views and invites the outdoors in. A detached garage with a living roof provides privacy and adds interest to the site. Capitalizing on the extraordinary existing boulders, Dennis E. Zirbel created a natural-looking in-ground spa with a waterfall feature visible from the master suite. Exterior spaces include an outdoor kitchen with a pizza oven, patios, and headed covered decks that integrate the home with the site and provide numerous opportunities for outdoor living. The upper level provides a tree-house-like bedroom with 360 degrees of views and access to a second living roof over the attached garage.

Les rochers, la pente raide, les vues, le glamour, l'amour du plein air étaient déjà existant lors de la première rencontre avec les clients, ces éléments maintenant font parti leur maison familiale du Martis Camp.

Un niveau inférieur en porte-à-faux, revêtu d'acier ondulé de grand format, a permis la conception de la maison, car une partie du site a été jugée non constructible en raison de sa pente prononcée. L'étage supérieur, recouvert d'une mosaïque de bois de récupération, capture les vues et invite à sortir à l'extérieur. Un garage détaché avec un toit végétal assure l'intimité et ajoute de l'intérêt au site. En tirant parti des extraordinaires rochers existants, Dennis E. Zirbel a créé un spa d'aspect naturel avec une chute d'eau visible depuis la suite principale. Les espaces extérieurs comprennent une cuisine avec un four à pizza, des patios et des terrasses couvertes s'intègrant à la maison et offrent de nombreuses possibilités de vie en plein air. Le niveau supérieur offre une chambre à coucher en forme de maison dans les arbres avec une vue à 360 degrés et un accès à un second toit au-dessus du garage attenant.

Die Felsen, der steile Hang, die Aussicht, der Glamour, die Liebe zur Natur waren schon da, als sie die Gäste zum ersten Mal trafen. Diese Elemente sind jetzt Teil ihres Familienhauses im Martis Camp.

Eine freitragende untere Ebene, die mit Wellstahl verkleidet war, veranlasste die Gestaltung des Hauses, da festgestellt wurde, dass ein Teil des Grundstücks aufgrund seines steilen Abhangs nicht zum Bauen geeignet war. Die obere Ebene, die mit einem Mosaik aus Altholz bedeckt ist, fängt die Aussicht ein und lädt Sie ein, nach draußen zu gehen. Eine separate Garage mit Dachgarten bietet Privatsphäre und erhöht das Interesse an der Anlage. Dennis E. Zirbel nutzte die außergewöhnlich vorhandenen Felsen und schuf ein natürlich aussehendes Spa mit einem Wasserfall, der von der Master Suite aus sichtbar ist. Zu den Außenbereichen gehören eine Außenküche mit Pizzaofen sowie Terrassen und Terrassen, die das Haus in die Landschaft integrieren und Möglichkeiten zum Leben im Freien bieten. Die obere Ebene umfasst ein Baumhaus Schlafzimmer mit 360-Grad-Blick und Zugang zu einem zweiten Deck über die angeschlossene Garage.

Las rocas, la fuerte pendiente, las vistas, el glamur, el amor al aire libre, todos estos temas estuvieron presentes en el primer encuentro con los clientes durante una reunión en lo que ahora es su casa en Martis Camp.

Un nivel inferior en voladizo, revestido de acero corrugado, impulsó el diseño de la casa, ya que se determinó que una parte del terreno no era apto para edificar debido a su pronunciada pendiente. El nivel superior, cubierto por un mosaico de madera recuperada, captura las vistas e invita a salir al exterior. Un garaje independiente con una cubierta ajardinada proporciona privacidad y añade interés al conjunto. Aprovechando las extraordinarias rocas existentes, Dennis E. Zirbel creó un spa de aspecto natural con una cascada visible desde la suite principal. Los espacios exteriores incluyen una cocina al aire libre con un horno para pizzas, así como patios y cubiertas que integran la casa con el paisaje, proporcionando oportunidades para la vida al aire libre. El nivel superior incluye un dormitorio a modo de casa en los árboles con vistas de 360 grados y acceso a una segunda cubierta sobre el garaje adjunto.

eos architecture inc.

eosarc.com

COASTAL MODERN

Architect: eos architecture, Inc.

Structural Engineer: David Thomas Engineering A.P.C.

Civil Engineer: Pasco Laret Engineering & Associates

Soils Engineer: Hetherington Engineering, Inc.

General Contractor: Hanley Construction CO.

Windows: Fleetwood Windows & Doors

Front Door: Creative Metal Industries, Inc./ Jensen Door Systems Inc.

Photographer: Chris Laughter

MISSION BEACH MODERN

Architect: eos architecture, Inc.

Exterior Design Team: eos architecture, Inc. and Frontis Studios LLC.

Interior Design Team: eos architecture, Inc. and GIGI Tile and Design

Furniture: Dawson Design Group

Structural Engineer: Patterson Engineering Ltd.

General Contractor: Four by Four Construction CO.

Windows and Doors: Fleetwood & Doors

Exterior Wood Cladding: Prodema Rustik

Photographer: Chris Laughter

MODERN HACIENDA

Architect: eos architecture, Inc.

Structural Engineer: David Thomas Engineering A.P.C.

Civil Engineer: Coffey Engineering, Inc.

Soils Engineer: Christian Wheeler Engineering

General Contractor: Wardell Builders, Inc.

Windows and Doors: Arcadia Steel

Exterior Stone: Modern Builders Supply Inc.

Interior Stone, Fit and Finish: eos architecture, Inc. and GIGI Tile and Design

Photographer: Chris Laughter

The name eos derives from Greek mythology and the origin of the sunrise. With a foundation firmly rooted in the classical perfection of form, eos architecture, inc. focuses on the importance of the plan, aspires to artistry in architecture, and a continual re-visitation of the Vitruvian concepts: Firmitas—Utilitas—Venustas (strength, usefulness, and beauty).

eos architecture specializes in a comprehensive design that elevates the architectural experience through planning excellence, technical development, beauty in detail, and execution. The firm was established in 2005 by Principal Architect Jennifer Bolyn; over the years, she has assembled a talented team of designers, engineers, and contractors to execute the firm's vision. Under her leadership, eos is highly versatile in style and possesses an exceptional ability to grasp a project's potential on a macro and micro scale. Her level of focus assures that projects are integrally designed, including the technical guidance for energy efficiency, lighting, thermal comfort, and the material quality for beauty and durability.

Le nom eos provient de la mythologie grecque et de l'origine du lever du soleil. Avec une base fermement ancrée dans la perfection classique de la forme, eos architecture, inc. se concentre sur l'importance du plan, aspire à l'art de l'architecture et à une révision continue des concepts vitruviens : Firmitas-Utilitas-Venustas (force, utilité et beauté).

eos architecture se spécialise dans une conception globale qui élève l'expérience architecturale par l'excellence de la planification, le développement technique, la beauté dans le détail et l'exécution. Le bureau a été créé en 2005 par l'architecte principale Jennifer Bolyn ; au fil des années, elle a réuni une équipe talentueuse de concepteurs, d'ingénieurs et d'entrepreneurs pour réaliser la vision du bureau. Sous sa direction, eos est très polyvalent dans son style et possède une capacité exceptionnelle à saisir le potentiel d'un projet à l'échelle macro et micro. Son niveau de concentration garantit que les projets sont conçus intégralement, y compris les conseils techniques pour l'efficacité énergétique, l'éclairage, le confort thermique et la qualité des matériaux pour la beauté et la durabilité.

Der Name eos leitet sich aus der griechischen Mythologie und dem Ursprung des Sonnenaufgangs ab. Mit einem Fundament, das fest in der klassischen Perfektion der Form verwurzelt ist, konzentriert sich eos architecture, inc., auf die Bedeutung des Planes, strebt nach Kunstfertigkeit in der Architektur und einer ständigen Wiederbesinnung auf die vitruvianischen Konzepte: Firmitas-Utilitas-Venustas (Stärke, Nützlichkeit und Schönheit).

eos architecture ist auf ein umfassendes Design spezialisiert, das die architektonische Erfahrung durch hervorragende Planung, technische Entwicklung, Schönheit im Detail und Ausführung erhöht. Das Büro wurde 2005 von der leitenden Architektin Jennifer Bolyn gegründet; im Laufe der Jahre hat sie ein talentiertes Team von Designern, Ingenieuren und Bauunternehmern zusammengestellt, um die Vision des Büros umzusetzen. Unter ihrer Leitung ist eos stilistisch sehr vielseitig und verfügt über die außergewöhnliche Fähigkeit, das Potenzial eines Projekts auf Makro- und Mikroebene zu erfassen. Ihr Schwerpunkt gewährleistet, dass Projekte ganzheitlich konzipiert werden, einschließlich der technischen Anleitung für Energieeffizienz, Beleuchtung, thermischen Komfort und die Materialqualität für Schönheit und Haltbarkeit.

El nombre eos deriva de la mitología griega y del origen del amanecer. Con una base firmemente arraigada en la perfección clásica de la forma, eos Architecture, Inc. se centra en la importancia de la planificación, aspira al arte en la arquitectura y a una continua re visitación de los conceptos de Vitruvio: Firmitas-Utilitas-Venustas (fuerza, utilidad y belleza).

eos architecture se especializa en un diseño integral que eleva la experiencia arquitectónica a través de la excelencia en la planificación, el desarrollo técnico, la belleza en detalle y la ejecución. El estudio fue fundado en 2005 por la arquitecta jefa Jennifer Bolyn. A lo largo de los años ha reunido un talentoso equipo de diseñadores, ingenieros y contratistas para llevar a cabo la visión del estudio. Bajo su dirección, eos se distingue por un estilo muy versátil y por una capacidad excepcional para captar el potencial de un proyecto a escala macro y micro. Su nivel de atención asegura que los proyectos se diseñen de forma integral, incluyendo la orientación técnica para la eficiencia energética, la iluminación, el confort térmico y la calidad de unos materiales que aportan belleza y durabilidad.

COASTAL MODERN

SOLANA BEACH, CALIFORNIA

Lot size: 0.5 acre
Project size: 6,200 sq ft

Solana Beach is a vibrant coastal town with a forward-looking urban plan. A thoughtful zoning ordinance ensures view protection and an appropriate scale for the homes that rise from the Pacific Ocean to the East. At the Western base of the hills, the house sits on a large lot. Its open floor plan changes with the seasons, a porous building envelope that engages the site. The bold use of vast dual window walls opens the great room to nature and creates an awe-inspiring expanse of space from the Eastern winter garden, through the home, to the western vanishing edge pool. The house lives inside out, blurring boundaries. The architect reduced the plan to simple axes, with a wide, open riser stairway connecting three levels and funneling light to the basement. Blue-grey stonewalls, Alaskan yellow cedar ceilings, large format porcelain tile, and planked oak flooring are understated materials reflecting the colors of the Pacific. Deepened eaves and covered patios with recessed heaters provide year-round comfort and shelter from the sun. The home's simple concepts embrace the location, with a frame to the view and a celebration of the surroundings.

Solana Beach est une ville côtière animée avec un plan urbain qui assure la protection des vues et une échelle appropriée pour les maisons qui s'élèvent du Pacifique à l'est. Cette maison à la base ouest des collines offre un plan ouvert qui change avec les saisons, une enveloppe poreuse qui capture le terrain. Les vastes fenêtres ouvrent la grande salle sur l'environnement naturel et créent un espace étonnant du jardin d'hiver de l'est, à travers la maison, jusqu'à la piscine à débordement à l'ouest. La maison est à la fois intérieure et extérieure avec des limites floues. L'architecte a réduit le plan à de simples axes, avec un grand escalier à contremarche qui relie trois niveaux et canalise la lumière vers le sous-sol. Les murs en pierre bleu-gris, les plafonds en cèdre jaune d'Alaska, les carreaux de porcelaine et les planchers de bois franc en chêne reflètent les couleurs du Pacifique. Les avant-toits profonds et les patios couverts avec radiateurs encastrés offrent un confort tout au long de l'année et un abri du soleil. Les concepts de maison simples englobent l'emplacement, avec un cadre pour la vue et une célébration de l'environnement.

Solana Beach ist eine pulsierende Küstenstadt mit einem Stadtplan, der den Schutz der Aussicht gewährleistet, und einem angemessenen Maßstab für die Häuser, die sich vom Pazifik nach Osten erheben. Diese Wohnung am westlichen Fuß der Hügel bietet einen offenen Grundriss, der sich mit den Jahreszeiten ändert, eine poröse Hülle, die das Gelände einfängt. Breite Öffnungen öffnen den großen Raum für die natürliche Umgebung und schaffen einen atemberaubenden Raum vom östlichen Wintergarten aus durch das Haus zum Infinity-Pool im Westen. Das Haus ist sowohl innen als auch außen mit verschwommenen Grenzen. Der Architekt reduzierte den Plan auf einfache Achsen mit einer weit geöffneten Steigtreppe, die drei Ebenen verbindet und Licht in den Keller leitet. Blaugraue Steinmauern, Decken aus alaskischer gelber Zeder, Porzellanfliesen und Eichenparkett spiegeln die Farben des Pazifiks wider. Tiefe Traufe und überdachte Terrassen mit vertieften Heizkörpern bieten das ganze Jahr über Komfort und Schutz vor der Sonne. Einfache Wohnkonzepte umfassen die Lage mit einem Rahmen für die Aussicht und die Feier der Umgebung.

Solana Beach es una vibrante ciudad costera con un plan urbanístico que asegura la protección de las vistas y una escala apropiada para las casas que se levantan desde el Pacífico hacia el este. Esta vivienda en la base occidental de las colinas ofrece una planta abierta que cambia con el paso de las estaciones, una envoltura porosa que capta el terreno. Amplios ventanales abren la gran sala al entorno natural y crea un impresionante espacio desde el jardín de invierno oriental, a través de la casa, hasta la piscina infinita al oeste. La casa es a la vez interior y exterior con límites difuminados. La arquitecta redujo el plan a ejes simples, con una amplia escalera de contrahuellas abierta que conecta tres niveles y canaliza la luz al sótano. Las paredes de piedra de color gris azulado, los techos de cedro amarillo de Alaska, los azulejos de porcelana y los suelos de madera de roble reflejan los colores del Pacífico. Los aleros profundos y los patios cubiertos con radiadores empotrados brindan comodidad durante todo el año y refugio del sol. Los conceptos simples de la casa abarcan la ubicación, con un marco para la vista y una celebración del entorno.

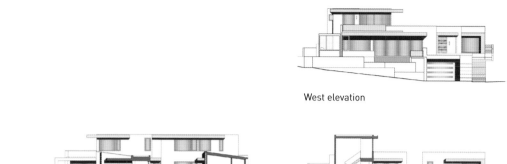

West elevation

Section AA

Section BB

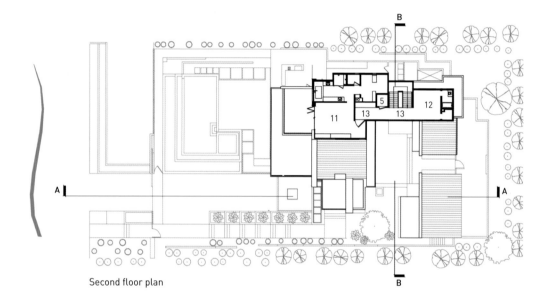

Second floor plan

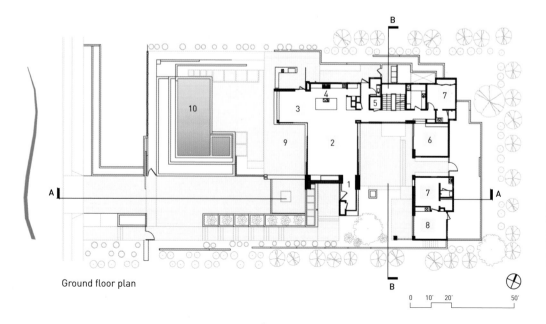

Ground floor plan

1. Entry
2. Living area
3. Dining area
4. Kitchen
5. Elevator
6. Family room
7. Bedroom
8. Art Studio
9. Covered patio
10. Pool
11. Owner's suite
12. Gym/office
13. Hall

0   10'   20'   50'

MISSION BEACH MODERN

SAN DIEGO, CALIFORNIA

Lot size: 4,500 sq ft
Project size: 4,600 sq ft

The Mission Beach boardwalk is a San Diego icon, famous for sandy beaches, beautiful walks, restaurants, bars, and people watching. This dynamic urban context motivated the architect to embrace the site's boisterous and public nature while elevating the more private and serene spaces above the fray. The prominent corner lot on the Westernmost edge of the Mission Beach peninsula inspired the team to create a modern abstract gesture that would add identity and character to the boardwalk and develop a floor plan that plays on the West and South exposures. A public, indoor/outdoor beach level engages the boardwalk, with the home's common spaces. The uppermost level is an oasis giving residents private access to the oceanfront, with the master bedroom sitting front and center. The team selected materials that could withstand prolonged exposure to saltwater. These materials, including a Prodema wood cladding, a titanium metal facade, large glass expanses, cast-in-place concrete, and stainless steel, ensure durability while making this home a unique design statement embodying the site's public and the home's private nature.

La promenade de Mission Beach est une icône de San Diego, célèbre pour ses plages, ses belles promenades, ses restaurants, ses bars et ses visiteurs. Ce contexte urbain dynamique a motivé l'architecte à embrasser la nature bruyante et publique du site, tout en élevant les espaces plus privés au-dessus de la mêlée. Le terrain d'angle proéminent à l'extrémité ouest de la péninsule de Mission Beach a inspiré l'équipe à créer un geste abstrait et moderne, qui ajouterait de l'identité et du caractère à la promenade et à élaborer un plan d'étage qui joue sur les expositions sud ouest. Un niveau de plage public, engage la promenade avec les espaces communs de la maison. Le niveau supérieur est une oasis donnant aux résidents un accès privé à l'océan, avec la chambre principale située à l'avant et au centre. L'équipe a sélectionné des matériaux pouvant résister à une exposition prolongée à l'eau salée. Ces matériaux, dont un revêtement en bois Prodema, une façade métallique en titane, de grandes surfaces vitrées, du béton coulé sur place et de l'acier inoxydable, garantissent la durabilité tout en faisant de cette maison un modèle unique qui incarne la nature publique du site et la nature privée de la maison.

Der Mission Beach Boardwalk ist eine Ikone von San Diego, berühmt für seine Strände, Promenaden, Restaurants, Bars und Menschen. Dieser dynamische urbane Kontext motivierte den Architekten, die geschäftige Natur des Ortes zu nutzen und gleichzeitig die privatesten Räume über das geschäftige Treiben zu heben. Das höchste Grundstück am westlichsten Rand der Mission Beach-Halbinsel inspirierte das Team, ein modernes und abstraktes Projekt zu erstellen, das der Promenade Identität und Charakter verleiht und einen Plan entwickelt, der mit der West- und Südausrichtung spielt. Ein öffentlicher Strandbereich verbindet die Promenade mit den Gemeinschaftsräumen des Hauses. Die obere Ebene ist eine Oase, die den Bewohnern einen privaten Zugang zur Küste ermöglicht. Das Hauptschlafzimmer befindet sich im Zentrum. Das Team wählte Materialien aus, die einer längeren Exposition gegenüber Salzwasser standhalten konnten. Diese Materialien, zu denen eine Prodema-Holzverkleidung, eine Titan-Metallfassade, eine große Verglasung, Beton und Edelstahl gehören, gewährleisten Haltbarkeit und verleihen dem Haus ein einzigartiges Design, das den öffentlichen und privaten Charakter des Ortes verkörpert.

El paseo marítimo de Mission Beach es un icono de San Diego, famoso por sus playas, sus paseos, sus restaurantes, sus bares y su gente. Este dinámico contexto urbano motivó a la arquitecta a abrazar la naturaleza bulliciosa del lugar, mientras elevaba los espacios más privados por encima del bullicio. La parcela más elevada en el borde más occidental de la península de Mission Beach inspiró al equipo a crear un proyecto moderno y abstracto que añadiera identidad y carácter al paseo marítimo y desarrollara un plano que jugara con las orientaciones a oeste y sur. Un espacio de playa pública conecta el paseo marítimo con los espacios comunes de la casa. El nivel superior es un oasis que permite a los residentes un acceso privado a la costa, con el dormitorio principal en el centro. El equipo seleccionó materiales que pudieran soportar una exposición prolongada al agua salada. Estos materiales, que incluyen un revestimiento de madera Prodema, una fachada de metal de titanio, grandes acristalamientos, hormigón y acero inoxidable, aseguran la durabilidad mientras que proporcionan a la casa con un diseño único que encarna la naturaleza pública y privada del lugar.

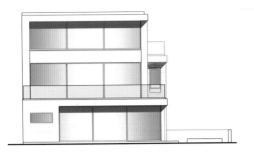

West elevation

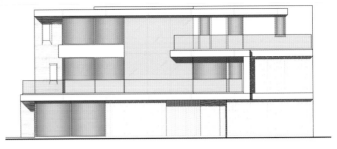

South elevation

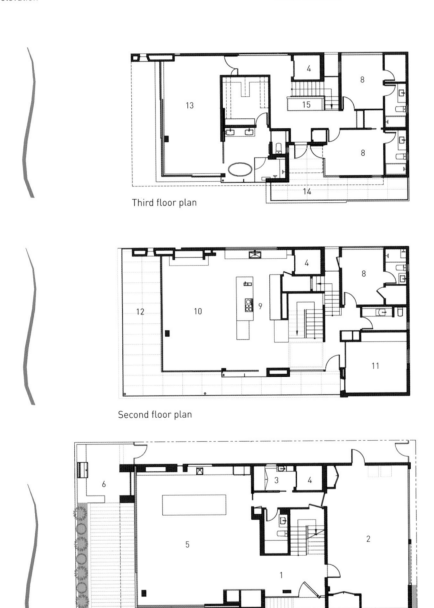

Third floor plan

Second floor plan

Ground floor plan

0   5'   10'   20'

1. Entry
2. Garage
3. Laundry room
4. Elevator
5. Entertainment
6. Barbecue
7. Firepit
8. Bedroom
9. Kitchen
10. Great room
11. Office
12. Covered balcony
13. Owner's suite
14. Balcony
15. Open

MODERN HACIENDA

RANCHO SANTA FE, CALIFORNIA

The owners discovered a beautiful vacant site overlooking a verdant canyon with views to the Pacific Ocean accidentally. They had just completed the construction of a new coastal home but felt drawn to this location nestled in the hills of Historic Rancho Santa Fe. The lot presented an engineering challenge when the soils investigation found the slope was failing; the architect, civil, and geotechnical engineers devised a plan to return the canyon to a natural but stabilized condition. Like the city of Santa Barbara, Rancho Santa Fe's identity is born from Spanish Hacienda-inspired architecture. With careful planning, execution, and materials selection, the home integrates the Spanish influence with modern features. Inspired by Hadrian's villa's planning, the architect angled the plan along the hill's crest to face the westerly views, and embedded the second floor into the hillside. A predominately hip roof with flat clay tiles and a formal courtyard entry embody the Southern California's Spanish architecture. The deepened eaves, straight box gutters, window massing, lighting design, and water elements create the contemporary feel.

Les propriétaires ont découvert par hasard un beau terrain surplombant un canyon verdoyant avec vue sur l'océan Pacifique. Ils venaient d'achever la construction d'une nouvelle maison côtière mais, se sont sentis attirés par cet endroit niché dans les collines de l'historique Rancho Santa Fe. Une enquête sur les sols avait révélé que la pente était dangereuse; ceci a ammené l'architecte et les ingénieurs à concevoir un plan pour remettre le canyon dans un état naturel stabilisé. Comme la ville de Santa Barbara, l'identité du Rancho Santa Fe a été influencée par l'architecture de l'Hacienda espagnole. Grâce à une planification, une exécution et une sélection de matériaux minutieuses, la maison intègre l'influence espagnole aux caractéristiques modernes. Inspiré par le plan de la villa d'Hadrien, l'architecte a orienté le plan le long de la crête de la colline vers les vues de l'ouest, et a encastré le deuxième étage dans le flanc de la colline. Un toit en croupe avec des tuiles plates en terre cuite et une entrée avec une cour formelle incarnent l'architecture espagnole de la Californie du Sud, tandis qu'un profond avant-toit, les gouttières droites, la masse des fenêtres, la conception de l'éclairage et les éléments d'eau créent une impression de modernité.

Die Eigentümer entdeckten versehentlich ein schönes Grundstück mit Blick auf eine grüne Schlucht mit Blick auf den Pazifik. Sie hatten gerade ein neues Küstenhaus gebaut, wurden aber von diesem Ort in den Hügeln des historischen Rancho Santa Fe angezogen. Eine Bodenuntersuchung ergab, dass der Hang gefährlich war; Dies veranlasste den Architekten und die Ingenieure, einen Plan zu entwickeln, um den Canyon in einen stabilisierten natürlichen Zustand zu versetzen. Wie die Stadt Santa Barbara zeigt auch die Identität von Rancho Santa Fe Einflüsse der spanischen Hacienda. Durch sorgfältige Planung, Ausführung und Auswahl der Materialien verbindet das Haus spanischen Einfluss mit modernen Merkmalen. Inspiriert vom Plan von Hadrians Villa orientierte der Architekt den Plan entlang der Spitze des Hügels in Richtung Westen und bettete die zweite Etage in den Hang ein. Ein Satteldach mit Terrakottafliesen und ein formeller Eingang zum Innenhof verkörpern die spanische Architektur Südkaliforniens, während eine tiefe Traufe, gerade Dachrinnen, eine Vielzahl von Fenstern, das Design von Beleuchtung und Wasserelementen einen Eindruck hinterlassen. der Moderne.

Los propietarios descubrieron casualmente un hermoso terreno con vista a un cañón verde con vistas al Pacífico. Acababan de construir una nueva casa costera, pero se sintieron atraídos por este lugar en las colinas del histórico Rancho Santa Fe. Una investigación del suelo reveló que la pendiente era peligrosa; esto llevó a la arquitecta y los ingenieros a diseñar un plan para restaurar el cañón a un estado natural estabilizado. Como la ciudad de Santa Bárbara, la identidad de Rancho Santa Fe muestra influencias de la Hacienda española. A través de una cuidadosa planificación, ejecución y selección de materiales, la casa incorpora la influencia española con características modernas. Inspirado por el plano de la Villa de Adriano, la arquitecta orientó el plano a lo largo de la cima de la colina hacia las vistas occidentales y empotró el segundo piso en la ladera. Un tejado a cuatro aguas con tejas de terracota y una entrada con un patio formal encarnan la arquitectura española del sur de California, mientras que un alero profundo, canalones rectos, una masa de ventanas, diseño de los elementos de iluminación y agua crean una impresión de modernidad.

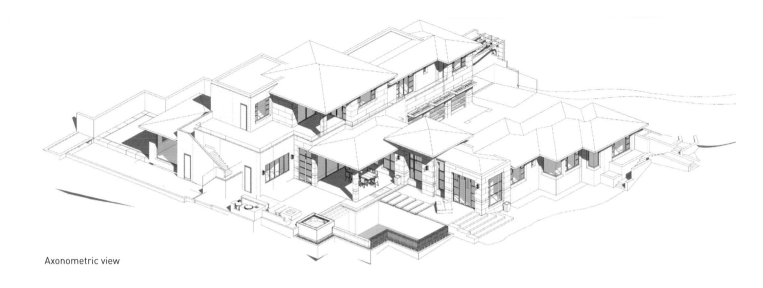

Axonometric view

North elevation

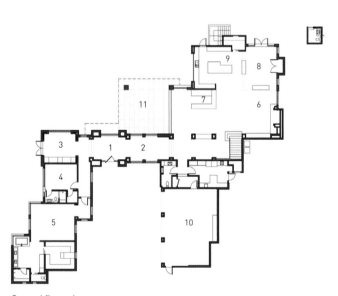

Ground floor plan

Second floor plan

1. Entry
2. Hall
3. Office
4. Bedroom
5. Owner's suite
6. Living room
7. Bar
8. Dining room
9. Kitchen
10. Garage
11. Outdoor room
12. Bedroom
13. Gym
14. Music room
15. Entertainment room
16. Covered deck

0   10'   20'   40'

HORIZON HOUSE I

Architecture team: Geoffrey von Oeyen Design / von Oeyen Architects

Landscape Architect: Geoffrey von Oeyen Design

Geologist: Landphases, Inc.

Structural Engineer: Weidlinger Associates, Inc

Civil Engineers: LC Engineering, Grading / DK Engineer Corp, Drainage

General Contractor: G&H Constructors, Inc

MEP Engineer: TTG Engineers

Pool Consultant: Avanti Pools

Photographer: Geoffrey von Oeyen

CASE ROOM

Architecture Team: Geoffrey von Oeyen Design / von Oeyen Architects

Landscape Architect: Geoffrey von Oeyen Design

General Contractor: G&H Constructors, Inc.

Structural Engineer: Parker Resnick

Civil Engineer: Parker Resnick

MEP Engineer: G&H Constructors, Inc.

Photographer: Kyle Monk

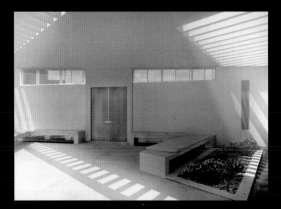

Y-HOUSE

Architecture Team: Geoffrey von Oeyen Design / von Oeyen Architects

Landscape Architect: Geoffrey von Oeyen Design

Renderings: Geoffrey von Oeyen Design

Geoffrey von Oeyen Design, based in Los Angeles, leverages geometric relationships and site conditions to create visually, environmentally, and culturally resilient works. Current projects in North America and Asia represent familiar contexts in unanticipated ways and are designed as geometric realignments that redirect daylight and reframe views. In the words of Preston Scott Cohen, the firm discovers "new possibilities within the intractable givens, turning otherwise functionally necessary forms into optical devices that produce spatial experiences."

Principal Geoffrey von Oeyen has received multiple national awards, including the Architectural League Prize, Next Progressives, and a MacDowell Fellowship, and the firm's built architectural projects have been widely featured in publications such as Architect, Architectural Record, Archinect, Architizer, and the Architect's Newspaper. In 2019, Geoffrey von Oeyen Design was internationally longlisted by Dezeen for "Emerging Architect of the Year" and was selected by the Dezeen readers as one of the top ten firms in architecture, design, and landscape architecture.

Geoffrey von Oeyen Design, basé à Los Angeles, exploite les relations géométriques et les conditions du site pour créer des œuvres visuellement, écologiquement et culturellement résilientes. Les projets actuels en Amérique du Nord et en Asie représentent des contextes familiers de manière imprévue et sont conçus comme des réalignements géométriques qui redirigent la lumière du jour et recadrent les vues. Pour reprendre les mots de Preston Scott Cohen, le cabinetel estudio découvre « de nouvelles possibilités dans les données intraitables, transformant des formes autrement fonctionnellement nécessaires en dispositifs optiques qui produisent des expériences spatiales. »

L'architecte en chef, Geoffrey von Oeyen, a reçu de nombreux prix nationaux, notamment le prix de la Ligue architecturale, Next Progressives et la MacDowell Fellowship, et les projets architecturaux construits de l'entreprise ont été largement présentés dans des publications telles que Architect, Architectural Record, Archinect, Architizer, and the Architect's Journal. En 2019, Geoffrey von Oeyen Design a été choisi à l'échelle internationale par Dezeen pour « Architecte émergent de l'année » et a été sélectionné par les lecteurs de Dezeen comme l'un des dix meilleurs cabinets d'architecture, de design et d'architecture de paysage.

Geoffrey von Oeyen Design aus Los Angeles nutzt geometrische Beziehungen und Standortbedingungen, um visuell, ökologisch und kulturell belastbare Werke zu schaffen. Aktuelle Projekte in Nordamerika und Asien stellen vertraute Kontexte unvorhergesehener Formen dar und sind als geometrische Neuausrichtungen konzipiert, die das Tageslicht umleiten und die Ansichten überdenken. Mit den Worten von Preston Scott Cohen deckt die Studie „neue Möglichkeiten innerhalb des unüberwindlichen Offensichtlichen auf und verwandelt funktional notwendige Formen in optische Geräte, die räumliche Erfahrungen erzeugen".

Der Chefarchitekt Geoffrey von Oeyen hat mehrere nationale Auszeichnungen erhalten, darunter den Architectural League Prize, Next Progressives und das MacDowell Fellowship. Die vom Studio errichteten Architekturprojekte wurden in Fachzeitschriften wie Architect, Architectural Record, Archinect, Architizer und veröffentlicht Architektenzeitung. Im Jahr 2019 wurde Geoffrey von Oeyen Design von Dezeen international als „Emerging Architect of the Year" und von Dezeen-Lesern als eines der zehn besten Architektur-, Design- und Landschaftsarchitekturbüros ausgewählt.

Geoffrey von Oeyen Design, con sede en Los Ángeles, aprovecha las relaciones geométricas y las condiciones del sitio para crear obras visual, ambiental y culturalmente resilientes. Los proyectos actuales en América del Norte y Asia representan contextos familiares de formas imprevistas y están diseñados como realineamientos geométricos que redirigen la luz del día y replantean las vistas. En palabras de Preston Scott Cohen, el estudio descubre «nuevas posibilidades dentro de lo obvio insuperable, convirtiendo formas funcionalmente necesarias en dispositivos ópticos que producen experiencias espaciales».

El arquitecto jefe, Geoffrey von Oeyen, ha recibido múltiples premios nacionales, incluido el Architectural League Prize, Next Progressives y MacDowell Fellowship, y los proyectos arquitectónicos construidos del estudio han sido publicados ampliamente en revistas especializadas como Architect, Architectural Record, Archinect, Architizer y Architect's Periódico. En 2019, Geoffrey von Oeyen Design fue seleccionado internacionalmente por Dezeen como «Arquitecto emergente del año» y fue seleccionado por los lectores de Dezeen como una de los diez mejores estudios de arquitectura, diseño y arquitectura paisajista.

HORIZON HOUSE I

MALIBU, CALIFORNIA

Lot size: 23,306 sq ft
Project size: 4,317 sq ft (renovation plus 996 sq ft addition)

This significant addition and remodel was designed to geometrically transform a generic 1960s ranch house into an optical device for framing panoramic views of the Pacific horizon in Malibu, California. The space in the intersection of the original L-shaped house, where two wings met in closest proximity to the ocean, lacked unobstructed ocean views, space for large gatherings and performances by the musician owners, and outdoor space. The design reconciles the two wings with a third east-west axis, uniting the two halves of the house to reframe the horizon above an infinity pool. The existing ranch house ceiling was removed, and its roof bisected, reconstructed in steel, lifted, and reoriented due south. The horizon is mirrored by horizontal framing devices, such as the 57-ft clear-span truss in parallel with the pool. Operable skylights modulate daylight and passive ventilation and animate the roofscape as an archipelago of extrusions against the horizon. Cantilevered aluminum frames, supporting operable fabric shade canopies, create visual and physical extensions outward.

Un considerable ajout et rénovation ont été conçus pour transformer géométriquement une maison de ranch des années 1960 en un dispositif optique pour encadrer des vues panoramiques de l'horizon du Pacifique à Malibu, en Californie. L'espace à l'intersection de la maison originale en forme de L, où deux ailes se rencontraient le plus près de l'océan, manquait de vue sur l'océan, d'espace pour de grands rassemblements et performances des propriétaires musiciens, et d'espace extérieur. La conception réconcilie les deux ailes avec un troisième axe est-ouest, unissant les deux moitiés de la maison pour recadrer l'horizon au-dessus d'une piscine à débordement. Le plafond de la maison du ranch a été enlevé et son toit coupé en deux, reconstruit en acier, soulevé et réorienté plein sud. L'horizon est reflété par des dispositifs de charpente horizontaux, tels que la ferme à portée libre d'environ 17 mètres en parallèle avec la piscine. Les lanterneaux opérables modulent la lumière du jour et la ventilation passive et animent la toiture comme un archipel d'extrusions contre l'horizon. Les cadres en aluminium en porte-à-faux, soutenant les auvents en tissu fonctionnels, créent des extensions visuelles et physiques vers l'extérieur.

Eine massive Erweiterung und Renovierung wurde entworfen, um ein Ranchhaus aus den 1960er Jahren geometrisch in ein optisches Gerät zu verwandeln, das einen Panoramablick auf die pazifische Skyline in Malibu, Kalifornien, bietet. Der Raum an der Kreuzung des ursprünglichen L-förmigen Hauses, in dem sich zwei Flügel näher am Meer trafen, hatte keinen Blick auf das Meer, Platz für große Versammlungen und Aufführungen der Musikerbesitzer sowie Platz im Freien. Das Design versöhnt die beiden Flügel mit einer dritten Ost-West-Achse und verbindet die beiden Hälften des Hauses, um den Horizont über einem Infinity-Pool auszuschneiden. Das Dach des Hauses wurde entfernt und in zwei Hälften geschnitten, in Stahl umgebaut, angehoben und nach Süden ausgerichtet. Der Horizont wird von horizontalen Rahmengeräten wie einem 17-Meter-Strahl parallel zum Pool reflektiert. Oberlichter modulieren das Tageslicht und die passive Belüftung und beleben das Dach wie ein Archipel von Extrusionen gegen den Horizont. Die freitragenden Aluminiumrahmen, die die Stoffüberdachungen tragen, schaffen visuelle und physische Erweiterungen nach außen.

Se diseñó una considerable extensión y renovación para transformar geométricamente una casa de planta única de la década de 1960 en un dispositivo óptico para enmarcar vistas panorámicas del Pacífico en Malibú, California. El espacio en la intersección de la casa original en forma de L, donde dos alas se unían más cerca del océano, carecía de vistas al mar, espacio para grandes reuniones y actuaciones de los propietarios músicos y espacio al aire libre. El diseño reconcilia las dos alas con un tercer eje este-oeste, uniendo las dos mitades de la casa para recortar el horizonte sobre una piscina infinita. Se quitó el techo de la casa y se cortó por la mitad, se reconstruyó en acero, se levantó y se reorientó hacia el sur. El horizonte se refleja mediante dispositivos de encuadre horizontales, como una viga de 17 metros en paralelo con la piscina. Los tragaluces modulan la luz del día y la ventilación pasiva y animan el tejado como un archipiélago de extrusiones contra el horizonte. Los marcos de aluminio en voladizo que sostienen los toldos de tela crean extensiones visuales y físicas hacia el exterior.

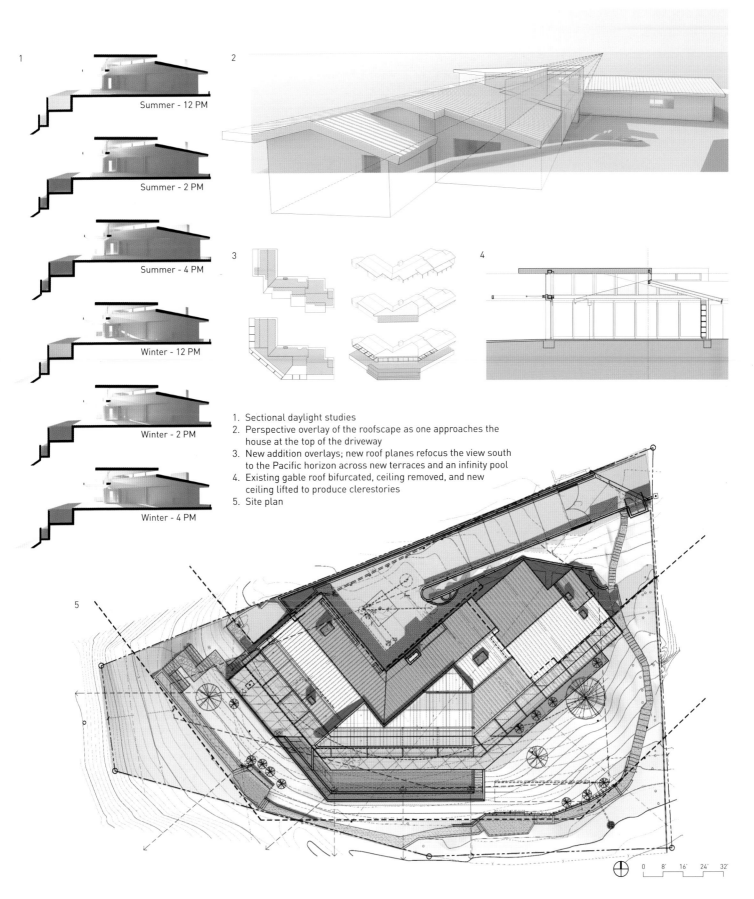

1. Sectional daylight studies
2. Perspective overlay of the roofscape as one approaches the house at the top of the driveway
3. New addition overlays; new roof planes refocus the view south to the Pacific horizon across new terraces and an infinity pool
4. Existing gable roof bifurcated, ceiling removed, and new ceiling lifted to produce clerestories
5. Site plan

Summer - 12 PM

Summer - 2 PM

Summer - 4 PM

Winter - 12 PM

Winter - 2 PM

Winter - 4 PM

0 8' 16' 24' 32'

CASE ROOM

MALIBU, CALIFORNIA

Lot size: 3.3 acres
Project size: 650 sq ft (addition)

The clients, two attorneys who are partners in life and law, commissioned a 650 square-foot addition to their Malibu, California residence for use as a satellite office away from their Downtown Los Angeles headquarters. Since the global pandemic, the concept of work-from-home has taken on new urgency, and the owners have utilized the Case Room as their primary workspace. Architecturally, clerestories diffuse the north light at the foot of the hillside, orient the space, and frame views up the hill. The massing of the project is designed as a series of blocks obliquely sliced and assembled in a descending sectional sequence. The symmetrical roof gables, which step down one foot at each progression from the maximum city-defined height limit, align in plan with the major programmatic divisions of the space. The new second-floor elevator landing and adjacent clerestory lightwell frame views into the double-height room and toward the hillside. The interplay of reflected daylight on the folding ceiling surfaces throughout the day provides a gently modulating, diffused top lighting for contemplative work.

Les clients, deux avocats partenaires dans la vie et le droit, ont commandé un ajout d'environ 60 mètres carrés à leur résidence de Malibu, en Californie, pour l'utiliser comme bureau satellite loin de leur siège social du centre-ville de Los Angeles. Depuis la pandémie mondiale, le concept de travail à domicile a pris une nouvelle urgence et les propriétaires ont utilisé la Case Room comme leur principal espace de travail. Sur le plan architectural, les claires-voies diffusent la lumière du nord au pied de la colline, orientent l'espace et encadrent les vues sur la colline. Le volume du projet est conçu comme une série de blocs tranchés obliquement et assemblés dans une séquence de coupe descendante. Les pignons de toit symétriques, qui descendent trente centimètres à chaque progression à partir de la limite de hauteur maximale définie par la ville, s'alignent en plan avec les principales divisions programmatiques de l'espace. Le nouveau palier d'ascenseur au deuxième étage et le puit de lumière adjacent encadrent les vuessur la salle à double hauteur et vers la colline. L'interaction de la lumière du jour réfléchie sur les surfaces pliées du plafond tout au long de la journée fournit un éclairage supérieur légèrement modulant et diffus pour un travail contemplatif.

Die Mandanten, zwei Anwälte, Partner im Privat- und Berufsleben, haben eine Erweiterung ihres Wohnsitzes in Malibu, Kalifornien, um etwa 60 Quadratmeter in Auftrag gegeben, um ihn als Satellitenbüro außerhalb ihres Hauptsitzes in der Innenstadt von Los Angeles zu nutzen. Seit der globalen Pandemie hat das Konzept der Telearbeit eine neue Dringlichkeit erhalten, und die Eigentümer haben den Fallraum als primären Arbeitsbereich genutzt. Architektonisch streuen Triforien am Fuße des Hügels Nordlicht, orientieren den Raum und rahmen den Blick auf den Hügel ein. Das Volumen des Projekts besteht aus einer Reihe von schräg geschnittenen Blöcken, die in absteigender Reihenfolge angeordnet sind. Die symmetrischen Giebel des Daches, die in jedem Verlauf von der von der Stadt festgelegten maximalen Höhengrenze um etwa einen Fuß abfallen, sind planmäßig auf die Hauptabteilungen des Raums ausgerichtet. Die neue Aufzugslandung im zweiten Stock und die angrenzende helle Terrasse rahmen den Blick auf den Raum mit doppelter Höhe und den Hang hinunter. Tageslicht, das von den facettierten Deckenflächen reflektiert wird, sorgt für eine diffuse, weich modulierende Deckenbeleuchtung für kontemplatives Arbeiten.

Los clientes, dos abogados, pareja en la vida personal y laboral, encargaron una ampliación de unos 60 metros cuadrados a su residencia en Malibú, California, para usarla como oficina satélite lejos de su sede en el centro de Los Ángeles. Desde la pandemia global, el concepto de teletrabajo ha adquirido una nueva urgencia y los propietarios han utilizado Case Room como su espacio de trabajo principal. Arquitectónicamente, los triforios difunden la luz del norte al pie de la ladera, orientan el espacio y enmarcan las vistas de la colina. La volumetría del proyecto está diseñada como una serie de bloques cortados oblicuamente y ensamblados en una secuencia seccional descendente. Los frontones simétricos del tejado, que bajan unos treinta centímetros en cada progresión desde el límite de altura máximo definido por la ciudad, se alinean en planta con las principales divisiones del espacio. El nuevo rellano del ascensor en el segundo piso y el patio de luces adyacente enmarcan vistas a la sala de doble altura y hacia la ladera. La luz del día reflejada en las superficies del techo facetado proporciona una iluminación superior difusa y de modulación suave para el trabajo contemplativo.

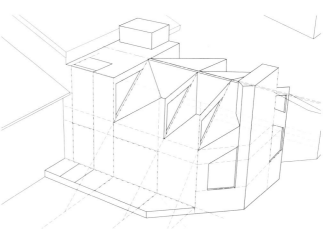

Axonometric diagram

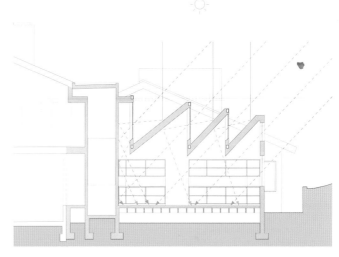

Section with daylighting overlay

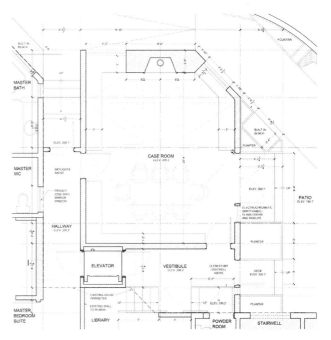

Partial floor plan

The vast expanse of West Texas and proximity to the Chinati Foundation inform the massing and parti of this Marfa retreat for a London family. A covered southern front courtyard and open rear northern courtyard, partially shaded by the building itself, provide privacy from neighboring parcels while shaping expansive views to distant mountain ranges on the horizon. Water elements in this house, including evaporative cooling ponds in the entry court and the swimming pool in the rear, draw from an on-site well. Subtle plays with siting and perspective are achieved by mirroring the ground topography at the outer roof edge, while the inner rear courtyard roof remains horizontal. The house thus performs differently as an object in the landscape than as an optical device for viewing the landscape. Daylighting is a primary overlay, shaping circulation, program, and facades. The architectural promenade, beginning with the vehicular approach and including an enfilade arrangement of entry court, living room, and rear courtyard, is an orchestrated sequence that situates this house in the landscape.

La vaste étendue de l'ouest du Texas et la proximité de la Fondation Chinati informent le volume et le parti pris de cette retraite de Marfa pour une famille londonienne. Une cour avant sud couverte et une cour arrière nord ouverte, partiellement ombragée par le bâtiment lui-même, offrent une intimité des parcelles voisines tout en façonnant des vues imprenables sur les chaînes de montagnes lointaines à l'horizon. Les éléments d'eau de cette maison, y compris les bassins de refroidissement par évaporation dans la cour d'entrée et la piscine à l'arrière, puisent dans un puits sur place. Des jeux subtils avec l'emplacement et la perspective sont obtenus en reflétant la topographie du sol au bord extérieur du toit, tandis que le toit de la cour arrière intérieure reste horizontal. La maison se comporte donc différemment en tant qu'objet dans le paysage que comme dispositif optique de visualisation du paysage. La lumière du jour est une superposition principale, façonnant la circulation, le programme et les façades. La promenade architecturale, commençant par l'approche véhiculaire et comprenant un agencement en enfilade de la cour d'entrée, du salon et de la cour arrière, est une séquence orchestrée qui situe cette maison dans le paysage.

Die Weite von West-Texas und die Nähe zur Chinati Foundation prägen das Volumen und den Aufbau dieses Marfa-Retreats für eine Londoner Familie. Eine überdachte Terrasse nach Süden und eine offene Terrasse nach Norden, die teilweise vom Gebäude selbst beschattet wird, bieten Privatsphäre vor benachbarten Parzellen und bieten einen atemberaubenden Blick auf die Bergketten am Horizont. Es nutzte einen Brunnen vor Ort, um die Verdunstungskühlteiche im Vorgarten und den Pool im hinteren Bereich zu versorgen. Subtile Spiele mit Standort und Perspektive werden erreicht, indem die Topographie vom Boden bis zur Außenkante des Daches gespiegelt wird, während das Dach des Innenhofs horizontal bleibt. Daher verhält sich das Haus anders, eher wie ein Objekt in der Landschaft als wie ein optisches Gerät zur Betrachtung der Landschaft. Tageslicht ist eine Hauptüberlappung, die Zirkulation, Räume und Fassaden prägt. Der architektonische Spaziergang, der vom Fahrzeugansatz ausgeht und eine miteinander verbundene Anordnung der Eingangsterrasse, des Wohnzimmers und des Hinterhofs umfasst, ist eine orchestrierte Sequenz, die dieses Haus in die Landschaft einfügt.

La vasta extensión del oeste de Texas y la proximidad a la Fundación Chinati informa el volumen y el diseño de este retiro de Marfa para una familia de Londres. Un patio delantero sur cubierto y un patio trasero norte abierto, parcialmente sombreado por el edificio en sí, brindan privacidad de las parcelas vecinas mientras enmarcan las impresionantes vistas de las cadenas montañosas en el horizonte. Un pozo *in situ* suministra agua a los estanques de enfriamiento por evaporación en el patio delantero y a la piscina en la parte trasera. Los juegos sutiles con la ubicación y la perspectiva se logran reflejando la topografía desde el suelo hasta el canto exterior del tejado, mientras que el tejado del patio interior permanece horizontal. Por lo tanto, la casa se comporta de manera diferente, más como un objeto en el paisaje que como un dispositivo óptico para ver el paisaje. La luz del día es una superposición principal, dando forma a la circulación, los espacios y las fachadas. El paseo arquitectónico, a partir del enfoque vehicular y que abarca una disposición interconectada del patio de entrada, la sala de estar y el patio trasero, es una secuencia orquestada que sitúa esta casa en el paisaje.

Summer 11 AM

Summer 12 PM

Summer 1 PM

Summer 2 PM

Summer 3 PM

Summer 4 PM

Summer 12 PM

Summer 2 PM

Summer 4 PM

Winter 12 PM

Winter 2 PM

Winter 4 PM

Entry court and sectional daylight studies

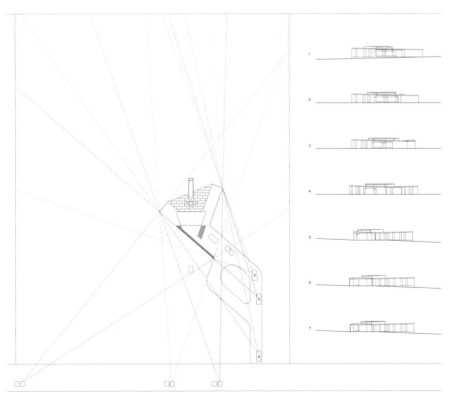

Auto approach sequence: Elevation views

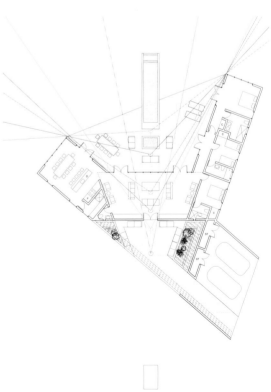

Floor plan with entry view sequence overlay

184

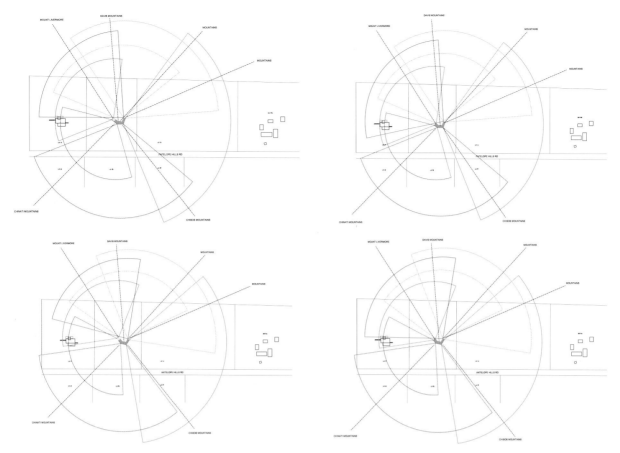

Siting and massing strategies per mountain viewsheds

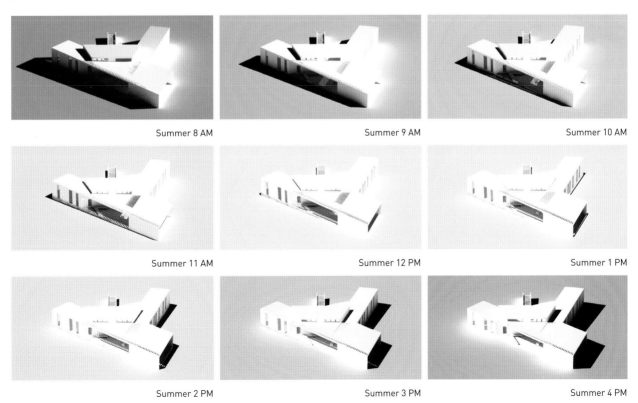

Summer 8 AM	Summer 9 AM	Summer 10 AM
Summer 11 AM	Summer 12 PM	Summer 1 PM
Summer 2 PM	Summer 3 PM	Summer 4 PM

Exterior daylight studies

Jeff Svitak Inc.

jeffsvitak.com

REDWOOD HOUSE

Structural Engineer: Omar Mobayed

Landscape Architect: Aaron Nussbaum

Photographer: Onnis Luque and Tomoko Matsubayashi

1941 COLUMBIA

Structural Engineer: DCI Engineers

Developer: Jeff Svitak, Inc.

Construction Management: Jeff Svitak, Inc.

Photographer: Yoshi Koitani

THE LOUISIANA

Production Architects: Trachtenberg Architects

Structural Enginner: DCG Structural Engineers

Landscape Architect: Aaron Nussbaum Studio

Developer: Morley, LLC.

General Contractor: RGB Group, Inc.

Construction Management: Jeff Svitak, Inc.

Photographer: Onnis Luque

Jeff Svitak Inc. is an all-inclusive studio focusing primarily on architectural design, while simultaneously integrating both real estate development and construction management into its practice. The studio prides itself on creating unique and inspired human environments that engage with the senses of the user. While each project has its own individual inspiration and concept, Svitak believes heavily in the role of spatial organization and its influence on human emotions. By intimately studying this relationship, Jeff Svitak Inc. looks to enhance the emotional quality of its building's inhabitants; thoughtfully integrating aspects of privacy and intimacy within the interior environment, connecting exterior living spaces, and inviting an overall sense of community through crafted and welcoming public and circulatory spaces.

The studio actively pursues and engages with a diverse range of project typologies and sizes, from an 800 square-foot art studio to a 20-story residential high rise. This openness allows the studio to critically re-think with a fresh perspective, how it can improve upon and better engage the project experience, with a focus on activating the sensitivity of the human being.

Jeff Svitak Inc. est un studio tout compris qui se concentre principalement sur la conception architecturale, tout en intégrant simultanément le développement immobilier et la gestion de la construction dans sa pratique. Le studio est fier de créer des environnements humains uniques et inspirés qui font appel aux sens de l'utilisateur. Bien que chaque projet ayant sa propre inspiration et son propre concept, Svitak croit fortement au rôle de l'organisation spatiale et à son influence sur les émotions humaines. En étudiant de près cette relation, Jeff Svitak Inc. cherche à améliorer la qualité émotionnelle des occupants de son bâtiment ; en intégrant de manière réfléchie les aspects de la vie privée et de l'intimité dans l'environnement intérieur, en reliant les espaces de vie extérieurs et en invitant à un sentiment général de communauté, grâce à des espaces publics et circulatoires bien conçus et accueillants.

Le studio poursuit et s'engage activement dans une gamme variée de typologies et de tailles de projets, allant d'un studio d'art d'environ 75 métres carrés à une tour résidentielle de 20 étages. Cette flexibilité permet au studio de repenser de manière critique, avec une nouvelle perspective, la manière dont il peut améliorer et mieux engager l'expérience du projet, en mettant l'accent sur l'activation de la sensibilité de l'être humain.

Jeff Svitak Inc. ist ein Studio, das sich hauptsächlich auf architektonisches Design konzentriert und sowohl die Immobilienentwicklung als auch das Baumanagement integriert. Das Studio ist stolz darauf, einzigartige und inspirierte menschliche Umgebungen zu schaffen, die die Sinne des Benutzers ansprechen. Während jedes Projekt seine eigene individuelle Inspiration und sein eigenes Konzept hat, glaubt Svitak stark an die Rolle der räumlichen Organisation und deren Einfluss auf menschliche Emotionen. Indem Jeff Svitak diese Beziehung eingehend untersucht, versucht er, die emotionale Qualität der Bewohner seines Gebäudes zu verbessern, indem er Aspekte der Privatsphäre und Intimität in die innere Umgebung integriert, die äußeren Lebensräume miteinander verbindet und durch gestaltete und einladende öffentliche Räume und Verkehrskreisläufe zu einem allgemeinen Gemeinschaftsgefühl einlädt.

Das Studio verfolgt und beschäftigt sich aktiv mit einer Vielzahl von Projekttypologien und -größen, von einem 75 Quadratmeter großen Kunststudio bis zu einem 20-stöckigen Wohngebäude. Diese Flexibilität ermöglicht es dem Studio, mit einer neuen Perspektive kritisch zu überdenken, wie es die Projekterfahrung verbessern und sich darauf einlassen kann, wobei der Schwerpunkt auf der Aktivierung der menschlichen Sensibilität liegt.

Jeff Svitak Inc. es un estudio que se centra principalmente en el diseño arquitectónico, a la vez que integra tanto el desarrollo inmobiliario como la gestión de la construcción. El estudio se enorgullece de crear ambientes humanos únicos e inspirados que se conectan con los sentidos del usuario. Mientras que cada proyecto tiene su propia inspiración y concepto individual, Svitak cree firmemente en el papel de la organización espacial y su influencia en las emociones humanas. Estudiando íntimamente esta relación, Jeff Svitak Inc. busca mejorar la calidad emocional de los habitantes de su edificio integrando cuidadosamente aspectos de privacidad e intimidad dentro del ambiente interior, conectando los espacios vitales exteriores e invitando a un sentido general de comunidad a través de espacios públicos y circulatorios elaborados y acogedores.

El estudio persigue activamente y se compromete con una diversa gama de tipologías y tamaños de proyectos, desde un estudio de arte de 75 metros cuadrados hasta un edificio residencial de 20 pisos. Esta flexibilidad permite que el estudio se replantee críticamente con una perspectiva fresca, cómo puede mejorar y comprometerse con la experiencia del proyecto, centrándose en la activación de la sensibilidad del ser humano.

REDWOOD HOUSE

SAN DIEGO, CALIFORNIA

Project size: 2,000 sq ft

A house and an architect's office are nestled into a unique canyon running through the city of San Diego. The canyon creates an essence for the house to work around and integrate with. The house is divided into separate massing elements, which allow the canyon to enter into the house and studio through a slim courtyard.

The house is accessed across a floating steel bridge and through a sliding cedar door, revealing various spaces with panoramic views of the canyon beyond. The living room is a cantilevered room floating above the natural elements of the canyon, which opens up completely to the life outside. The circulation flows inside and out; access to the bedrooms is through an outdoor vestibule and then into a wooden box, where trees are the only visual element. The basement has another outdoor private access and is utilized as the architect's office. The architectural footprint, while small, is vertically integrated to offer a wide array of living opportunities, which all address the canyon from various perspectives.

Une maison et un bureau d'architecte sont nichés dans un canyon unique qui traverse la ville de San Diego. Le canyon crée une essence dans laquelle la maison peut se développer et s'intégrer. La maison est divisée en éléments de masse séparés, ce qui permet au canyon d'entrer dans la maison et le studio par une mince cour.

On accède à la maison par un pont flottant en acier et par une porte coulissante en cèdre, révélant divers espaces avec des vues panoramiques sur le canyon au-delà. Le salon est une pièce en porte-à-faux flottant, au-dessus des éléments naturels du canyon, qui s'ouvre complètement sur la vie à l'extérieur. La circulation se fait à l'intérieur et à l'extérieur ; l'accès aux chambres se fait par un vestibule extérieur, puis dans une boîte en bois, où les arbres sont le seul élément visuel. Le sous-sol a un autre accès extérieur privé et sert de bureau d'architecte. L'empreinte architecturale, bien que petite, est intégrée verticalement pour offrir un large éventail de possibilités de vie, qui toutes abordent le canyon sous des angles différents.

Das architektonische Haus- und Büroprojekt befindet sich in einer Schlucht, die durch die Stadt San Diego verläuft und eine Grundlage schafft, auf der sich das Haus entwickeln und integrieren kann. Die Wohnung ist in separate Elemente unterteilt, die es der Kanone ermöglichen, das Haus zu betreten und durch einen engen Innenhof zu studieren.

Der Zugang zum Haus erfolgt über eine schwebende Stahlbrücke und durch eine Schiebetür aus Zedernholz, die verschiedene Räume mit Panoramablicken auf den dahinter liegenden Canyon freigibt. Das Wohnzimmer ist ein freitragender Raum, der über den natürlichen Elementen der Schlucht schwebt und sich vollständig dem Leben draußen öffnet. Der Zugang zu den Zimmern erfolgt über eine Außenlobby und anschließend über eine Holzkonstruktion, in der Bäume das einzige visuelle Element sind. Das Untergeschoss hat einen weiteren privaten Zugang im Freien und wird als Architekturbüro genutzt. Die architektonische Grundfläche ist zwar klein, aber vertikal integriert, um eine breite Palette von Wohnmöglichkeiten zu bieten, die alle aus verschiedenen Perspektiven auf die Schlucht ausgerichtet sind.

El proyecto de casa y oficina de arquitectura se encuentra en un cañón que atraviesa la ciudad de San Diego creando una base en la que la casa puede evolucionar e integrarse. La vivienda está dividida en elementos separados, que permiten al cañón entrar en la casa y el estudio a través de un estrecho patio.

El acceso se realiza a través de un puente de acero en voladizo y de una puerta corrediza de cedro, revelando varios espacios con vistas panorámicas. La sala de estar es una habitación también en voladizo sobre los elementos naturales exteriores. El acceso a las habitaciones se realiza a través de un vestíbulo exterior y luego a través de una estructura de madera, donde los árboles son el único elemento visual. El sótano tiene otro acceso privado por el exterior y se utiliza como despacho de arquitectura. La huella arquitectónica, aunque pequeña, está integrada verticalmente en el paisaje, ofreciendo varias perspectivas del paisaje.

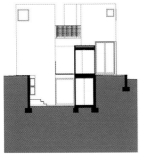

Section A

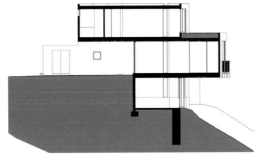

Section B

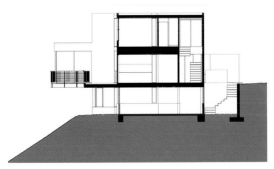

Section C

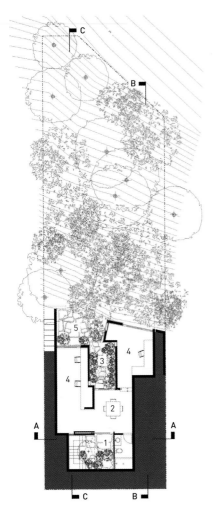

Basement floor plan

1. Entry courtyard
2. Meeting room
3. Courtyard
4. Studio
5. Patio
6. Bridge
7. Entry
8. Dining area
9. Living area

10. Deck
11. Patio
12. Kitchen
13. Storage
14. Outdoor vestibule
15. Bedroom
16. Master bedroom
17. Green roof patio

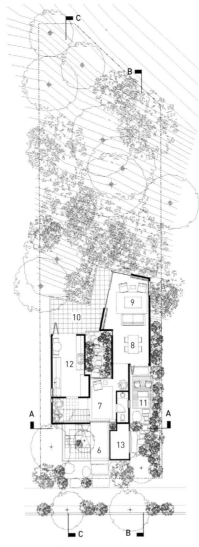

Ground floor plan

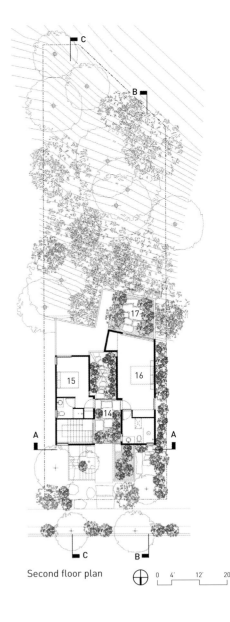

Second floor plan

0   4'   12'   20'

1941 COLUMBIA

Located on a narrow, 50' x 100' mid-block site in Little Italy, an expanding and architecturally significant neighborhood in downtown San Diego, 1941 Columbia adapts to the site's constraints through fragmentation. This fragmentation of buildings allows the maximum amount of light and ventilation to flow through the units. Inspired by the narrow and winding streets of Venice, 1941 Columbia contains 18 apartments, which are separated by delicately carved voids, creating internal courtyards that compress and expand. These shared common spaces further the environment of community and evoke a sense of calm as one gradually fades from the public realm to the private. With only 50 minutes of daylight facing the street and being walled-in on all the other three sides, the concept came to design six small "towers" instead of one single monolithic structure. The staggering of walls and floor plates allow all 18 units to existing in extremely tight proximity to one another while still maintaining a sense of openness and privacy within each unit.

Situé sur un site étroit d'environ 15 x 30 mètres au milieu d'un site de mi-bloc dans Little Italy, un quartier en expansion et important sur le plan architectural dans le centre-ville de San Diego, 1941 Columbia s'adapte aux contraintes du site par la fragmentation. Cette fragmentation des bâtiments permet à la quantité maximale de lumière et de ventilation, de circuler dans les unités. Inspiré par les rues étroites et sinueuses de Venise, 1941 Columbia comprend 18 appartements, qui sont séparés par des vides délicatement sculptés, créant ainsi des cours intérieures qui se compriment et s'agrandissent. Ces espaces communs partagés renforcent l'environnement de la communauté et évoquent un sentiment de calme alors que l'on passe progressivement du domaine public au domaine privé. Avec seulement 50 minutes de lumière du jour donnant sur la rue et étant murée sur les trois autres côtés, le concept en est venu à concevoir six petites « tours » au lieu d'une seule structure monolithique. L'échelonnement des murs et des plaques de sol permet aux 18 unités d'exister à proximité les unes des autres tout en conservant un sentiment d'ouverture et d'intimité au sein de chaque unité.

1941 Columbia liegt auf einem schmalen, 15 x 30 Meter großen Grundstück in Little Italy, einem expandierenden und architektonisch bedeutsamen Viertel in der Innenstadt von San Diego. 1941 Columbia passt sich durch Fragmentierung den Vorgaben des Geländes an. Diese Fragmentierung der Gebäude ermöglicht es, ein Maximum an Licht und Belüftung durch die Einheiten fließen zu lassen. Inspiriert von den engen und gewundenen Gassen Venedigs, enthält Columbia 18 Wohnungen, die durch fein gestaltete Hohlräume voneinander getrennt sind, wodurch Innenhöfe entstehen, die sich verdichten und ausdehnen. Diese gemeinsam genutzten Räume fördern die Umgebung der Gemeinschaft und rufen ein Gefühl der Ruhe hervor, während man allmählich vom öffentlichen Bereich in den privaten Bereich übergeht. Mit nur 50 Minuten Sonnenlicht pro Tag und umgeben von Mauern auf den anderen drei Seiten sah das Konzept vor, sechs kleine Türme anstelle einer einzigen monolithischen Struktur zu entwerfen. Durch die Staffelung der Wände und der Bodenplatten können die 18 Apartments sehr nahe beieinander liegen und gleichzeitig ein Gefühl von Offenheit und Privatsphäre in jedem von ihnen bewahren.

Situado en un estrecho terreno de 15 por 30 metros, junto a Little Italy, un barrio en expansión y arquitectónicamente significativo en el centro de San Diego, 1941 Columbia se adapta a las limitaciones del lugar a través de la fragmentación de los edificios que permite la máxima cantidad de luz y ventilación entre volúmenes. Inspirado por las estrechas y sinuosas calles de Venecia, 1941 Columbia contiene 18 apartamentos, separados por vacíos delicadamente tallados, creando patios internos que se comprimen y expanden. Estos espacios comunes compartidos fomentan el entorno de la comunidad y evocan una sensación de calma a medida que uno pasa gradualmente del ámbito público al privado. Con sólo 50 minutos al día de luz solar y rodeado de muros por los otros tres lados, el concepto concibió diseñar seis pequeñas torres en lugar de una única estructura monolítica. El escalonamiento de las paredes y las losas del suelo permite que los 18 apartamentos existan muy próximos entre sí, a la vez que se mantiene una sensación de apertura y privacidad dentro de cada una de ellas.

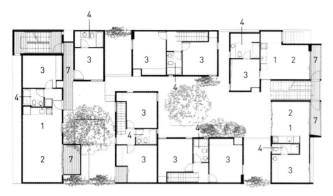

Level 2 plan

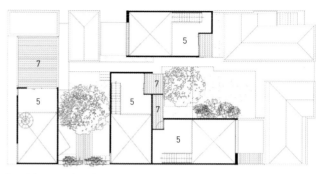

Level 4 mezzanine plan

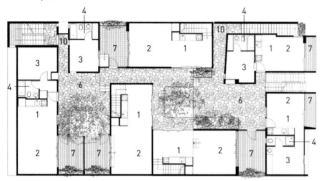

Level 1 plan

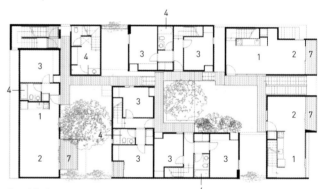

Level 4 plan

Ground floor plan

Level 3 plan

1. Kitchen   6. Courtyard
2. Living area 7. Patio
3. Bedroom   8. Garage
4. Bathroom   9. Studio
5. Mezzanine   10. Entry

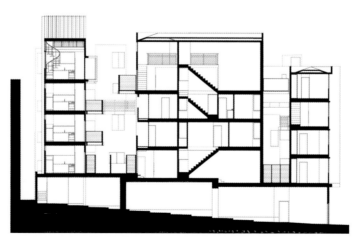

Section

THE LOUISIANA

SAN DIEGO, CALIFORNIA

Project size: 20,338 sq ft

The Louisiana is an apartment building designed around a series of court-yards, which serve as a dissolvent for the structure as it projects upward, and bring light and ventilation to the 15 units in the building. These court-yards generate functional outdoor rooms, which become as important to the dwellings as any of their interior rooms. They are meant to harness repose and quietness while acting as an escape from the pressures of the outside environment and the daily routine. Such a quality is a much-needed life component that is often forgotten in the ordinary apartment buildings of our urban environment.

Each unit is unique and reacts spatially to its specific location on the site and within the building. The units all work around a large central community courtyard, which is utilized as the main circulatory component. Instead of the common elevator and corridor, the circulation is conceived as an informal and engaging social space for casual encounters.

La Louisiane est un immeuble d'appartements conçu autour d'une série de cours, qui servent d'ouverture à la structure lorsqu'elle se projette vers le haut, et apportent lumière et ventilation aux 15 unités de l'im-meuble. Ces cours génèrent des pièces extérieures fonctionnelles, qui deviennent aussi importantes pour les logements que n'importe laquelle de leurs pièces intérieures. Elles sont destinées à favoriser le repos et la tranquillité, tout en servant de refuge contre les pressions de l'environ-nement extérieur et la routine quotidienne. Cette qualité est un élément indispensable de la vie qui est souvent oublié dans les immeubles d'habi-tation ordinaires de notre environnement urbain.

Chaque unité est unique et réagit spatialement à son emplacement spéci-fique sur le site et dans le bâtiment. Les unités fonctionnent toutes autour d'une grande cour communautaire centrale, qui est utilisée comme élé-ment circulatoire principal. Au lieu de l'ascenseur et du couloir communs, la circulation est conçue comme un espace social informel et engageant pour des rencontres informelles.

Das Louisiana ist ein Apartmentgebäude, das um eine Reihe von Höfen herum entworfen wurde, die als Lösungsmittel für die nach oben ragen-de Struktur dienen und Licht und Belüftung in die 15 Einheiten des Ge-bäudes bringen. Diese Höfe erzeugen funktionale Außenräume, die für die Wohnungen ebenso wichtig werden wie jeder ihrer Innenräume. Sie sollen Ruhe und Stille ermöglichen und gleichzeitig als Flucht vor dem Druck der äußeren Umgebung und der täglichen Routine dienen. Eine sol-che Qualität ist eine dringend benötigte Lebenskomponente, die in den gewöhnlichen Mehrfamilienhäusern unserer städtischen Umwelt oft ver-gessen wird.

Jede Einheit ist einzigartig und reagiert räumlich auf ihre spezifische Lage auf dem Grundstück und innerhalb des Gebäudes. Die Einheiten arbeiten alle um einen großen zentralen Gemeinschaftshof herum, der als Hauptkomponente des Kreislaufs genutzt wird. Anstelle des gemein-samen Aufzugs und Korridors ist die Zirkulation als ein informeller und ansprechender sozialer Raum für zwanglose Begegnungen konzipiert.

The Louisiana es un edificio de apartamentos diseñado alrededor de una serie de patios, que disuelven la estructura a medida que se proyecta hacia arriba y aportan luz y ventilación a las 15 viviendas del edificio. Estos patios generan espacios exteriores funcionales, que adquieren tanta importancia para las viviendas como cualquiera de sus estancias interiores. Están dise-ñados para fomentar el reposo y la tranquilidad mientras actúan como un escape de las presiones del entorno exterior y la rutina diaria. Tal calidad es un componente vital muy necesario que a menudo se olvida en los comu-nes edificios de apartamentos de nuestro entorno urbano.

Cada vivienda es única y reacciona espacialmente a su ubicación específica en el lugar y en el edificio. Todas las viviendas funcionan alrededor de un gran patio comunitario central, que se utiliza como el componente circula-torio principal. En lugar del ascensor y el pasillo comunes, la circulación se concibe como un espacio social informal para encuentros casuales.

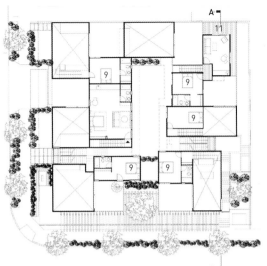

Third floor plan

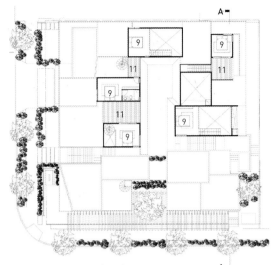

Fourth floor mezzanine plan

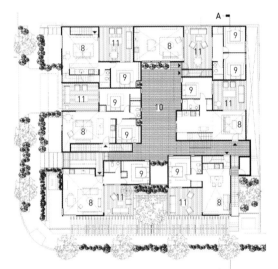

Second floor plan

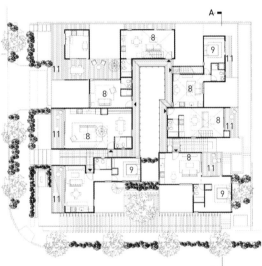

Fourth floor plan

1. Parking garage
2. Shop keeper space
3. Restaurant
4. Kitchen
5. Patio seating
6. Patio
7. Mechanical room
8. Living space
9. Bedroom
10. Community courtyard
11. Deck

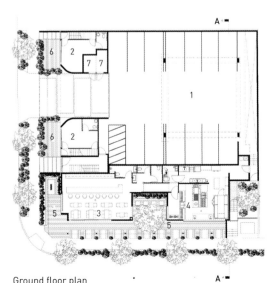

Ground floor plan

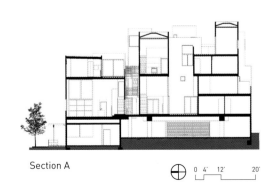

Section A

0 4' 12' 20'

Kevin Tsai
Architecture

kevin-tsai.com

GLASS HOUSE

Landscape Designer: OCAMPO's Landscape Development, INC

Structural Engineer: Thang Le & Associates

General Contractor: Space Construction

Photographer: Tara Wujcik Photography

M HOUSE

Landscape Architect: Melinda Wood Designs

Structural Engineer: Thang Le & Associates

General Contractor: Space Construction

Milwork Design and Build: td[s]

Photographer: Sherri J. Photography

McKUIN RESIDENCE

Landscape Architect: Bionic

Structural Engineer: IDG Structural Engineering

General Contractor: Space Construction

Milwork Design and Build: td[s]

Photographer: Dakota Witzenburg

Founded in 2012, Kevin Tsai Architecture is a Los Angeles-based architectural design studio with a multi-disciplinary team of 26 talented architects, graphic artists, industrial designers, interior designers, and brand practitioners. Collaboration is the cornerstone of KTA's process. The team works in tandem with clients to deliver unique and enduring work, ranging from single-family homes to large mixed-use developments.

In an era where mimicking trends are increasingly taking priority over design integrity, KTA neither follows trends nor allows itself to be defined by a distinct style, choosing instead a tenet that fosters innovation, elegance, versatility, and social consciousness to create timeless spaces that enrich human lives.

Fondé en 2012, Kevin Tsai Architecture est un studio de conception architecturale basé à Los Angeles avec une équipe multidisciplinaire de 26 talentueux architectes, graphistes, designers industriels, designers d'intérieur et praticiens de la marque. La collaboration est la pierre angulaire du processus de KTA. L'équipe travaille en tandem avec les clients pour fournir un travail unique et durable, allant des maisons unifamiliales aux grands développements à usage mixte.

À une époque où l'imitation des tendances prend de plus en plus la priorité sur l'intégrité du design, KTA ne suit ni les tendances ni ne se laisse définir par un style distinct, choisissant à la place un principe qui favorise l'innovation, l'élégance, la polyvalence et la conscience sociale pour créer des espaces intemporels qui enrichissent les vies humaines.

Kevin Tsai Architecture ist ein 2012 in Los Angeles gegründetes Architekturbüro mit einem multidisziplinären Team von 26 talentierten Architekten, Grafikern, Industriedesignern, Innenarchitekten und Markenfachleuten. Zusammenarbeit ist der Eckpfeiler des KTA-Prozesses. Das Team arbeitet eng mit Kunden zusammen, um eine einzigartige und dauerhafte Arbeit zu leisten, die von Einfamilienhäusern bis zu großen gemischt genutzten Entwicklungen reicht.

In einer Zeit, in der die Nachahmung von Trends zunehmend Vorrang vor der Integrität des Designs hat, folgt KTA keinen Trends oder wird nicht durch einen bestimmten Stil definiert, sondern wählt stattdessen ein Prinzip, das Innovation, Eleganz, Vielseitigkeit und Flexibilität fördert soziales Bewusstsein, um zeitlose Räume zu schaffen, die das menschliche Leben bereichern.

Kevin Tsai Architecture es un estudio de diseño de arquitectura fundado en 2012 en Los Ángeles con un equipo multidisciplinar de 26 talentosos arquitectos, artistas gráficos, diseñadores industriales, diseñadores de interiores, y profesionales de la marca. La colaboración es la piedra angular del proceso de KTA. El equipo trabaja en conjunto con los clientes para ofrecer un trabajo único y duradero, que va desde viviendas unifamiliares hasta grandes desarrollos de uso mixto.

En una era en la que imitar las tendencias tiene cada vez más prioridad sobre la integridad del diseño, KTA no sigue las tendencias ni se deja definir por un estilo particular, eligiendo en cambio un principio que fomenta la innovación, la elegancia, la versatilidad y la conciencia social para crear espacios atemporales que enriquecen las vidas humanas.

GLASS HOUSE

PLAYA DEL REY, CALIFORNIA

Lot size: 5,000 sq ft
Project size: 2,500 sq ft

This project features an elevated three-room suite perched atop an open carport structure. The house was redesigned as a series of open and connected spaces with the dining room, living room, and kitchen as one large, single space.

A sense of transparency flows through the home, which is illuminated by ample windows and a glass-paneled staircase in the middle of the space, giving the design a modern yet understated feel without sacrificing privacy. The upstairs master bedroom is an open, light-filled space that is wrapped in floor-to-ceiling glass, giving the illusion that the room is floating above the first floor.

Ce projet comprend une suite de trois pièces perchée au dessus d'un carport. La maison a été repensée en une série d'espaces ouverts et connectés avec la salle à manger, le salon et la cuisine comme un seul grand espace. Une sensation de transparence traverse la maison, qui est éclairée par de grandes fenêtres et un escalier vitré au milieu de l'espace, donnant au design une sensation moderne mais sobre sans sacrifier l'intimité. La chambre principale à l'étage supérieur est un espace ouvert et lumineux, enveloppé de verre du sol au plafond, donnant l'illusion que la pièce flotte au-dessus du premier étage.

Dieses Projekt umfasst eine Drei-Zimmer-Suite über einem Carport. Das Haus wurde als eine Reihe offener und miteinander verbundener Räume umgestaltet, wobei Esszimmer, Wohnzimmer und Küche einen großen Raum bilden.

Ein Gefühl der Transparenz zieht sich durch das Haus, das von großen Fenstern und einer verglasten Treppe in der Mitte des Raums beleuchtet wird und dem Design ein modernes und dennoch zurückhaltendes Gefühl verleiht, ohne die Privatsphäre zu beeinträchtigen. Das Hauptschlafzimmer auf der oberen Ebene ist ein heller, offener Raum, der mit raumhohen Gläsern umwickelt ist und die Illusion vermittelt, dass der Raum über dem ersten Stock schwebt.

Este proyecto cuenta con una *suite* de tres habitaciones construida sobre una cochera. La casa fue rediseñada como una serie de espacios abiertos y conectados con el comedor, la sala de estar y la cocina formando un solo espacio amplio.

Una sensación de transparencia fluye a través de la casa, que está iluminada por amplias ventanas y una escalera con paneles de cristal como elemento central, lo que le da al diseño un aspecto moderno pero sobrio sin sacrificar la privacidad. El dormitorio principal de la planta superior es un espacio abierto y lleno de luz que está envuelto en cristal del suelo al techo, creando la impresión de que la habitación sobrevuela el primer piso.

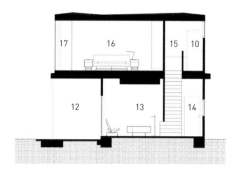

Cross section

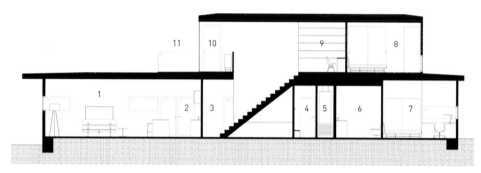

Longitudinal section

1. Living room
2. Kitchen
3. Family room beyond
4. Mud room
5. Closet
6. Bathroom 1
7. Bedroom 1
8. Bedroom 2
9. Den
10. Upper hallway
11. Balcony
12. Carport
13. Family room
14. Lower hallway
15. Den beyond
16. Master bedroom
17. Master bathroom beyond

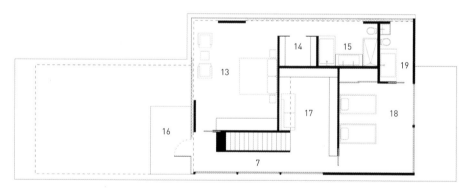

Roof plan

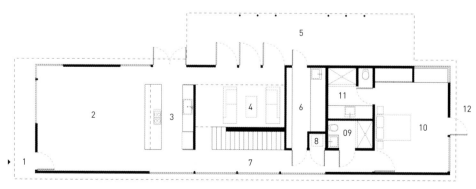

Ground floor plan

1. Main entry
2. Living room
3. Kitchen
4. Family room
5. Carport
6. Mud room
7. Hallway
8. Closet
9. Powder room
10. Bedroom 1
11. Bathroom 1
12. Rear yard
13. Master bedroom
14. Walk-in closet
15. Master bathroom
16. Balcony
17. Den
18. Bedroom 2
19. Bathroom 2

M HOUSE
ROLLING HILLS, CALIFORNIA

Lot size: 78,410 sq ft
Project size: 5,500 sq ft

M House is a reworked mid-century modern California ranch house. This restoration project included updating the open-plan layout while preserving the integrity of the exposed beam and rafter structure. Clean lines, modern execution, and a natural material palette connect the space with the original mid-century identity. The interior features sweeping rooflines, angular openings, and floor-to-ceiling glass that both accentuate the building's pure form and engulf the space in natural light. A soft, earth-tone terrazzo extends to the exterior spaces and landscaping. Along with the floor-to-ceiling glass wall panels, these elements seamlessly blend the interior with the exterior, enhancing its connection with nature. The master bathroom is an elongated minimalist space drawing on the beauty of simplicity that many mid-century homes embody. A wall-mounted bench further articulates the length of the space and continues into the shower room, where a large skylight fills the room with natural light.

La maison M est le résultat de la rénovation d'une maison de ranch moderne californienne du milieu du siècle dernier. Ce projet de restauration comprenait la mise à jour du plan ouvert tout en préservant l'intégrité de la structure en bois exposée. Des lignes épurées, une exécution moderne et une palette de matériaux naturels relient l'espace à l'identité originale du milieu du siècle. L'intérieur présente des lignes de toit larges, des ouvertures angulaires et du verre du sol au plafond qui, à la fois, accentuent la forme pure du bâtiment et engloutissent l'espace dans la lumière naturelle. Un terrazzo d'une douce couleur terre s'étend aux espaces extérieurs et à l'aménagement paysager. Avec les panneaux muraux en verre du sol au plafond, ces éléments fondent parfaitement l'intérieur avec l'extérieur, renforçant sa connexion avec la nature.La salle de bain principale est un espace minimaliste allongé s'inspirant de la splendide simplicité que de nombreuses maisons du milieu du siècle incarnent. Un banc bâti contre un mur articule davantage la longueur de l'espace et se poursuit dans la salle de douche, où un grand puits de lumière remplit la pièce de lumière naturelle.

M Haus ist das Ergebnis einer Renovierung einer kalifornischen Ranch in der Mitte des Jahrhunderts. Dieses Restaurierungsprojekt beinhaltete die Aktualisierung des offenen Plans unter Wahrung der Integrität des freiliegenden Holzrahmens. Klare Linien, moderne Ausführung und eine Palette natürlicher Materialien verbinden den Raum mit der ursprünglichen Identität der Mitte des Jahrhunderts. Der Innenraum verfügt über breite Dachlinien, eckige Öffnungen und verglaste Wände, die die reine Form des Hauses betonen und den Raum in natürliches Licht hüllen. Ein weicher erdfarbener Terrazzo erstreckt sich auf Außenbereiche und Landschaftsgestaltung. Zusammen mit den Glasgehäusen verbinden diese Elemente das Innere perfekt mit dem Äußeren und verstärken so die Verbindung zur Natur. Das Hauptbadezimmer ist ein länglicher, minimalistischer Raum, der sich von der großartigen Einfachheit inspirieren lässt, die viele Häuser aus der Mitte des Jahrhunderts verkörpern. Eine gegen eine Wand gebaute Bank artikuliert die Länge des Raums und führt weiter in die Dusche hinein, wo ein großes Oberlicht den Raum mit natürlichem Licht füllt.

La Casa M es el resultado de una renovación de un rancho estilo moderno de California de mediados del siglo pasado. Este proyecto de restauración incluyó la actualización del diseño de planta abierta al tiempo que se preservó la integridad de la estructura de madera expuesta. Las líneas limpias, la ejecución moderna y una selección de materiales naturales funden el espacio con la identidad original de mediados de siglo. El interior cuenta con amplios techos, aberturas angulares y paramentos acristalados que acentúan la forma pura de la casa y envuelven el espacio en luz natural. Un terrazo suave en tono tierra se extiende a los espacios exteriores y al paisajismo. Junto con los cerramientos de cristal, estos elementos combinan a la perfección el interior con el exterior, mejorando su conexión con la naturaleza. El baño principal es un espacio minimalista alargado que se inspira en la espléndida simplicidad que encarnan muchas casas de mediados de siglo. Un banco construido a lo largo de la pared acentúa aún más la longitud del espacio y se proyecta hacia la ducha, donde un gran tragaluz llena el espacio de luz natural.

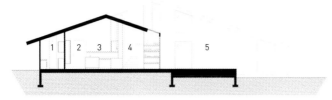

Section

1. Laundry room
2. Family room beyond
3. Kitchen
4. Library beyond
5. Terrace

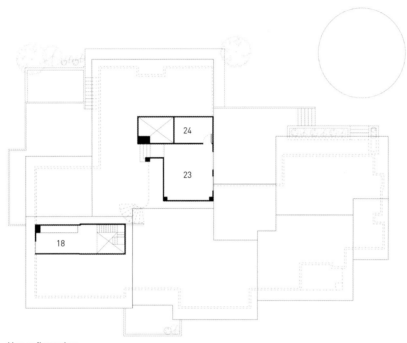

Upper floor plan

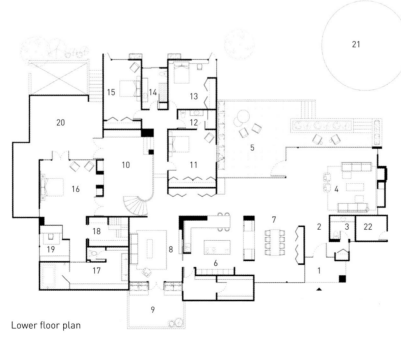

Lower floor plan

1. Main entry
2. Foyer
3. Powder room
4. Living room
5. Terrace
6. Kitchen
7. Dining room
8. Family room
9. Courtyard
10. Library
11. Bedroom 1
12. Bathroom 1
13. Bedroom 2
14. Bathroom 2
15. Bedroom 3
16. Master bedroom
17. Master bathroom
18. Walk-in closet
19. Vanity room
20. Patio
21. Pool
22. Equipment room
23. Study den
24. Attic storage

McKUIN RESIDENCE

OJAI, CALIFORNIA

Designed in collaboration with our client, McKuin Design, Ojai House is a vacation home built for McKuin and their family. This weekend getaway home is set in Ojai, California, a tranquil and rural town just outside the city of Los Angeles, and features four bedrooms, four and a half baths, plus a separate guest house.

The main house is a U shape with the main wing on one side and the bedroom wing on the other, boasting floor to ceiling cathedral style windows throughout and offering sweeping views of the upper Topatopa Mountains. The shape of the house and the exterior wood siding help the home blend in with the natural beauty of the surrounding landscape.

The 700 square-foot guest house sits in front of an expansive pool. The walls feature gabions sourced from local Ojai rocks that were dug up during construction. The rocks help insulate the rooms against heat during the day and the cold at night while creating the perfect unison between house and nature.

Conçue en collaboration avec notre client McKuin Design, Ojai House est une maison de vacances construite pour McKuin et sa famille. Cette maison est situé à Ojai, en Californie, un cadre tranquille et la ville rurale dans la banlieue de la ville de Los Angeles et dispose de quatre chambres, quatre et demi bains, plus une maison d'hôtes séparée.

La maison principale est en forme de U avec l'aile principale d'un côté et l'aile de la chambre de l'autre, bénéficiant de fenêtres de style cathédrale du sol au plafond et offrant une vue imprenable sur les montagnes de Topatopa. La forme de la maison et le revêtement extérieur en bois aident la maison à se fondre dans la beauté naturelle du paysage environnant.

La maison d'hôtes de 65 mètres carrés se trouve en face d'une grande piscine. Les murs comportent des gabions provenant de roches locales d'Ojai qui ont été déterrées pendant la construction. Les roches aident à isoler les pièces de la chaleur pendant la journée et du froid la nuit tout en créant l'unisson parfait entre la maison et la nature.

Das Ojai House wurde in Zusammenarbeit mit unserem Kunden McKuin Design entworfen und ist ein Ferienhaus, das für McKuin und seine Familie gebaut wurde. Dieses Haus befindet sich in Ojai, Kalifornien, einer ruhigen und ländlichen Stadt außerhalb von Los Angeles. Es verfügt über vier Schlafzimmer, viereinhalb Bäder sowie ein separates Gästehaus.

Das Haupthaus ist U-förmig mit dem Hauptflügel auf der einen Seite und dem Schlafzimmerflügel auf der anderen Seite. Es verfügt über raumhohe Fenster im Kathedralenstil und bietet einen weiten Blick auf die Topatopa-Berge. Die Form des Hauses und die hölzerne Außenverkleidung tragen dazu bei, dass sich das Haus in die natürliche Schönheit der umgebenden Landschaft einfügt.

Das 65 Quadratmeter große Gästehaus befindet sich vor einem weitläufigen Pool. Die Wände sind mit Gabionen aus Ojai-Felsen versehen, die während des Baus ausgegraben wurden. Die Felsen schützen die Räume tagsüber vor Hitze und nachts vor Kälte und schaffen die perfekte Verbindung zwischen Haus und Natur.

Diseñada en colaboración con nuestro cliente, McKuin Design, Ojai House es una casa de vacaciones construida para McKuin y su familia. Esta casa está ubicada en Ojai, California, un pueblo tranquilo y rural a las afueras de la ciudad de Los Ángeles, y cuenta con cuatro dormitorios, cuatro baños y medio, además de una casa de huéspedes separada.

La casa principal tiene forma de U con el ala principal en un lado y el ala del dormitorio en el otro, con ventanas de piso a techo estilo catedral en todas partes y con vistas panorámicas de las montañas superiores de Topatopa. La forma de la casa y el revestimiento exterior de madera ayudan a que la casa se mezcle con la belleza natural del paisaje circundante.

La casa de huéspedes de 65 metros cuadrados se encuentra frente a una gran piscina. Las paredes cuentan con gaviones de rocas de Ojai que fueron excavadas durante la construcción. Las rocas ayudan a aislar las habitaciones del calor durante el día y del frío por la noche, creando el unísono perfecto entre la casa y la naturaleza.

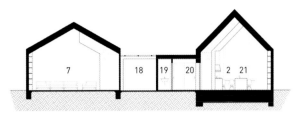

Section 1

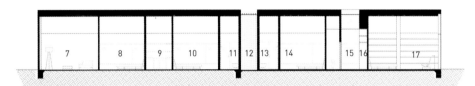

Section 2

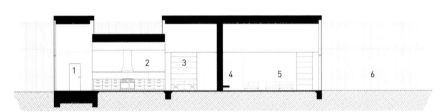

Section 3

1. Foyer
2. Kitchen
3. Dining area
4. Fire place
5. Living room
6. Courtyard
7. Family room
8. Bedroom 1
9. Laundry room
10. Bedroom 2
11. Bathroom 2

12. Outdoor shower
13. Bathroom 3
14. Bedroom 3
15. Bathroom 4
16. Closet
17. Bedroom 4
18. Outdoor storage
19. Powder room
20. Mud room
21. Dining room
    beyond

Main house floor plan

1. Main entry
2. Foyer
3. Kitchen
4. Dining room
5. Living room
6. Terrace
7. Courtyard
8. Mudroom
9. Hallway
10. Family room

11. Bedroom 1
12. Bathroom 1
13. Laundry room
14. Bedroom 2
15. Bathroom 2
16. Outdoor garden
17. Bedroom 3
18. Bathroom 3
19. Bedroom 4
20. Bathroom 4

Guest house floor plan

1. Pool cabana
2. Kitchenette
3. Terrace
4. Courtyard

5. Bathroom 1
6. Bathroom 2
7. Outdoor shower
8. Equipment room

SANTA MONICA RESIDENCE

Structural Engineer: Steve Mezey

General Contractor: LETTER FOUR

Photographer: Anthony Barcelo

PACIFIC PALISADES RESIDENCE

Interior Designer: Carolyn Miller

Kitchen Designer: Kitchens on Montana

Landscape Designer: AP&Co. Landscaping

Structural Engineer: Steve Mezey

MEP Engineer: Shamim Engineering

General Contractor: LETTER FOUR

Photorgrapher: Marcia Prentice

VIEW PARK RESIDENCE

Interior Designer: LETTER FOUR

Landscape Designer: LETTER FOUR

Structural Engineer: Gerald Joo

General Contractor: LETTER FOUR

Photorgrapher: Alen Lin

LETTER FOUR is a full-service design-build firm offering the seamless integration of in-house, licensed architectural and general contracting services that are specifically tailored to the diverse goals of their clientele. Lauren and Jeremy each grew up with artists, contractors, and fine woodworkers, and as a result, have been able to draw upon those life lessons to form the backbone of what they call LETTER FOUR today, a diverse, collaborative practice.

Located in Culver City, California, the firm prides itself on successfully working in many different architectural styles, site typologies, and project programs to address the unique architectural landscape of southern California. While LETTER FOUR's primary focus is new high-end residential construction, they often recommend maintaining a certain portion of the existing building and design details, both to expand upon its strengths and in an effort to reduce the environmental impact. With the firm's attention to detail, transparent communication, focus on quality design, and maximum constructability, they effectively and efficiently deliver each project, from start to finish.

LETTER FOUR est une entreprise de conception-construction offrant un service complet qui intègre de manière transparente des services d'architecture et d'entreprise générale en interne, sous licence, qui sont spécifiquement adaptés aux divers objectifs de leur clientèle. Lauren et Jeremy ont tous deux grandi avec des artistes, des entrepreneurs et des menuisiers d'art. Ils ont donc pu tirer des leçons de leur vie pour former l'épine dorsale de ce qu'ils appellent aujourd'hui LETTER FOUR, une pratique diversifiée et collaborative.

Situé à Culver City, en Californie, le cabinet est fier de travailler avec succès dans de nombreux styles architecturaux, typologies de sites et programmes de projets différents pour répondre au paysage architectural unique du sud de la Californie. Bien que LETTER FOUR se concentre principalement sur les nouvelles constructions résidentielles haut de gamme, elle recommande souvent de conserver une certaine partie du bâtiment existant et des détails de conception, à la fois pour développer ses points forts et dans un effort pour réduire l'impact environnemental. Grâce à son souci du détail, à une communication transparente, à l'accent mis sur la qualité de la conception et à une constructibilité maximale, l'entreprise réalise chaque projet avec efficacité et efficience, du début à la fin.

LETTER FOUR ist eine Full-Service-Design-Build-Firma, die die nahtlose Integration von hausinternen, lizenzierten Architektur- und Generalunternehmerleistungen anbietet, die speziell auf die unterschiedlichen Ziele ihrer Kunden zugeschnitten sind. Lauren und Jeremy sind beide mit Künstlern, Bauunternehmern und Kunsttischlern aufgewachsen und konnten so aus diesen Lebenserfahrungen schöpfen, um das Rückgrat dessen zu bilden, was sie heute LETTER FOUR nennen, eine vielfältige, gemeinschaftliche Praxis.

Die Firma mit Sitz in Culver City, Kalifornien, ist stolz darauf, erfolgreich in vielen verschiedenen Architekturstilen, Typologien von Standorten und Projektprogrammen zu arbeiten, um die einzigartige architektonische Landschaft Südkaliforniens zu thematisieren. LETTER FOUR konzentriert sich zwar in erster Linie auf den Bau neuer hochwertiger Wohngebäude, empfiehlt jedoch häufig die Beibehaltung eines bestimmten Teils des bestehenden Gebäudes und der Designdetails, sowohl um seine Stärken auszubauen als auch in dem Bemühen, die Umweltbelastung zu reduzieren. Mit der Liebe zum Detail, der transparenten Kommunikation, dem Schwerpunkt auf qualitativ hochwertigem Design und maximaler Konstruierbarkeit liefern sie jedes Projekt effektiv und effizient von Anfang bis Ende.

LETTER FOUR es una empresa de diseño y construcción de servicios completos que ofrece la integración perfecta de servicios de arquitectura y contratación general internos y autorizados que se adaptan específicamente a los diversos objetivos de su clientela. Lauren y Jeremy crecieron cada uno con artistas, contratistas y carpinteros, y como resultado, han sido capaces de aprovechar esas lecciones de vida para formar la columna vertebral de lo que hoy llaman LETTER FOUR, un estudio diverso y colaborativo.

Ubicado en Culver City, California, el estudio se enorgullece de trabajar con éxito en estilos arquitectónicos diferentes, tipologías de solares y programas de proyectos para abordar el paisaje arquitectónico único del sur de California. Aunque el enfoque principal de LETTER FOUR es la construcción de nuevas viviendas de alta gama, a menudo recomiendan mantener una parte del edificio existente y detalles de diseño, tanto para realzar sus puntos fuertes como para reducir el impacto ambiental. Con gran atención al detalle, a la comunicación transparente y al enfoque en la calidad del diseño, cada proyecto se entrega de manera efectiva y eficiente, de principio a fin.

SANTA MONICA RESIDENCE

SANTA MONICA, CALIFORNIA

Lot size: 5,266 sq ft
Project size: 3,306 sq ft

LETTER FOUR was hired for full design-build services to create this beautiful eclectic-modern three-level home with a rooftop entertaining area. The firm used varied textures and materials with a nod to the mid-century modern era. The central stair is the main design element that ties together all levels with a slatted wood vertical feature, visible from all open areas of the home. Each level of the home engages with the outdoors as the house carefully terraces, circulating around the courtyard and central staircase and working up to the roof deck. The kitchen and bathrooms are appointed with finishes, plumbing fixtures, cabinetry, lighting, and hardware to create the eclectic style requested by the clients. The firm installed basalt tile inside and out on the main living level and central patio to unify the spaces and blur the distinction between interior and exterior when the sliding glass-paneled walls are opened. This allows the homeowners to spend much of their time outdoors and take full advantage of the perfect weather in southern California.

LETTER FOUR a été engagée pour des services complets de conception-construction afin de créer cette belle maison éclectique et moderne à trois niveaux avec un espace de divertissement sur le toit. Le cabinet d'architectes a utilisé des textures et des matériaux variés avec un clin d'œil à l'époque moderne du milieu du siècle passé. L'escalier central est le principal élément de conception qui relie tous les niveaux grâce à un élément vertical en bois à lattes, visible depuis toutes les zones ouvertes de la maison. Chaque niveau de la maison s'ouvre sur l'extérieur, car la maison se transforme en terrasses, circulant autour de la cour et de l'escalier central et allant jusqu'au toit. La cuisine et les salles de bain sont aménagées avec de nouvelles finitions, des appareils de plomberie, des armoires, des luminaires et de la quincaillerie pour créer le style éclectique demandé par les clients. Le cabinet a installé de nouvelles tuiles de basalte à l'intérieur et à l'extérieur du niveau principal et du patio central pour unifier les espaces et estomper la distinction entre intérieur et extérieur lorsque les murs coulissants vitrés sont ouverts. Cela permet aux propriétaires de passer une grande partie de leur temps à l'extérieur et de profiter pleinement du temps parfait qui règne dans le sud de la Californie.

LETTER FOUR wurde mit umfassenden Design-Build-Dienstleistungen beauftragt, um dieses schöne, vielseitig-moderne dreistöckige Haus mit einem Unterhaltungsbereich auf dem Dach zu schaffen. Die Firma verwendete verschiedene Texturen und Materialien mit einer Anspielung auf die Moderne der Mitte des Jahrhunderts. Die zentrale Treppe ist das Hauptgestaltungselement, das alle Ebenen mit einem vertikalen Lattenholzelement verbindet, das von allen offenen Bereichen des Hauses aus sichtbar ist. Jede Ebene des Hauses befasst sich mit der Natur, während das Haus sorgfältig terrassiert, um den Innenhof und die zentrale Treppe zirkuliert und bis zur Dachterrasse arbeitet. Die Küche und die Badezimmer sind mit Oberflächen, Armaturen, Schränken, Beleuchtung und Hardware ausgestattet, um den von den Kunden gewünschten eklektischen Stil zu schaffen. Die Firma installierte Basaltfliesen innen und außen auf der Hauptwohnebene und der zentralen Terrasse, um die Räume zu vereinheitlichen und die Unterscheidung zwischen Innen und Außen zu verwischen. So können die Hausbesitzer einen Großteil ihrer Zeit im Freien verbringen und das perfekte Wetter in Südkalifornien voll ausnutzen.

LETTER FOUR fue contratada para servicios completos de diseño y construcción con el objetivo de crear esta hermosa, ecléctica y moderna casa de tres niveles con zona de estar en la azotea. El estudio utilizó texturas y materiales con un guiño a la era moderna de mediados del siglo pasado. La escalera central es el principal elemento de diseño que une todos los niveles con una estructura vertical de listones de madera, visible desde todas las áreas abiertas de la casa. Cada nivel se conecta con el exterior, circulando alrededor del patio y la escalera central y subiendo hasta la azotea. La cocina y los baños están acabados con nuevos materiales, accesorios de fontanería, armarios, iluminación y herrajes para conseguir el estilo ecléctico solicitado por los clientes. El estudio instaló nuevas baldosas de basalto en el exterior e interior del nivel principal, en la sala de estar y en el patio central, unificando así los espacios y permitiendo distinguir entre el interior y el exterior al abrirse los cerramientos acristalados deslizantes. Esto permite a los propietarios pasar gran parte de su tiempo al aire libre y aprovechar al máximo el clima perfecto del sur de California.

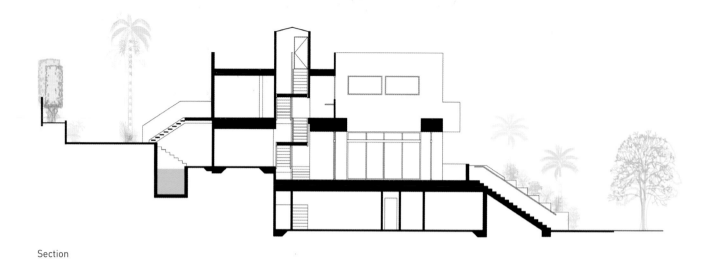

Section

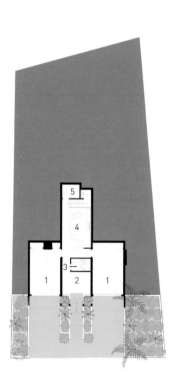

First floor plan

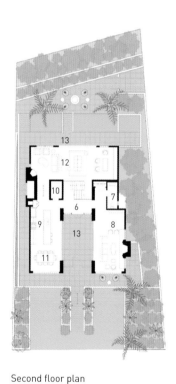

Second floor plan

Third floor plan

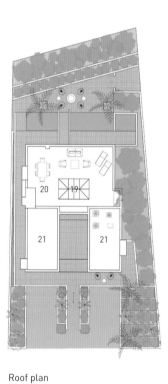

Roof plan

1. Garage
2. Bedroom
3. Bathroom
4. Den
5. Storage
6. Entry
7. Powder room
8. Formal living room
9. Kitchen
10. Pantry
11. Dining area
12. Family room
13. Patio
14. Study
15. Master bedroom
16. Master closet
17. Laundry room
18. Master bathroom
19. Stair solarium
20. BBQ dining area
21. Mechanical room

PACIFIC PALISADES RESIDENCE

PACIFIC PALISADES, CALIFORNIA

Lot size: 4,949 sq ft
Project size: 2,942 sq ft

For this project, LETTER FOUR worked closely with the homeowners to more than double the square footage of an existing non-descript 1950s Spanish bungalow and fully transform it into a beautiful, airy, light-filled modern Spanish home. It was important for the client to stay true to the Spanish style that is so close to the heart of authentic Californian architecture. LETTER FOUR chose to create a circular entry tower, pulling from historic curvilinear Spanish inspiration, with handpainted tile around a custom made arched-top door and authentic terracotta tile flooring. The firm added a second story and an expansive roof deck with an ocean view. The firm also reconfigured the first floor and fully modernized the finishes, fixtures, flow, function, and feel of the home, creating a strong connection with the outdoors and plenty of space for a growing family. LETTER FOUR carefully balanced the scope of the project with code limitations to secure an exemption from California Coastal Commission requirements and expedite the project timeline.

Pour ce projet, LETTER FOUR a travaillé en étroite collaboration avec les propriétaires pour plus que doubler la superficie d'un bungalow espagnol des années 1950 existant, non décrit, et le transformer entièrement en une belle maison espagnole moderne, aérée et lumineuse. Il était important pour le client de rester fidèle au style espagnol qui est si proche du cœur de l'architecture californienne authentique. LETTER FOUR a choisi de créer une tour d'entrée circulaire, en s'inspirant de l'architecture curviligne historique espagnole, avec des carreaux peints à la main autour d'une porte en arche faite sur mesure et un authentique sol en carreaux de terre cuite. L'entreprise a ajouté un deuxième étage et un vaste toit-terrasse avec vue sur l'océan. L'entreprise a également reconfiguré le premier étage et a entièrement modernisé les finitions, les installations, la circulation, la fonction et l'atmosphère de la maison, créant un lien fort avec l'extérieur et beaucoup d'espace pour une famille grandissante. LETTER FOUR soigneusement équilibré la portée du projet avec les limites du code pour obtenir une exemption des exigences de la California Coastal Commission et accélérer le calendrier du projet.

Bei diesem Projekt arbeitete LETTER FOUR eng mit den Hausbesitzern zusammen, um die Quadratmeterzahl eines bestehenden, nicht näher beschriebenen spanischen Bungalows aus den 1950er Jahren mehr als zu verdoppeln und ihn vollständig in ein schönes, luftiges, lichtdurchflutetes modernes spanisches Haus zu verwandeln. Für den Bauherrn war es wichtig, dem spanischen Stil treu zu bleiben, der dem Herzen der authentischen kalifornischen Architektur so nahe steht. LETTER FOUR entschied sich für einen runden Eingangsturm nach historischer, kurvenförmiger spanischer Inspiration, mit handbemalten Fliesen um eine maßgefertigte Bogentür herum und einem authentischen Terrakottafliesenboden. Die Firma fügte eine zweite Etage und eine weitläufige Dachterrasse mit Meerblick hinzu.Sie gestaltete auch die erste Etage um und modernisierte vollständig die Oberflächen, Einbauten, den Fluss, die Funktion und das Wohngefühl des Hauses, wodurch eine starke Verbindung mit der Natur und viel Platz für eine wachsende Familie geschaffen wurde. LETTER FOUR wog den Umfang des Projekts sorgfältig mit den Beschränkungen des Codes ab, um eine Befreiung von den Anforderungen der California Coastal Commission zu erreichen und den Zeitplan des Projekts zu beschleunigen.

Para este proyecto, LETTER FOUR trabajó estrechamente con los propietarios para duplicar los metros cuadrados de unbungaló de estilo español de los años 50 y transformarlo completamente en una hermosa, espaciosa y luminosa casa moderna. Era importante que el cliente se mantuviera fiel al estilo español, tan cercano al corazón de la auténtica arquitectura californiana. LETTER FOUR eligió crear una torre de entrada circular, de inspiración curvilínea, con azulejos pintados a mano alrededor de una puerta en forma de arco hecha a medida y un suelo de azulejos de terracota. Se añadió un segundo piso y una amplia cubierta con vista al mar. También se reconfiguró el primer piso y se modernizaron completamente los acabados, las instalaciones, la circulación, la la función y la sensación de hogar, creando una fuerte conexión con el exterior y mucho espacio para una familia en crecimiento. LETTER FOUR equilibró cuidadosamente el alcance del proyecto para asegurar una exención de los requisitos de la Comisión Costera de California y acelerar el calendario de construcción.

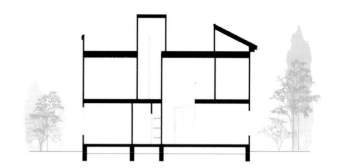

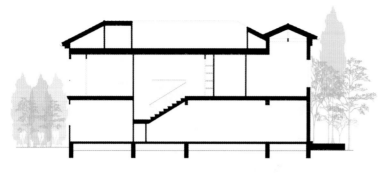

Sections

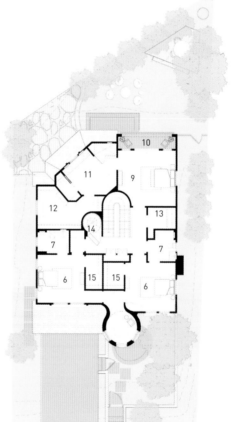

First floor plan

Second floor plan

Roof plan

1. Entry
2. Living room
3. Dining area
4. Kitchen
5. Family room
6. Bedroom
7. Bathroom
8. Garage
9. Master bedroom
10. Master bedroom deck
11. Master bathroom
12. Master closet
13. Laundry room
14. Stair to roof
15. Closet
16. BBQ area
17. Living area
18. Dining area
19. Mechanical room

VIEW PARK RESIDENCE

VIEW PARK, CALIFORNIA

Lot size: 17,504 sq ft
Project size: 4,080 sq ft

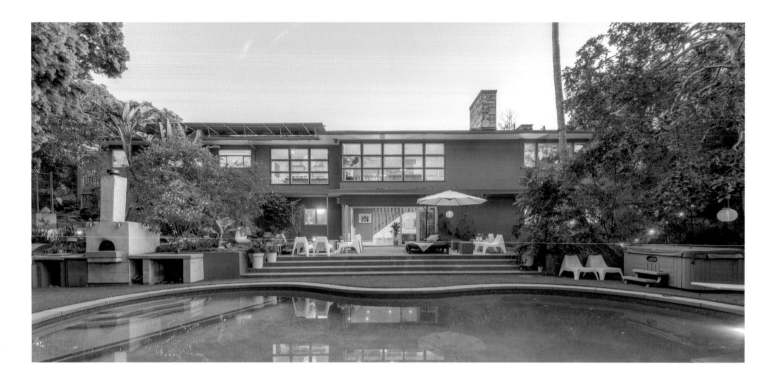

In the historic Los Angeles neighborhood of View Park and built-in 1952, this mid-century Modern gem needed some polishing. With five bedrooms and four-and-a-half bathrooms, the homeowners did not need additional square footage, but certain refinements were in order. The main focus was to open up the home to allow for more natural light by reconfiguring the layout and creating large communal spaces. LETTER FOUR took what was previously a small, dark kitchen and butler's pantry and completely transformed it by orienting the layout towards the back yard and adding skylights to create an open, functional, light-filled space. The downstairs entertaining area is set up perfectly for indoor-outdoor use and engagement with the lush landscaping, with new slide-fold doors out to the newly updated pool, patio, and landscaping. The house transitions into the landscape where one is surrounded by vegetation with such privacy that it feels impossible to be in the center of Los Angeles.

Dans le quartier historique de View Park à Los Angeles, ce joyau moderne du milieu du siècle dernier avait besoin d'être poli. Avec cinq chambres, quatre salles de bains et un cabinet de toilette, les propriétaires n'avaient pas besoin de superficie supplémentaire, mais certains raffinements s'imposaient. L'objectif principal était d'ouvrir la maison pour permettre plus de lumière naturelle en reconfigurant l'agencement et en créant de grands espaces communs. LETTER FOUR a pris ce qui était auparavant une petite cuisine sombre et un garde-manger de majordome et l'a complètement transformé en orientant la disposition vers la cour arrière et en ajoutant des puits de lumière pour créer un espace ouvert, fonctionnel et rempli de lumière. L'espace de divertissement du bas est parfaitement aménagé pour une utilisation intérieur-extérieur et un engagement dans le luxuriant aménagement paysager, avec de nouvelles portes coulissantes rabattables donnant sur la piscine, le patio et l'aménagement paysager récemment mis à jour. La maison se fond dans le paysage où l'on est entouré de végétation avec une telle intimité qu'il semble impossible de se trouver au centre de Los Angeles.

Im historischen Stadtteil View Park in Los Angeles, der 1952 erbaut wurde, musste dieser moderne Edelstein aus der Mitte des Jahrhunderts noch etwas poliert werden. Mit fünf Schlafzimmern und viereinhalb Badezimmern brauchten die Hausbesitzer keine zusätzliche Quadratmeterzahl, aber gewisse Verfeinerungen waren angebracht. Das Hauptaugenmerk lag auf der Öffnung des Hauses für mehr natürliches Licht, indem der Grundriss neu gestaltet und große Gemeinschaftsräume geschaffen wurden. LETTER FOUR nahm eine zuvor kleine, dunkle Küche und Vorratskammer und verwandelte sie vollständig, indem es den Grundriss zum Hinterhof hin ausrichtete und Oberlichter hinzufügte, um einen offenen, funktionalen, lichtdurchfluteten Raum zu schaffen. Der Entertainmentbereich im Erdgeschoss ist mit neuen Schiebe-Falttüren zum neu gestalteten Pool, zur Terrasse und zur Landschaft perfekt auf die Nutzung im Innen- und Außenbereich und die Auseinandersetzung mit der üppigen Landschaftsgestaltung ausgerichtet. Das Haus geht in die Landschaft über, in der man von Vegetation umgeben ist, mit einer solchen Privatsphäre, dass es sich unmöglich anfühlt, sich im Zentrum von Los Angeles zu befinden.

En el histórico barrio de View Park (Los Ángeles) y construido en 1952, esta gema moderna de mediados de siglo necesitaba ser pulida. Con cinco dormitorios y cuatro baños y medio, los propietarios no necesitaban más metros cuadrados, pero sí ciertos refinamientos. El objetivo principal era abrir la casa para permitir más luz natural, reconfigurando la distribución y creando grandes espacios comunes. LETTER FOUR tomó lo que antes era una pequeña y oscura cocina con despensa y la transformó completamente, orientando la distribución hacia el patio trasero y añadiendo tragaluces para crear un espacio abierto, funcional y lleno de luz. La zona de entretenimiento de la planta baja está perfectamente preparada para el uso interior-exterior integrándose con el exuberante paisaje. La piscina, el patio y el jardín fueron renovados con la instalación de nuevas puertas corredizas. La casa permite ahora la transición al exterior, donde uno está rodeado de vegetación pero con tal privacidad que parece imposible estar en el centro de Los Ángeles.

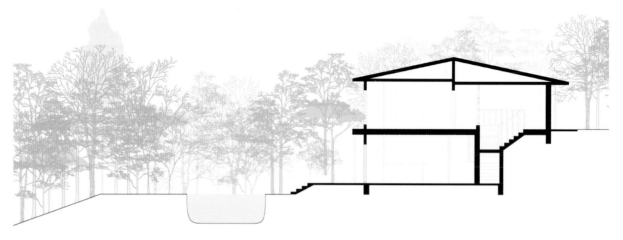

Section

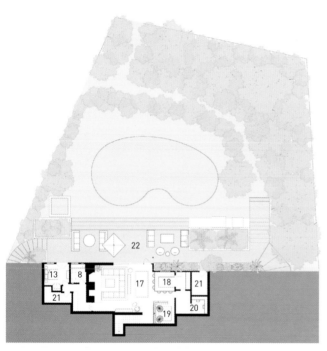

Lower floor plan

Main floor plan

1. Entry
2. Formal living room
3. Dining area
4. Kitchen
5. Laundry room
6. Garage
7. Mudroom
8. Bathroom
9. Closet
10. Guest bedroom/office
11. Powder room
12. Utility closet
13. Bedroom
14. Master bedroom
15. Master bathroom
16. Master closet
17. Family room
18. Bar
19. Playroom
20. Office
21. Mechanical room
22. Patio

LOC
Architects

loc-arch.com

CANYON HOUSE

Design Team: Ali Jeevanjee, Poonam Sharma, Vedi Vartani, Yumin Zeng Structural Engineer: MMC Associates

Civil Engineer: The Eden Group

Geotechnical Consultant: Schick Geotechnical

General Contractor: Evergreen Construction and Design

Photographer: Nico Marques

MONTECITO HOUSE

Design Team: Ali Jeevanjee, Poonam Sharma, Ara Hovsepyan, Naif Altouri

Structural Engineer: Barry Cohan

Civil Engineer: The Eden Group

Geotechnical Consultant: Braun and Associates

General Contractor: Evergreen Construction and Design

Photographer: Ali Jeevanjee

CROSSROADS ARTS AND ATHLETICS FACILITIES

Design Team: Poonam Sharma, Ali Jeevanjee, and Tessa Forde

Structural Engineer: Miyamoto International

Civil Engineer: KPFF

MEP Engineer: GMEP

General Contractor: Douglass Design Build

Photographer: Nico Marques

Founded in 2006 by partners Poonam Sharma and Ali Jeevanjee, LOC is an award-winning, process-driven, and socially responsive architecture practice committed to the creation of transformative experiences through the built environment. LOC's focus, in both its work process and product, is a human experience and the role of design in shaping that experience. The universality of this focus and commitment to process enables LOC to be versatile in its work and to successfully engage in projects as varied as homes, workplaces, schools, and civic art. Through the process of bringing people together for listening, collaboration, and investigation, LOC is able to gain a deeper understanding of the issues at stake to generate unconventional and unexpected solutions. Finished projects are intended to be places that can be transformative in how users experience a site, the surrounding environment, the activities they engage in there, and the communities with whom they share these experiences. LOC has received many awards and its work has been published widely.

Fondé en 2006 par les partenaires Poonam Sharma et Ali Jeevanjee, LOC est un cabinet d'architecture primé, axé sur les processus et socialement réactif, qui s'engage à créer des expériences transformatrices à travers l'environnement bâti. LOC met l'accent, tant dans son processus de travail que dans son produit, sur l'expérience humaine et le rôle de la conception dans la formation de cette expérience. L'universalité de cette orientation et de cet engagement envers le processus permet à LOC d'être polyvalent dans son travail et de s'engager avec succès dans des projets aussi variés que les maisons, les lieux de travail, les écoles et l'art civique. En réunissant des personnes pour écouter, collaborer et enquêter, LOC est en mesure de mieux comprendre les enjeux et de générer des solutions non conventionnelles et inattendues. Les projets achevés sont conçus comme des lieux qui peuvent transformer la façon dont les utilisateurs vivent un site, dans un cadre environnemental pour les activités qu'ils y mènent et les communautés avec lesquelles ils partagent ces expériences. LOC a reçu de nombreux prix et ses travaux ont été largement publiés.

LOC wurde 2006 von den Partnern Poonam Sharma und Ali Jeevanjee gegründet. LOC ist ein preisgekröntes, prozessorientiertes und sozial verantwortliches Architekturbüro, das sich der Schaffung von transformativen Erfahrungen durch die gebaute Umwelt verschrieben hat. Im Mittelpunkt von LOC steht sowohl im Arbeitsprozess als auch im Produkt die menschliche Erfahrung und die Rolle des Designs bei der Gestaltung dieser Erfahrung. Die Universalität dieses Fokus und das Engagement für den Prozess ermöglichen es LOC, in ihrer Arbeit vielseitig zu sein und sich erfolgreich an so unterschiedlichen Projekten wie Wohnungen, Arbeitsräumen, Schulen und bürgerlicher Kunst zu beteiligen. Durch den Prozess, Menschen zum Zuhören, zur Zusammenarbeit und zum Kennenlernen zusammenzubringen, ist LOC in der Lage, ein tieferes Verständnis für die anstehenden Probleme zu erlangen, um unkonventionelle und unerwartete Lösungen zu finden. Abgeschlossene Projekte sollen Orte sein, die in Bezug auf die Art und Weise, wie Benutzer einen Ort, die Umgebung und die Aktivitäten, die sie dort durchführen, erleben, die Menschen und die Gemeinschaften, mit denen sie diese Erfahrungen teilen, verändern können. LOC hat viele Auszeichnungen erhalten und die Arbeit des Büros wurde umfassend veröffentlicht.

Fundada en 2006 por los socios Poonam Sharma y Ali Jeevanjee, LOC es un estudio de arquitectura galardonado, socialmente sensible y comprometido con la creación de experiencias transformadoras a través del entorno construido. El enfoque de LOC, tanto en su proceso de trabajo como en su producto, es una experiencia humana donde el papel del diseño es la confirmación de esa experiencia. La universalidad de este enfoque y el compromiso permite a LOC ser versátil en su trabajo y participar con éxito en proyectos tan variados como viviendas, lugares de trabajo, escuelas y espacios de arte cívico. A través del proceso de reunir a la gente para escuchar, colaborar e investigar, LOC es capaz de obtener una comprensión más profunda de los temas en juego para generar soluciones no convencionales e inesperadas. Los proyectos terminados pretenden ser espacios que puedan ser transformadores en la forma en que los usuarios experimentan un lugar, el entorno que lo rodea, las actividades que realizan en él y las comunidades con las que comparten estas experiencias. LOC ha recibido muchos premios y su trabajo ha sido publicado ampliamente.

CANYON HOUSE

LOS ANGELES, CALIFORNIA

In 1971, Reyner Banham described four ecologies in Los Angeles: the beaches, the freeways, the flats, and the foothills. Today one can add to that the downtown core and a growing network of subways feeding into that. But Los Angeles is a city of topography, and the foothills are its quintessential neighborhoods.

A production creative director and family purchased a small cabin in Mount Washington, a hilltop neighborhood that is a twenty-minute subway ride from downtown Los Angeles but has all of the qualities of living in the country. They approached LOC with the goal of expanding the one-bedroom cabin despite its precarious location at the top of a steep drop, capitalizing on the views of downtown to the south and the San Gabriel Mountains to the north. LOC Architects introduced a series of concrete and stucco wedges to transform the cabin into a home deeply connected to the experience of the lush canyon it inhabits.

En 1971, Reyner Banham a décrit quatre écologies à Los Angeles : les plages, les autoroutes, les appartements et les contreforts. Aujourd'hui, on peut ajouter à cela le centre-ville et un réseau de métro croissant qui l'alimente. Mais Los Angeles est une ville de topographie, et dont les collines en sont la quintessence.

Un directeur de production et sa famille ont acheté une petite cabane à Mount Washington, un quartier en haut d'une colline qui se trouve à vingt minutes en métro du centre-ville de Los Angeles mais qui a toutes les qualités de la vie à la campagne. Ils ont approché LOC dans le but d'agrandir la cabane d'une chambre à coucher malgré son emplacement précaire, au sommet d'une pente raide, en profitant de la vue sur le centre-ville au sud et sur les montagnes de San Gabriel au nord. Les architectes de LOC ont introduit une série de cales en béton et en stuc pour transformer la cabane en une maison profondément liée à l'expérience du canyon luxuriant qu'elle habite.

1971 beschrieb Reyner Banham vier Ökologien in Los Angeles: die Strände, die Autobahnen, die Ebenen und die Vorgebirge. Heute kann man dem noch den Stadtkern und ein wachsendes Netz von U-Bahnen hinzufügen, die in diesen hineinführen. Aber Los Angeles ist eine Stadt mit einer Topographie, und die Ausläufer sind die wichtigsten Stadtviertel.

Ein kreativer Regisseur und seine Familie kauften eine kleine Hütte in Mount Washington, einem auf einem Hügel gelegenen Viertel, das zwanzig U-Bahn-Minuten von der Innenstadt von Los Angeles entfernt ist, aber alle Lebensqualitäten des Landes aufweist. Sie wandten sich an LOC mit dem Ziel, die Einzimmerhütte trotz ihrer prekären Lage an der Spitze eines steilen Gefälles zu erweitern und dabei die Aussicht auf die Innenstadt im Süden und die San-Gabriel-Berge im Norden zu nutzen. LOC Architects führten eine Reihe von Beton- und Stuckkeilen ein, um die Hütte in ein Zuhause zu verwandeln, das tief mit der Erfahrung des üppigen Canyons, den es bewohnt, verbunden ist.

En 1971, Reyner Banham describió cuatro ecologías en Los Ángeles: las playas, las autopistas, los llanos y las colinas. Hoy en día se puede añadir a eso el centro de la ciudad y una creciente red de metro que se alimenta de eso. Pero Los Ángeles es una ciudad topográfica, y las colinas son sus vecindarios por excelencia.

Un director creativo de producción y su familia compraron una pequeña cabaña en el monte Washington, un barrio en la cima de la colina que está a veinte minutos en metro del centro de Los Ángeles pero que tiene todas las cualidades de la vida del país. Se acercaron a LOC con el objetivo de ampliar la cabaña de un dormitorio, a pesar de su precaria ubicación en la cima de una colina, aprovechando las vistas del centro de la ciudad al sur y de las montañas de San Gabriel al norte. Los arquitectos del LOC introdujeron una serie de cuñas de hormigón y estuco para transformar la cabaña en un hogar profundamente conectado a la experiencia del exuberante cañón en el que habita.

Existing house

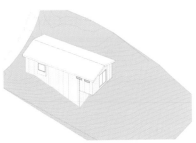

Existing house demo

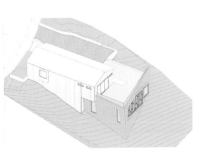

Lower volume addition

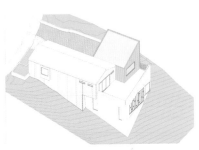

Upper volume addition

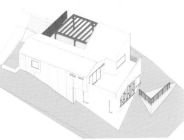

Carport and
lower deck addition

Complete

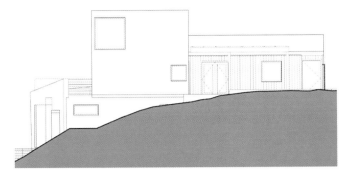

North elevation

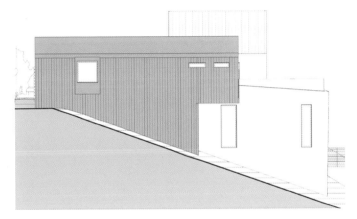

South elevation

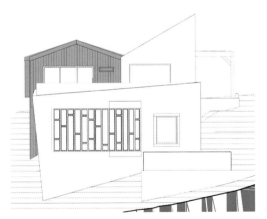

East elevation

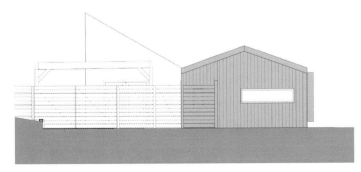

West elevation

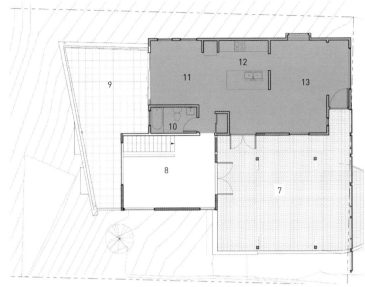

Upper floor plan

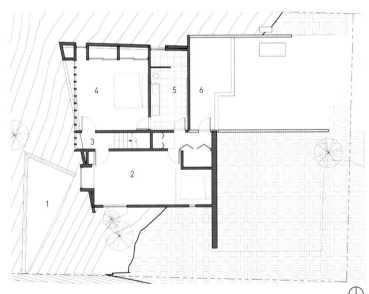

Lower floor plan

1. Exterior terrace
2. Bedroom
3. Corridor
4. Master bedroom
5. Bathroom
6. Crawl space
7. Carport/exterior courtyard
8. Dining room
9. Deck
10. Existing bathroom
11. Existing den
12. Existing kitchen
13. Existing living room

MONTECITO HOUSE

MONTECITO, CALIFORNIA

Project size: 2,530 sq ft

The Montecito House is formed by a series of bold, shifting volumes that respond to the unusual geometry of its hillside site in relation to the street. These volumes frame a courtyard and create a series of terraces to better experience the dramatic views and topography. The courtyard flows seamlessly into the living areas on the lower level, with the main private spaces located above to capitalize on the expansive view of the mountains and ocean. The garage volume is excavated into the hillside, and the experience of approaching the house occurs along a lushly landscaped path and arriving in the courtyard before entering the home. The massing of the house is expressed in varying shades of neutral stucco cladding to highlight their materiality and differentiate them from one another. The neutral tones stand in further contrasts to the lush native landscaping on the surrounding hill.

La maison du Montecito est formée par une série de volumes audacieux et changeants qui répondent à la géométrie inhabituelle de son site à flanc de colline par rapport à la rue. Ces volumes encadrent une cour et créent une série de terrasses pour mieux profiter des vues spectaculaires et de la topographie. La cour s'intègre harmonieusement dans les espaces de vie du niveau inférieur, les principaux espaces privés étant situés au-dessus pour profiter de la vue étendue sur les montagnes et l'océan. Le volume du garage est creusé dans le flanc de la colline, et l'expérience de l'approche de la maison se fait le long d'un chemin luxuriant et paysager et en arrivant dans la cour avant d'entrer dans la maison. La masse de la maison s'exprime par des revêtements en stuc neutre de différentes nuances pour mettre en valeur leur matérialité et les différencier les uns des autres. Les tons neutres contrastent encore avec le luxuriant aménagement paysager indigène de la colline environnante.

Das Haus Montecito besteht aus einer Reihe kühner, sich verschiebender Volumen, die auf die ungewöhnliche Geometrie seiner Hanglage im Verhältnis zur Straße reagieren. Diese Volumen rahmen einen Innenhof ein und bilden eine Reihe von Terrassen, um die dramatischen Ansichten und die Topographie besser zu erleben. Der Hof geht nahtlos in die Wohnbereiche auf der unteren Ebene über, wobei sich die wichtigsten Privaträume darüber befinden, um den weiten Blick auf die Berge und das Meer zu nutzen. Das Garagenvolumen ist in den Hang gegraben. Bei der Annäherung über einen üppig angelegten Weg gelangt man zunächst in den Hof, bevor man das Haus betritt. Die Masse des Hauses drückt sich in unterschiedlichen Schattierungen neutraler Stuckverkleidungen aus, um ihre Materialität hervorzuheben und sie voneinander zu unterscheiden. Die neutralen Töne stehen in weiterem Kontrast zu der üppigen einheimischen Landschaftsgestaltung auf dem umgebenden Hügel.

La Casa Montecito está formada por una serie de volúmenes audaces y cambiantes que responden a la inusual geometría de su ladera en relación con la calle. Estos volúmenes enmarcan un patio y crean una serie de terrazas para experimentar mejor las dramáticas vistas y la topografía. El patio fluye sin problemas hacia las zonas habitables del nivel inferior, con los principales espacios privados situados en la parte superior para aprovechar la amplia vista de las montañas y el océano. El volumen del garaje está excavado en la ladera, y la experiencia de acercarse a la casa se produce a lo largo de un sendero ajardinado exuberante que atraviesa un patio antes de entrar en la casa. La vivienda presenta diversos tonos de revestimiento de estuco neutro para resaltar su materialidad y diferenciarlos entre sí. Los tonos neutros contrastan aún más con el rico paisaje nativo de la colina circundante.

Site plan

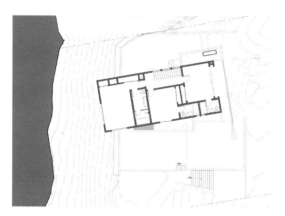

Second floor plan

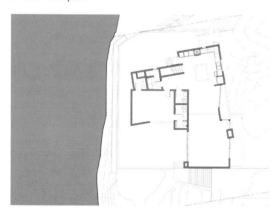

Ground floor plan

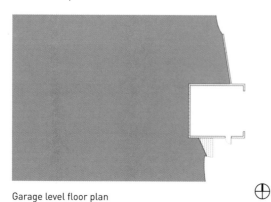

Garage level floor plan

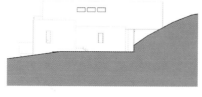

North elevation

East elevation

West elevation

South elevation

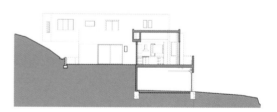

Longitudinal section

Cross section

CROSSROADS ARTS AND ATHLETICS FACILITIES

LOS ANGELES, CALIFORNIA

Project size: 12,000 sq ft

An urban landscape inside a former airplane parts storage warehouse accommodates an eclectic series of uses for a Los Angeles area private school with an emphasis on the fine and performing arts. Crossroads is unusual in that it does not have a campus that is clearly defined. The school's Santa Monica campus is, instead, a series of industrial buildings acquired over four-plus decades. As the school continues to grow it is acquiring buildings on the adjacent blocks. The original industrial aesthetic of the building was celebrated by honoring its dramatic open space. A series of distinct volumes containing the school's required program was inserted, simulating an urban landscape. The program included such diverse elements as jazz classrooms, photography lab, darkroom, a ceramics studio, and graphics classrooms, and a gym, which turned out to be the most dramatic large gathering space on the campus. It is now the place where events such as incoming students and parents are welcomed at the beginning of each school year.

Un paysage urbain à l'intérieur d'un ancien entrepôt de pièces d'avion, dispose d'une installation éclectique pour une école privée de la région de Los Angeles, avec un accent sur les beaux-arts et les arts du spectacle. Crossroads est inhabituel en ce sens qu'il ne dispose pas d'un campus clairement défini. Le campus de Santa Monica de l'école est, au contraire, une série de bâtiments industriels acquis au cours de plus de quatre décennies. Comme l'école continue à se développer, elle acquiert des bâtiments sur les blocs adjacents. L'esthétique industrielle originale du bâtiment a été célébrée en honorant son spectaculaire espace ouvert. Une série de volumes distincts contenant le programme obligatoire de l'école a été insérée, simulant un paysage urbain. Le programme comprenait des éléments aussi divers que des salles de jazz, un laboratoire de photographie, une chambre noire, un studio de céramique, des salles de graphisme et un gymnase, qui s'est avéré être le plus grand espace de rassemblement du campus. C'est désormais le lieu où des événements tels que l'arrivée des étudiants et des parents sont accueillis au début de chaque année scolaire.

Eine Stadtlandschaft in einem ehemaligen Lagerhaus für Flugzeugteile ist für eine Privatschule in der Gegend von Los Angeles mit Schwerpunkt auf bildenden und darstellenden Künsten nur eine der Nutzungsmöglichkeiten aus einer eklektische Reihe. Crossroads ist insofern ungewöhnlich, als es keinen klar definierten Campus hat. Das Werk in Santa Monica besteht aus einer Reihe von Industriegebäuden, die in mehr als vier Jahrzehnten erworben wurden. Während die Schule weiter wächst, erwirbt sie Gebäude in den angrenzenden Blöcken. Die ursprüngliche industrielle Ästhetik des Gebäudes wird gefeiert, indem der dramatische offene Raum geehrt wird. Es wurde eine Reihe unterschiedlicher Bände eingefügt, die das erforderliche Programm der Schule enthalten und eine Stadtlandschaft simulieren. Das Programm beinhaltet so unterschiedliche Elemente wie Jazz-Klassenzimmer, Fotolabor, Dunkelkammer, ein Keramikstudio und Grafikklassenräume sowie eine Turnhalle, die sich als der dramatischste große Versammlungsraum auf dem Campus erwies. Diese ist nun der Ort, an dem zu Beginn eines jeden Schuljahres Veranstaltungen wie die Ankunft von Schülern und Eltern stattfinden.

Un paisaje urbano en el interior de un antiguo almacén de piezas de aviones alberga una ecléctica serie de usos para una escuela privada del área de Los Ángeles con énfasis en las bellas artes y las artes escénicas. Crossroads es inusual en el sentido de que no tiene unas instalaciones claramente definidas. Las instalaciones en Santa Mónica consisten en una serie de edificios industriales adquiridos a lo largo de más de cuatro décadas. A medida que la escuela crece, va adquiriendo edificios en los bloques adyacentes. Su espectacular espacio abierto celebra la estética industrial original del edificio. Se insertaron una serie de volúmenes distintos que contenían el programa requerido por la escuela, simulando un paisaje urbano e incluyendo elementos tan diversos como aulas de jazz, laboratorio de fotografía, un cuarto oscuro de revelado, un estudio de cerámica, aulas de diseño gráfico y un gimnasio, que resultó ser el gran espacio de reunión en el recinto. Ahora es el lugar donde se celebran eventos como la llegada de estudiantes y padres al comienzo de cada año escolar.

Stripping the excess

The arts block

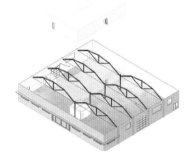

Plywood blocks

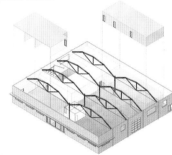

Slopped gym wall

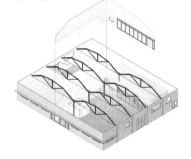

Gym block

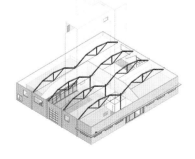

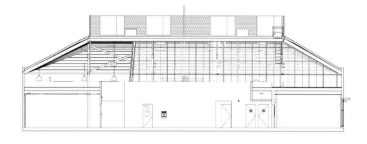

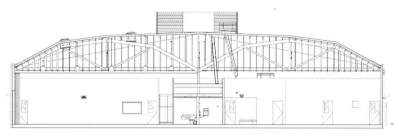

Sections

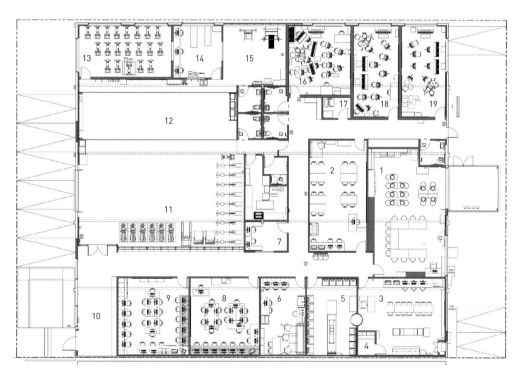

Ground floor furniture plan

1. Price
2. Digital photo
3. Photography
4. Film storage
5. Darkroom
6. Mini-lab/green screen
7. Office
8. Bass
9. Hopper
10. Corridor
11. Cardio/rowers
12. Robinson
13. Spinning
14. Office/training
15. Weights area
16. Fitzgerald
17. IT closet
18. Satchmo
19. Coltrane

Lucas & Lucas

lucas-lucas.com

MODERN HILLSIDE RESIDENCE

Landscape Builder: Siteworks Landscape

Pool Builder: Wine Country Pools

Builder: Benchmark Construction

Architect: Bevan + Associates

Photographer: Marion Brenner

SONOMA POOL HOUSE

Landscape Builder: Heaven on Earth Landscape

Pool Builder: Bertram Pools

Architect: Bevan + Associates

Photographers: Cesar Rubio and Doug Thomsen

NAPA POOL HOUSE

Landscape Builder: Oxbow Landscape and Pool

Pool Builder: Paradise Pools

Builder: Elder Lane Construction

Architect: Bevan + Associates

Photographer: Caitlin Atkinson

Lucas & Lucas is a multi-disciplinary landscape architecture practice deeply dedicated to the integration of architecture and landscape. With a service-oriented approach to residential design, we work closely with our clients to create highly individual custom residential projects throughout Northern California. Led by the husband and wife team of Jennifer and Mike Lucas, we bring together deep experience and well-honed skill sets in both land and structures to create holistic indoor-outdoor environments for very special clients.

Lucas & Lucas est un cabinet d'architecture paysagère pluridisciplinaire profondément dédié à l'intégration de l'architecture et du paysage. Avec une approche axée sur les services en matière de conception résidentielle, nous travaillons en étroite collaboration avec nos acquéreur, pour créer des projets personnalisés très individuels dans toute la Californie du Nord. Dirigés par l'équipe mari et femme de Jennifer et Mike Lucas, nous mettons en commun une expérience approfondie et des compétences bien rodées dans le domaine des terrains et des structures pour créer des environnements intérieurs et extérieurs holistiques pour des clients très spéciaux.

Lucas & Lucas ist ein multidisziplinäres Landschaftsarchitekturbüro, das sich der Integration von Architektur und Landschaft verschrieben hat. Mit einem dienstleistungsorientierten Ansatz bei der Wohnraumgestaltung arbeiten wir eng mit unseren Kunden zusammen, um höchst individuelle, maßgeschneiderte Projekte in ganz Nordkalifornien zu schaffen. Unter der Leitung des Ehepaars Jennifer und Mike Lucas vereinen wir profunde Erfahrung und ausgeprägte Fertigkeiten sowohl bei Grundstücken als auch bei Bauwerken, um ganzheitliche Innen- und Außenumgebungen für ganz besondere Kunden zu schaffen.

Lucas & Lucas es un estudio multidisciplinario de arquitectura paisajista profundamente dedicado a la integración de la arquitectura y el paisaje. Con un enfoque orientado al servicio en el diseño residencial, trabajamos estrechamente con nuestros clientes para crear proyectos personalizados muy individuales en todo el norte de California. Dirigido por el equipo formado por Jennifer y Mike Lucas, marido y mujer, reunimos una profunda experiencia y un conjunto de habilidades bien afinadas tanto en el terreno como en las estructuras para crear entornos holísticos de interior y exterior para clientes muy especiales.

MODERN HILLSIDE RESIDENCE

SONOMA, CALIFORNIA

Lot size: 8 acres
Building size: 6,000 sq ft

A collaborative approach to site planning and design lead to an integrated solution for this hillside modern home and landscape. Pragmatic considerations such as vehicular approach and arrival experience informed the overall layout and progression of spaces. Repetition of materials blends land and structure, blurring the lines between architecture and land. A ribbon of water defines the edge of the main level eliminating the need for guard rails while enhancing views. The swimming pool occupies a central court between the main living and the bedroom wing. Regionally appropriate Mediterranean plantings grace the hillside, soften the architectural lines, and work their way through the spaces and onto the building's roof. The overall effect becomes something like the hanging gardens of Babylon, but with a modern twist.

Une approche collaborative de la planification et de la conception du site a permis de trouver une solution intégrée pour cette maison et ce paysage modernes à flanc de colline. Des considérations pragmatiques telles que l'approche véhiculaire et l'expérience d'arrivée ont influencé l'aménagement global et la progression des espaces. La répétition des matériaux mélange le terrain et la structure, brouillant les lignes entre l'architecture et le terrain. Un ruban d'eau définit le bord du niveau principal, éliminant le besoin de garde-corps tout en améliorant les vues. La piscine occupe une cour centrale entre le salon principal et l'aile des chambres à coucher. Des plantations méditerranéennes adaptées à la région ornent le versant de la colline, adoucissent les lignes architecturales et se fraient un chemin à travers les espaces et sur le toit du bâtiment. L'effet d'ensemble ressemble aux jardins suspendus de Babylone, mais avec une touche de modernité.

Ein kooperativer Ansatz bei der Standortplanung und -gestaltung führte zu einer integrierten Lösung für dieses moderne Haus und die Landschaft am Hang. Pragmatische Erwägungen, wie z. B. die Annäherung mit dem Fahrzeug und die Erfahrung der Anreise, haben die Gesamtanordnung und den Verlauf der Räume bestimmt. Durch die Wiederholung der Materialien werden Land und Struktur miteinander verschmolzen und die Grenzen zwischen Architektur und Land verwischt. Ein Wasserband definiert den Rand der Hauptebene und macht Leitplanken überflüssig, während es gleichzeitig die Aussicht verbessert. Der Swimmingpool nimmt einen zentralen Hof zwischen dem Wohn- und dem Schlafzimmertrakt ein. Regional angepasste mediterrane Bepflanzungen schmücken den Hang, mildern die architektonischen Linien und arbeiten sich durch die Räume und auf das Dach des Gebäudes. Die Gesamtwirkung wird so etwas wie die hängenden Gärten von Babylon, aber mit einer modernen Wendung.

Un enfoque de colaboración para la planificación y el diseño del proyecto llevó a una solución integrada para esta vivienda y su paisajismo. Consideraciones pragmáticas como el tema del aparcamiento y el acceso decidieron la disposición general y la progresión de los espacios. La repetición de materiales desdibuja las líneas entre la arquitectura y el terreno. Una cinta de agua define el borde del nivel principal eliminando la necesidad de barandillas y mejorando las vistas. La piscina ocupa un patio central entre la sala principal y el ala de dormitorios. Las plantaciones mediterráneas autóctonas crecen en la ladera, suavizando las líneas arquitectónicas y abriéndose paso a través de los espacios hasta la cubierta del edificio. El efecto general recuerda a los jardines colgantes de Babilonia, pero con un toque moderno.

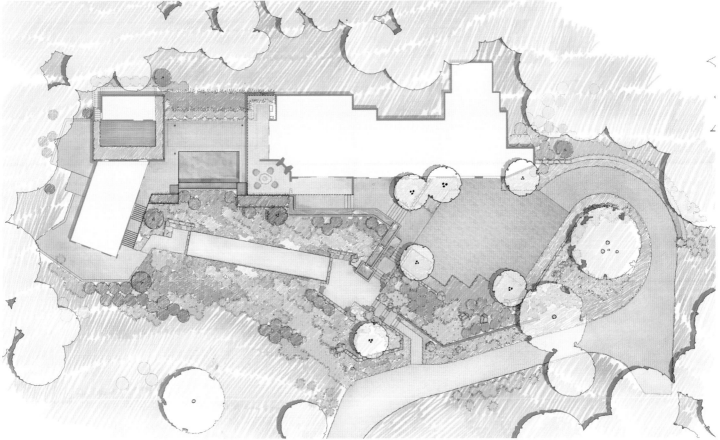

Site plan

This backyard garden was designed for an active family embodying a playful spirit for adults and children alike. The program was organized around the limits of a septic system, the majority of which resides below the central lawn. Permeable concrete pavers support outdoor dining and a linear fire pit. Japanese maples provide shade and a veil of privacy for overnight guests in the pool house. The white limestone terrace, white wall, and pool provide vibrancy and a clean, clear feeling to the architecture. Pool spoils were utilized for a raised lounge and fescue covered earthen forms. White oyster-shell trails support informal bocce. Round corrugated metal troughs contain Big timber bamboo providing vertical scale and depth while lending a more exotic Pacific Rim type vibe to the space. Raised beds for food production and a small orchard underplanted with a mass of Molinia grasses round out the program for this action-packed garden.

Ce jardin d'arrière-cour a été conçu pour une famille active incarnant un esprit ludique tant pour les adultes comme pour les enfants. Le programme a été organisé autour des limites d'une installation septique, dont la grande partie se trouve sous la pelouse centrale. Des pavés de béton perméables supportent les repas en plein air et un brasero de jardin linéaire. Des érables japonais offrent de l'ombre et un voile d'intimité aux invités qui passent la nuit dans le pool-house. La terrasse, le mur blanc et la piscine en pierre calcaire blanche donnent à l'architecture un aspect vibrant et une sensation de propreté et de clarté. Les déblais de la piscine ont été utilisés pour un salon surélevé et des formes de terre recouvertes de fétuque. Des pistes en coquilles d'huîtres blanches forment une pétanque informelle. Des abreuvoirs ronds en métal ondulé contiennent du bambou Big Timber, ce qui donne une échelle verticale et une profondeur, tout en conférant à l'espace une atmosphère plus exotique de type Pacific Rim. Des parterres surélevés pour la production alimentaire et un petit verger sous-planté d'une masse d'herbes Molinia complètent le programme de ce jardin plein d'action.

Dieser Garten im Hinterhof wurde für eine aktive Familie entworfen, die einen spielerischen Geist für Erwachsene und Kinder gleichermaßen verkörpert. Das Programm wurde um die Grenzen eines septischen Systems herum organisiert, das sich größtenteils unterhalb des zentralen Rasens befindet. Durchlässige Betonpflaster unterstützen das Essen im Freien und eine lineare Feuergrube. Japanische Ahorne spenden Schatten und geben den Übernachtungsgästen im Poolhaus einen Schleier der Privatsphäre. Die Terrasse aus weißem Kalkstein, die weiße Wand und der Pool verleihen der Architektur Lebendigkeit und ein sauberes, klares Gefühl. Der Pool wurde erhöht platziert und mit von Schwingel bedeckten irdenen Formen versehen. Weiße Muschelschalenwege unterstützen den informellen Boccia. Runde, gewellte Metalltröge enthalten großen hölzernen Bambus, der für vertikale Skala und Tiefe sorgt und dem Platz gleichzeitig eine exotischere, pazifikähnliche Ausstrahlung verleiht. Hochbeete für die Nahrungsmittelproduktion und ein kleiner Obstgarten, der mit einer Masse von Molinia-Gräsern unterbepflanzt ist, runden das Programm für diesen aktionsreichen Garten ab.

Este jardín trasero fue diseñado para una familia activa que encarna un espíritu lúdico tanto para adultos como para niños. El programa se organizó en torno a los límites de un sistema séptico, gran parte del cual se encuentra bajo el césped. Los adoquines de hormigón permeable dan soporte el comedor exterior y un brasero lineal. Unos arces japoneses proporcionan sombra y un velo de privacidad para los huéspedes que pasan la noche en la casa de la piscina. La terraza de piedra caliza blanca, la pared blanca y la piscina proporcionan vitalidad y una sensación de limpieza y claridad. Los senderos de conchas de ostras blancas forman unas pistas de petanca. Unos abrevaderos redondos de metal corrugado contienen grandes bambúes que proporcionan verticalidad y profundidad, a la vez que crean una atmósfera más exótica siguiendo el estilo de la costa del Pacífico. Parterres elevados para la producción de alimentos y un pequeño huerto con una masa de hierbas Molinia completan el programa de este jardín lleno de actividad.

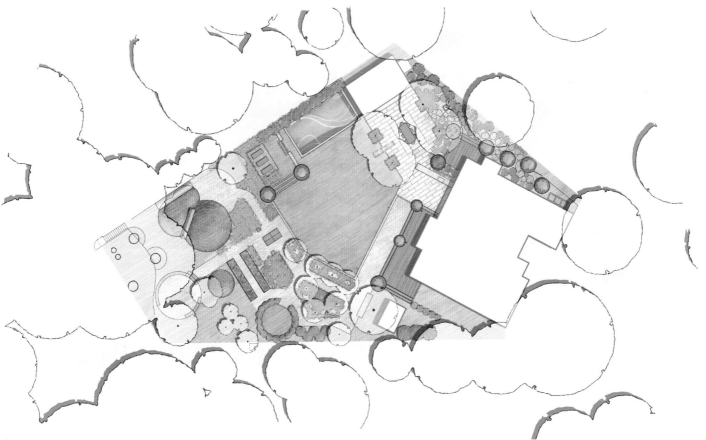

Site plan

NAPA POOL HOUSE

NAPA, CALIFORNIA

Majestic Valley Oaks grace this Napa Valley ranch residence, setting the tone for the pastoral landscape developed around a well-sited swimming pool and pool house. Block planting of bunch grasses and flowering perennials bracket the developed space and provide an ever-changing ethereal mass of plants that dance in the breeze and catch the sun's rays, creating a relaxed feeling in this destination environment. Cocktails and outdoor dining are supported and shaded by the pool house overhang while outdoor cooking abuts the interior kitchen of this crown jewel of a pool house. A bocce court bridges the walk back home with developed vegetable gardens and orchard, providing fresh produce for the elaborate meals that are regularly prepared and enjoyed in this outdoor getaway.

Majestic Valley Oaks orne cette résidence de ranch de la Napa Valley, donnant le ton au paysage pastoral qui s'est développé autour d'une piscine et d'un pool-house bien situés. Les plantations de touffes d'herbes et de plantes vivaces fleuries en bloc encadrent l'espace aménagé et fournissent une masse variée de plantes en constante évolution qui dansent dans la brise et captent les rayons du soleil, créant une sensation de détente dans cet environnement de destination. Les cocktails et les repas en plein air sont soutenus et ombragés par le surplomb du pool-house, tandis que la cuisine extérieure jouxte la cuisine intérieure de ce joyau de la couronne. Un terrain de pétanque fait le lien entre le chemin du retour et les jardins potagers et le verger aménagés, fournissant des produits frais pour les repas élaborés qui sont régulièrement préparés et dégustés dans cette escapade en plein air.

Die majestätischen Valley Oaks zieren diese Residenz der Napa Valley Ranch und geben den Ton für die pastorale Landschaft an, die sich um einen gut gelegenen Swimmingpool und ein Poolhaus herum ausbreitet. Blockpflanzungen aus Straußgräsern und blühenden Stauden umrahmen den bebauten Raum und sorgen für eine sich ständig verändernde ätherische Pflanzenmasse, die in der Brise tanzt und die Sonnenstrahlen einfängt, wodurch ein entspanntes Gefühl in dieser Zielumgebung entsteht. Cocktails und Essen im Freien werden durch den Überhang des Poolhauses unterstützt und beschattet, während die Außenküche an die Innenküche dieses Kronjuwels von Poolhaus angrenzt. Ein Bocciaplatz überbrückt den Rückweg nach Hause mit ausgebauten Gemüsegärten und Obstgärten und liefert frische Produkte für die aufwändigen Mahlzeiten, die regelmäßig an diesem Ausflugsziel im Freien zubereitet und genossen werden.

Los majestuosos robles adornan este rancho situado en el valle de Napa, estableciendo el tono de un paisaje de ambiente pastoral desarrollado en torno a una piscina y una casa de invitados bien orientados. La plantación de la zona verde y las plantas perennes en flor abrazan un espacio minuciosamente concebido proporcionando una masa etérea siempre cambiante de plantas que bailan con la brisa y atrapan los rayos del sol, creando una sensación de relajación. Los cócteles y las cenas al aire libre quedan protegidos del sol por el saliente de la casa, mientras que la cocina exterior, la joya de la corona del proyecto, colinda con una cocina interior. Una pista de petanca une el camino de regreso a casa con la zona de huerto, proporcionando productos frescos para las comidas elaboradas que se preparan y disfrutan regularmente en esta vivienda ideal para una escapada al aire libre.

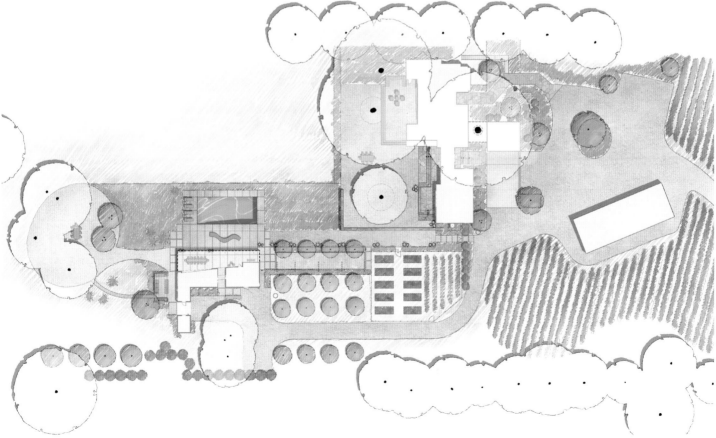

Site plan

ALTIPLANO

Structural Engineer: Nader Khoury, Engineering Structures

Civil Engineer: M&G

Soils Engineers & Geologist: Irvine Geotech

General Contractor: Silverlake Homes

Photographer: Meiwen See

COURTYARD HOUSE

Structural Engineer: Nader Khoury, Engineering Structures

Civil Engineer: CW Howe Partners

Soils Engineers & Geologist: Grover-Hollingsworth and Associates

General Contractor: Boswell Construction

Photographer: Meiwen See & Bethany Nauert

GABLE TOP

Structural Engineer: Nader Khoury, Engineering Structures

Civil Engineer: CW Howe Partners

Soils Engineers & Geologist: Grover-Hollingsworth and Associates

General Contractor: Boswell Construction

Photographer: Meiwen See & Bethany Nauert

Led by McShane and Cleo Murnane, Project M Plus is an award-winning, multi-disciplinary architecture and design agency building vibrant spaces, brands, and environments. We believe design shapes how we experience the world.

Dirigé par McShane et Cleo Murnane, Project M Plus est une agence d'architecture et de design multidisciplinaire primée qui crée des espaces, des marques et des environnements dynamiques. Nous croyons que le design façonne notre expérience du monde.

Unter der Leitung von McShane und Cleo Murnane ist Project M Plus eine preisgekrönte, multidisziplinäre Architektur- und Designagentur, die lebendige Räume, Marken und Umgebungen schafft. Wir glauben, dass Design die Art und Weise beeinflusst, wie wir die Welt erleben.

Dirigido por McShane y Cleo Murnane, Project M Plus es una agencia de arquitectura y diseño multidisciplinaria y galardonada que construye espacios, marcas y entornos vibrantes. Creemos que el diseño da forma a la forma en que experimentamos el mundo.

ALTIPLANO

LOS ANGELES, CALIFORNIA

Lot size: 8,400 sq ft
Project size: 3,460 sq ft

Perched above an Echo Park hilltop with expansive 360-degree views, this new modern home is situated to take in its unique surroundings. The home is designed at three-stories to best capture the incredible vistas and prevailing winds found on site. Once inside, the experience evolves into a series of view captures that include downtown LA, the Hollywood Sign, the San Gabriel Mountains, Catalina Island, and the ocean afar. A large operable glass window wall introduces the coveted indoor-outdoor Southern California lifestyle to the main living area. The home floats above the surrounding site transforming the parking area below as a flex space for outdoor living. At the rear of the house sits an informal living space, a guest house, a fire pit, and a pool. The unique vantage points were considered throughout to capture both the intimacy of refuge and the outward prospect of the dreamy LA landscape. The building is a neutral material palette with warm wood accents.

Perchée au-dessus d'une colline d'Echo Park avec une vue imprenable à 360 degrés, cette nouvelle maison moderne est située pour profiter de son environnement unique. La maison est conçue à trois étages pour capturer au mieux les vues incroyables et les vents dominants trouvés sur place. Une fois à l'intérieur, l'expérience évolue vers une série de prises de vue qui incluent le centre-ville de Los Angeles, le panneau Hollywood, les montagnes de San Gabriel, l'île Catalina et l'océan au loin. Un grand mur de fenêtre ouvrable introduit le style de vie convoité intérieur-extérieur du sud de la Californie dans le salon principal. La maison flotte au-dessus du site environnant, transformant le parking ci-dessous en un espace flexible pour la vie en plein air. À l'arrière de la maison se trouve un espace de vie informel, une maison d'hôtes, un foyer et une piscine. Les points de vue uniques ont été considérés partout pour capturer à la fois l'intimité du refuge et la perspective extérieure du paysage de rêve de Los Angeles. Le bâtiment est une palette de matériaux neutres avec des accents de bois chaleureux.

Dieses neue moderne Haus befindet sich auf einem Hügel im Echo Park und bietet einen weiten 360-Grad-Blick. Es bietet eine einzigartige Umgebung. Das dreistöckige Haus ist so gestaltet, dass es die unglaublichen Ausblicke und die vorherrschenden Winde vor Ort am besten einfängt. Einmal drinnen, entwickelt sich die Erfahrung zu einer Reihe von Ansichten, die die Innenstadt von LA, das Hollywood-Zeichen, die San Gabriel Mountains, Catalina Island und den Ozean in der Ferne umfassen. Eine große bedienbare Glasfensterwand bringt den begehrten südkalifornischen Lebensstil im Innen- und Außenbereich in den Hauptwohnbereich. Das Haus schwebt über dem umliegenden Grundstück und verwandelt den darunter liegenden Parkplatz in einen flexiblen Raum für das Leben im Freien. Auf der Rückseite des Hauses befinden sich ein informeller Wohnraum, ein Gästehaus, eine Feuerstelle und ein Pool. Die einzigartigen Aussichtspunkte wurden durchgehend berücksichtigt, um sowohl die Intimität der Zuflucht als auch die äußere Perspektive der verträumten Landschaft von LA einzufangen. Das Gebäude ist eine neutrale Materialpalette mit warmen Holzakzenten.

Situada sobre la cima de una colina de Echo Park con amplias vistas de 360 grados, esta nueva casa moderna está situada para disfrutar de su entorno único. La casa está diseñada en tres pisos para capturar mejor las increíbles vistas y los vientos dominantes que se encuentran en el lugar. Una vez dentro, la experiencia se convierte en una serie de capturas de vistas que incluyen el centro de Los Ángeles, el letrero de Hollywood, las montañas de San Gabriel, la isla Catalina y el océano a lo lejos. Una gran pared acristalada operable presenta el codiciado estilo de vida del sur de California en interiores y exteriores a la sala de estar principal. La casa flota sobre el sitio circundante transformando el área de estacionamiento debajo como un espacio flexible para la vida al aire libre. En la parte trasera de la casa se encuentra un espacio habitable informal, una casa de huéspedes, un brasero y una piscina. Los puntos de vista únicos se consideraron en todo momento para capturar tanto la intimidad del refugio como la perspectiva exterior del paisaje de ensueño de Los Ángeles. El edificio es una paleta de materiales neutros con cálidos acentos de madera.

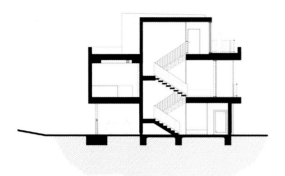

Cross section

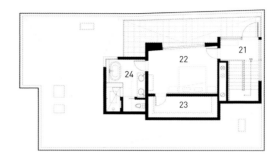

Third floor plan

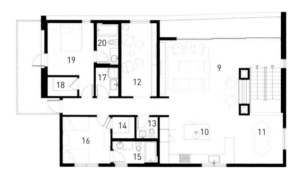

Second floor plan

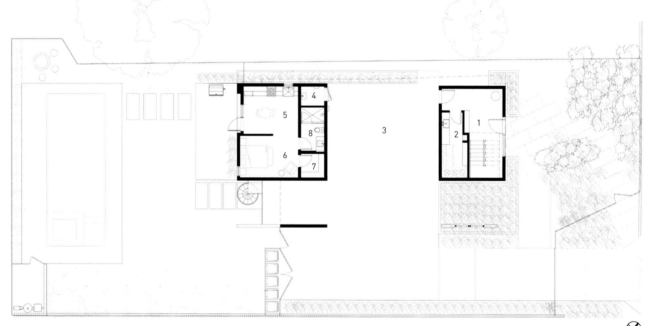

Ground floor plan

1. Entry	9. Living room	17. Laundry room
2. Laundry room	10. Kitchen	18. Closet
3. Carport	11. Dining room	19. Bedroom
4. Mechanical room	12. Library	20. Bathroom
5. Kitchen	13. Powder room	21. Stair
6. Bedroom	14. Closet	22. Owner's suite
7. Closet	15. Bathroom	23. Closet
8. Bathroom	16. Bedroom	24. Bathroom

COURTYARD HOUSE

LOS ANGELES, CALIFORNIA

The home is a series of horizontal volumes organized and stacked upon one another to create a courtyard and lawn on a LA hillside. The central premise of the home was to carve out an outdoor area that could be accessed from all parts of the house, promoting greater circulation and connecting the rooms to the pleasant Southern California weather. The upper level also has balconies for each bedroom.

The home is designed for a family of four and is a respite from urban life with an easy sense of coming and going, blurring the lines between inside and outside. Sliding glass doors pocket into the wall allowing a seamless opening to the yard. The white stucco is offset with carefully placed wood accents softening and warming up exterior areas. The staircase is located at the center of the home and creates the hinge point between all private and public spaces.

La maison est une série de volumes horizontaux disposés et empilés les uns sur les autres pour créer un patio et une pelouse sur une colline de Los Angeles. Le principe central de la maison était de créer un espace extérieur accessible de toutes les parties de la maison, favorisant une plus grande circulation et reliant les pièces au climat agréable du sud de la Californie. Le niveau supérieur dispose également de balcons pour chaque chambre.

La maison est conçue pour une famille de quatre personnes et est un répit de la vie urbaine avec un léger sens d'aller et venir, brouillant les lignes entre l'intérieur et l'extérieur. Les portes coulissantes en verre sont encastrées dans le mur, permettant un accès parfait au patio. Le stuc blanc est compensé par des accents de bois soigneusement placés qui adoucissent et apportent de la chaleur aux espaces extérieurs. L'escalier est situé au centre de la maison et devient un point d'articulation entre tous les espaces publics et privés.

Das Haus besteht aus einer Reihe horizontaler Bände, die organisiert und aufeinander gestapelt sind, um einen Innenhof und einen Rasen auf einem Hügel in LA zu schaffen. Die zentrale Prämisse des Hauses bestand darin, einen Außenbereich zu schaffen, der von allen Teilen des Hauses aus zugänglich war, eine größere Durchblutung zu fördern und die Räume mit dem angenehmen Wetter in Südkalifornien zu verbinden. Die obere Ebene hat auch Balkone für jedes Schlafzimmer.

Das Haus ist für eine vierköpfige Familie konzipiert und bietet eine Pause vom städtischen Leben mit einem leichten Gefühl des Kommens und Gehens, wodurch die Grenzen zwischen Innen und Außen verwischt werden. Die Glasschiebetüren sind in die Wand eingelassen und ermöglichen einen perfekten Zugang zur Terrasse. Der weiße Stuck wird durch sorgfältig platzierte Holzakzente ausgeglichen, die den Außenbereich erweichen und ihm Wärme verleihen. Die Treppe befindet sich in der Mitte des Hauses und wird zu einem Verbindungspunkt zwischen allen öffentlichen und privaten Räumen.

La casa es una serie de volúmenes horizontales organizados y apilados uno sobre otro para crear un patio y zona de césped en una ladera de Los Ángeles. La premisa central de la casa era crear un área al aire libre a la que se pudiera acceder desde todas las partes de la casa, promoviendo una mayor circulación y conectando las habitaciones con el agradable clima del sur de California. El nivel superior también tiene balcones para cada dormitorio.

La casa está diseñada para una familia de cuatro miembros y es un respiro de la vida urbana con una ligera sensación de ir y venir, difuminando las líneas entre el interior y el exterior. Las puertas corredizas de cristal se empotran en la pared, lo que permite un acceso perfecta al patio. El estuco blanco se compensa con acentos de madera cuidadosamente colocados que suavizan y aportan calor a las áreas exteriores. La escalera está ubicada en el centro de la casa y se convierte el un punto de articulación entre todos los espacios públicos y privados.

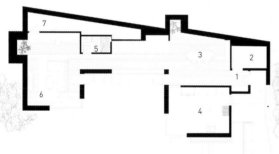

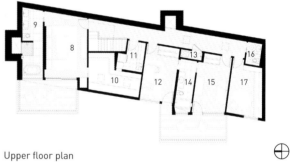

Upper floor plan

⊕

Main floor plan

1. Entry
2. Mechanical room
3. Dining room
4. Kitchen
5. Bathroom
6. Living room
7. Storage room
8. Owner's suite
9. Bathroom
10. Closet
11. Laundry room
12. Bedroom
13. Mechanical room
14. Bathroom
15. Bedroom
16. Powder room
17. Office

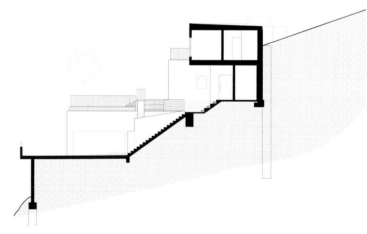

Cross section through exterior stair

GABLE TOP

LOS ANGELES, CALIFORNIA

Lot size: 7,280 sq ft
Project size: 2,450 sq ft

Located on a steep hillside lot in Los Angeles, the Gable Top house is a familiar form used in a modern application. The house is shaped with a singular gable mass atop a solid base to draw out the upper floor and is accentuated with a material change using heavy dark metal siding.
The lower level is small to reduce the impact on the site, while the upper level cantilevers outward to create a sense of floating over the hill. In addition, the house and gable form is positioned to face the Hollywood sign with a large glass and aluminum window system capturing wonderful hill views and the golden glow of the setting sun.

Située sur un terrain à flanc de colline escarpé à Los Angeles, la maison Gable Top est une forme familière utilisée dans une application moderne. La maison est formée avec une masse de pignon singulière au sommet d'une base solide pour tirer l'étage supérieur et est accentuée par un changement de matériau en utilisant un revêtement en métal foncé lourd. Le niveau inférieur est petit pour réduire l'impact sur le site, tandis que le niveau supérieur est en porte-à-faux vers l'extérieur pour créer une impression de flotter au-dessus de la colline. De plus, la forme de la maison et du pignon est positionnée pour faire face au panneau Hollywood avec un grand système de fenêtres en aluminium capturant une vue magnifique sur la colline et la lueur dorée du soleil couchant.

Das Gable Top House befindet sich in Hanglage in Los Angeles und ist eine bekannte Form, die in einer modernen Anwendung verwendet wird. Das Haus hat die Form einer einzigartigen Giebelmasse auf einem soliden Untergrund, um das Obergeschoss zu extrahieren, und wird durch einen Materialwechsel unter Verwendung einer schweren dunklen Metallverkleidung akzentuiert.
Die untere Ebene ist klein, um die Auswirkungen auf das Gelände zu verringern, während die obere Ebene nach außen ragt, um das Gefühl zu erzeugen, auf dem Hügel zu schweben. Darüber hinaus befinden sich das Haus und die Giebelform gegenüber dem Hollywood-Schild mit einem großen System von Aluminiumfenstern, die einen herrlichen Blick auf die Hügel und das goldene Leuchten der untergehenden Sonne bieten.

Ubicada en un terreno inclinado de la ladera en Los Ángeles, la casa Gable Top es una forma familiar utilizada en una aplicación moderna. La casa tiene la forma de un singular volumen a dos aguas sobre una base sólida para extraer el piso superior y se acentúa con un cambio de material utilizando un revestimiento de metal oscuro y pesado.
El nivel inferior es pequeño para reducir el impacto en el solar mientras que el nivel superior se proyecta hacia afuera para crear una sensación de flotar sobre la colina. Además, la casa y la forma del hastial están colocadas de cara al letrero de Hollywood con un gran sistema de ventanas de aluminio que capturan maravillosas vistas de las colinas y el brillo dorado del sol poniente.

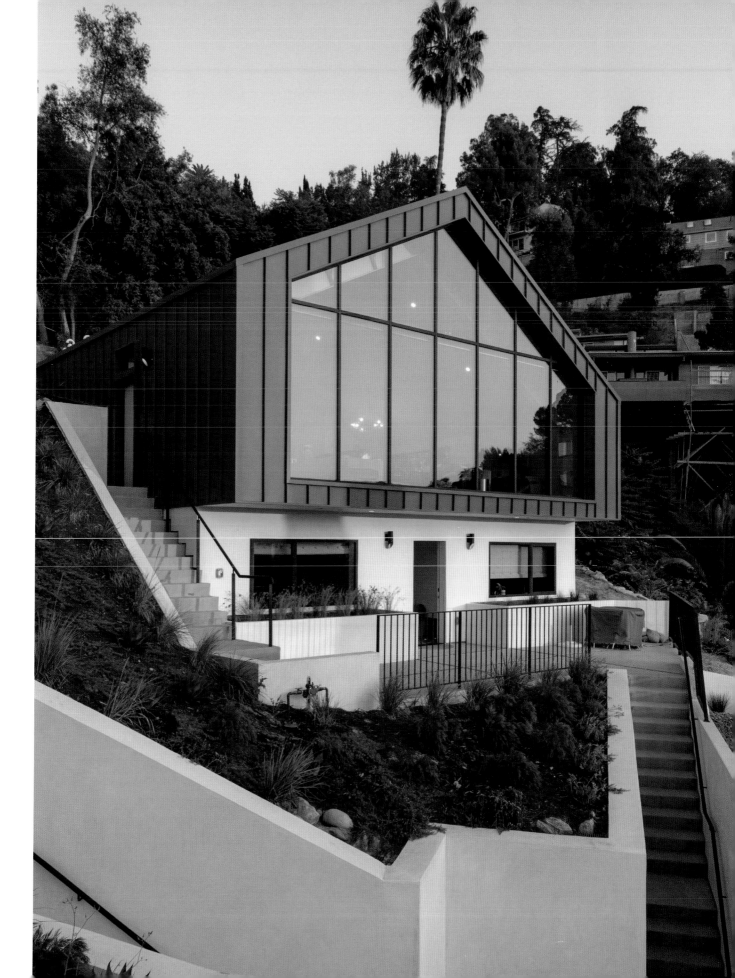

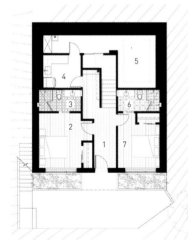

Lower floor plan

Upper floor plan

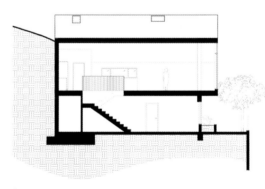

Section

1. Entry
2. Bedroom
3. Bathroom
4. Laundry room
5. Media room
6. Bathroom
7. Bedroom
8. Living room
9. Powder room
10. Nook
11. Kitchen
12. Pantry
13. Dining room

Marmol Radziner

marmol-radziner.com

MANDEVILLE CANYON RESIDENCE

Design Team:
Architecture: Ron Radziner, Design Partner; Leo Marmol, Managing Partner; Brad Williams; Caleb Reed; Alex Pettas

Interiors: Erika Montes, Sarah Netto

Landscape: Amy Smith, Joshua Leyva, Daniel Beck

Construction: James Dunne, Rob Schlief, Mari Kirsten

Interior Designer: Marmol Radziner

Landscape Architect: Marmol Radziner

Structural Engineer: Armen Melkonious, AMEC

Geotechnical Engineer: Grover Hollingsworth

Surveyor: Becker Miyamoto

General Contractor: Marmol Radziner

Photographers: Roger Davies, Sylvia Hardy, Laure Joliet, Richard Powers, Trevor Tondro

Leo Marmol, FAIA, and Ron Radziner, FAIA, formed Marmol Radziner in 1989, launching a unique design-build practice led by architects. Based in Los Angeles with offices in San Francisco and New York City, the firm offers architecture, construction, interior design, and landscape design. Marmol Radziner creates intimate, inviting spaces that connect the interior to the exterior. The firm's projects engage the surrounding environment and take a warm, textured approach to modernism that is elegant and timeless. Whether following the highest standards of sustainable design or creating outdoor rooms that extend daily living into the landscape, Marmol Radziner uses architecture to bring people closer to nature.

Leo Marmol, FAIA, et Ron Radziner, FAIA, ont créé Marmol Radziner en 1989, en lançant un cabinet de conception-construction unique en son genre, dirigé par des architectes. Basé à Los Angeles et disposant de bureaux à San Francisco et à New York, le cabinet propose des services d'architecture, de construction, de design d'intérieur et d'aménagement paysager. Marmol Radziner crée des espaces intimes et accueillants qui relient l'intérieur à l'extérieur. Les projets du cabinet s'inscrivent dans l'environnement et adoptent une approche chaleureuse et texturée du modernisme, élégante et intemporelle. Qu'il s'agisse de suivre les normes les plus élevées de conception durable ou de créer des pièces extérieures qui prolongent la vie quotidienne dans le paysage, Marmol Radziner utilise l'architecture pour rapprocher les gens de la nature.

Leo Marmol, FAIA, und Ron Radziner, FAIA, gründeten 1989 Marmol Radziner und starteten damit ein einzigartiges, von Architekten geleitetes Design- und Bauunternehmen. Das Büro mit Sitz in Los Angeles und Zweigstellen in San Francisco und New York City bietet Architektur, Konstruktion, Innenarchitektur und Landschaftsgestaltung. Marmol Radziner schafft intime, einladende Räume, die das Innere mit dem Äußeren verbinden. Die Projekte des Büros beziehen die Umgebung mit ein und widmen sich einer warmen, strukturierten Herangehensweise an die Moderne, die elegant und zeitlos ist. Ob sie den höchsten Standards für nachhaltiges Design folgen oder Außenräume schaffen, die das tägliche Leben in die Landschaft ausdehnen, Marmol Radziner nutzt Architektur, um den Menschen der Natur näher zu bringen.

Leo Marmol, FAIA, y Ron Radziner, FAIA, formaron Marmol Radziner en 1989, lanzando una empresa única de diseño y construcción dirigida por arquitectos. Con sede en Los Ángeles y oficinas en San Francisco y Nueva York, la firma ofrece arquitectura, construcción, diseño interior y diseño del paisaje. Marmol Radziner crea espacios íntimos y acogedores que conectan el interior con el exterior. Los proyectos del estudio se comprometen con el entorno y adoptan un enfoque cálido y texturizado de un modernismo elegante y atemporal. Ya sea siguiendo los más altos estándares de diseño sostenible o creando espacios exteriores que extienden la vida diaria al paisaje, Marmol Radziner utiliza la arquitectura para acercar a la gente a la naturaleza.

MANDEVILLE CANYON RESIDENCE

LOS ANGELES, CALIFORNIA

Lot size: 30,707 sq ft
Project size: 7,451 sq ft

The house is sited between a canyon road and a hillside in the Santa Monica Mountains. Using the footprint of the property to strengthen its connection to the site, the long rectangular forms of the house thread through the ancient native sycamore trees, following the gradual slope of the land. At its eastern end, the house floats three feet over the canyon floor. A pair of bridges provide access across a flood control channel that runs along the canyon road. The house, shrouded in shrubs and trees, gradually reveals a façade of dark gray brick and metal panels. Inside, a progression of spaces leads from dark to areas where light penetrates, to dark again. Floor-to-ceiling glazing and connected outdoor living spaces seamlessly integrate the architecture with the landscape. Skylights bring in additional natural light. Depending on the time of day, season, and weather, the experience of the home constantly changes. The dark colors and material palette of dark wood, brick, and metal were chosen to bring nature to the forefront.

La maison est située entre une route de canyon et une colline dans les montagnes de Santa Monica. Utilisant l'empreinte au sol de la propriété pour renforcer son lien avec le site, les longues formes rectangulaires de la maison se faufilent entre les anciens sycomores indigènes, suivant la pente graduelle du terrain. À son extrémité est, la maison flotte à un mètre au-dessus du fond du canyon. Deux ponts permettent l'accés à un canal de contrôle des inondations qui longe la route du canyon. La maison, entourée d'arbustes et d'arbres, révèle progressivement une façade de briques et de panneaux métalliques gris foncé. À l'intérieur, une progression d'espaces sombres conduisent à des zones où la lumière pénètre, pour revenir à l'obscurité. Les vitrages du sol au plafond et les espaces de vie extérieurs reliés entre eux intègrent parfaitement l'architecture au paysage. Les lucarnes apportent une lumière naturelle supplémentaire. Selon l'heure de la journée, la saison et le temps, l'expérience de la maison change constamment. Les couleurs sombres et la palette de matériaux de bois foncé, de brique et de métal ont été choisies pour mettre la nature au premier plan.

Das Haus liegt zwischen einer Canyonstraße und einem Berghang in den Santa Monica Mountains. Die langen, rechteckigen Formen des Hauses fädeln sich durch die uralten einheimischen Platanen und folgen der allmählichen Neigung des Grundstücks, indem sie die Beschaffenheit des Grundstücks nutzen, um die Verbindung zum Ort zu verstärken. An seinem östlichen Ende schwebt das Haus einen Meter über dem Canyonboden. Ein Brückenpaar ermöglicht den Zugang über einen Hochwasserschutzkanal, der entlang der Canyonstraße verläuft. Das von Sträuchern und Bäumen umhüllte Haus zeigt nach und nach eine Fassade aus dunkelgrauen Ziegelsteinen und Metallplatten. Im Inneren führt eine Abfolge von Räumen von Dunkelheit zu Bereichen, in die Licht eindringt, und wieder in die Dunkelheit. Eine raumhohe Verglasung und angeschlossene Außenwohnräume fügen die Architektur nahtlos in die Landschaft ein. Oberlichter bringen zusätzliches natürliches Licht herein. Je nach Tageszeit, Jahreszeit und Wetter ändert sich die Erfahrung des Hauses ständig. Die dunklen Farben und die Materialpalette aus dunklem Holz, Ziegel und Metall wurden ausgewählt, um die Natur in den Vordergrund zu rücken.

La casa está situada en un camino entre un cañón y una ladera en las montañas de Santa Mónica. Utilizando la propiedad original para reforzar su conexión con el terreno, las largas formas rectangulares de la casa se enhebran a través de los antiguos sicomoros, siguiendo la pendiente gradual del terreno. En su extremo este, la casa flota un metro sobre el suelo. Un par de puentes permiten el acceso a través de un canal de control de inundaciones que corre a lo largo del camino. La casa, rodeada de arbustos y árboles, revela gradualmente una fachada de ladrillo gris oscuro y paneles de metal. En el interior, una progresión de espacios lleva de la oscuridad a las áreas de más luz. Los vidrios de suelo a techo y los espacios exteriores conectados integran perfectamente la arquitectura con el paisaje. Los tragaluces aportan luz natural adicional. Dependiendo de la hora del día, la estación y el clima, el ambiente de la casa cambia constantemente. Se escogieron colores oscuros y una paleta de materiales como la madera oscura, el ladrillo y el metal.

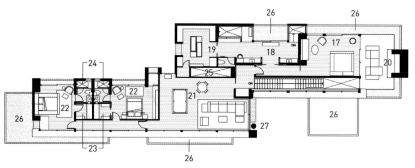

Second floor plan

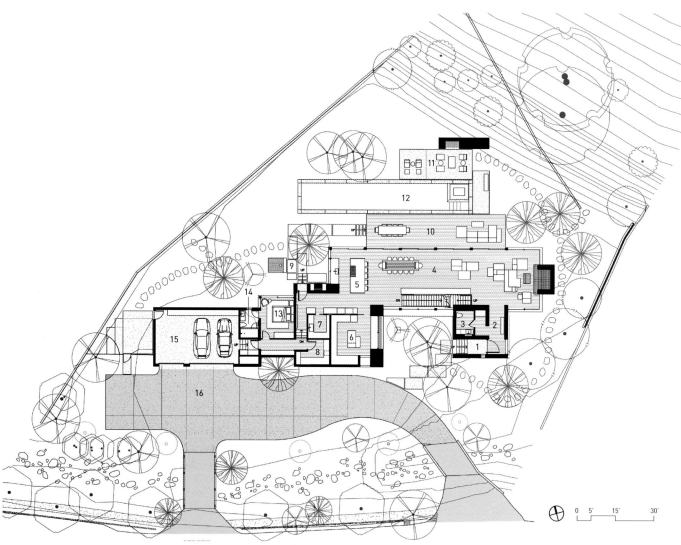

0 5' 15' 30'

Ground floor plan

1. Entry
2. Entry hall
3. Powder room
4. Great room
5. Kitchen
6. Office
7. Pantry
8. Laundry room
9. Outdoor kitchen
10. Outdoor living
11. Outdoor fireplace
12. Pool and spa
13. Guest bedroom
14. Guest bathroom
15. Garage
16. Driveway
17. Master bedroom
18. Master bathroom
19. Master closet
20. Master deck
21. Den
22. Bedroom
23. Closet
24. Bathroom
25. Light well open
    to below
26. Green roof
27. Existing sycamore

Martin Fenlon
Architecture

www.martinfenlon.com

ANGELUS HOUSE

Architect: Martin Fenlon Architecture

General Contractor: 509 Construction

Photographer: John Linden

FENLON HOUSE

Architect: Martin Fenlon Architecture

Photographer: John Linden, Zach Lipp

MORRIS HOUSE

Architect: Martin Fenlon Architecture

Landscape Designer: Joel Boulanger

General Contractor: Kevin Anderson

Photographer: Eric Staudenmaier

Martin Fenlon Architecture (MFA) is an award-winning architecture firm based in Los Angeles that was founded in 2004 by Martin Fenlon. Building upon the rich legacy of California Modernism and the Southern California Light & Space movement, MFA seeks a sustainable architecture of innovative space that is shaped by the unique qualities of the site and region, the logic and efficiency of construction, and the specific needs of the client.

Martin Fenlon is from Columbus Ohio and received Bachelors and Masters degrees in architecture from Ohio State University. During graduate school, Fenlon had the opportunity to work for the renowned firm Morphosis Architects before graduation, where he finished at the top of his class as recipient of the Faculty Prize in 1999. After working for Zago Architecture in Detroit for three years, he relocated to Los Angeles to establish his own practice. Fenlon is a licensed architect in California and Michigan.

Martin Fenlon Architecture (MFA) est un cabinet d'architecture primé, basé à Los Angeles, qui a été fondé en 2004 par Martin Fenlon. S'appuyant sur le riche héritage du modernisme californien et du mouvement Light & Space de Californie du Sud, MFA recherche une architecture durable d'un espace innovant qui soit façonnée par les qualités uniques du site et de la région, la logique et l'efficacité de la construction, et les besoins spécifiques du client.

Martin Fenlon est originaire de Columbus Ohio et a obtenu une licence et un master en architecture à l'université d'État de l'Ohio. Pendant ses études supérieures, M. Fenlon a eu l'occasion de travailler pour le célèbre cabinet Morphosis Architects avant d'obtenir son diplôme, où il a terminé premier de sa classe en tant que lauréat du prix de la faculté en 1999. Après avoir travaillé pour Zago Architecture à Detroit pendant trois ans, il a déménagé à Los Angeles pour créer son propre cabinet. Fenlon est un architecte agréé en Californie et dans le Michigan.

Martin Fenlon Architecture (MFA) ist ein preisgekröntes Architekturbüro mit Sitz in Los Angeles, das 2004 von Martin Fenlon gegründet wurde. Aufbauend auf dem reichen Erbe der kalifornischen Moderne und der Southern California Light-&-Space-Bewegung sucht MFA eine nachhaltige Architektur innovativer Räume, die von den einzigartigen Qualitäten des Ortes und der Region, der Logik und Effizienz der Konstruktion und den spezifischen Bedürfnissen des Kunden geprägt ist.

Martin Fenlon stammt aus Columbus, Ohio, und erhielt Bachelor- und Master-Abschlüsse in Architektur von der Ohio State University. Während seines Studiums hatte Fenlon die Gelegenheit, vor seinem Abschluss für das renommierte Büro Morphosis Architects zu arbeiten, wo er 1999 als Klassenbester mit dem Fakultätspreis ausgezeichnet wurde. Nachdem er drei Jahre lang für Zago Architecture in Detroit gearbeitet hatte, zog er nach Los Angeles um, um sein eigenes Büro zu gründen. Fenlon ist ein lizenzierter Architekt in Kalifornien und Michigan.

Martin Fenlon Architecture (MFA) es una galardonada firma de arquitectura con sede en Los Ángeles que fue fundada en 2004 por Martin Fenlon. Construyendo sobre el rico legado del Modernismo Californiano y el movimiento de Luz y Espacio del Sur de California, MFA busca una arquitectura sostenible de espacio innovador que se forme por las cualidades únicas del sitio y la región, la lógica, la eficiencia de la construcción y las necesidades específicas del cliente.

Martin Fenlon es de Columbus, Ohio, y recibió una licenciatura y una maestría en Arquitectura de la Universidad del Estado de Ohio. Durante la escuela de posgrado, Fenlon tuvo la oportunidad de trabajar para la renombrada firma Morphosis Architects antes de graduarse, donde terminó en la cima de su clase como ganador del Premio de la Facultad en 1999. Después de trabajar para Zago Architecture en Detroit durante tres años, se trasladó a Los Ángeles para establecer su propio estudio. Fenlon es un arquitecto licenciado en California y Michigan.

FENLON HOUSE

HERMON, LOS ANGELES, CALIFORNIA

Once a crowded property with an aging bungalow and a commercial storefront, this live/work complex accommodates the architect's growing family and practice. An expansion to the recently remodeled bungalow includes a new family room, exterior courtyard and deck, an attic conversion, and a stair hall. The storefront building, with its several bootleg additions, previously took up half of the site, exceeding the allowable floor area for the property and leaving little open space. In order to make space for a new yard and the 620 square feet of additions to the original house, over 600 square feet of the storefront was demolished. The expansion transitions the original house to the new yard, making one integral with the other. It maintains a separate identity from the original house while obscuring the boundaries of inside and outside.

Autrefois une propriété surpeuplée avec un bungalow vieillissant et une vitrine commerciale, ce complexe de vie et de travail accueille la famille et le cabinet de l'architecte, en pleine expansion. L'extension du bungalow récemment rénové comprend une nouvelle salle familiale, une cour et une terrasse extérieures, un grenier aménagé et un hall d'escalier. Le bâtiment de la façade, avec ses nombreux ajouts en contrebande, occupait auparavant la moitié du site, dépassant la surface de plancher autorisée pour la propriété et laissant peu d'espace libre. Afin de faire de la place pour une nouvelle cour et les 620 pieds soit 60 mètres carrés d'ajouts à la maison d'origine, plus de 600 pieds soit 56 mètres carrés de la façade du magasin ont été démolis. L'agrandissement fait la transition entre la maison d'origine et la nouvelle cour, rendant l'une solidaire de l'autre. Elle conserve une identité distincte de la maison d'origine tout en masquant les limites entre l'intérieur et l'extérieur.

Einst ein überfülltes Anwesen mit einem alternden Bungalow und einer kommerziellen Geschäftsfassade, beherbergt dieser Wohn-/Arbeitskomplex die wachsende Familie und Geschäftsräume des Architekten. Eine Erweiterung des kürzlich umgebauten Bungalows umfasst ein neues Familienzimmer, einen Außenhof und ein Deck, einen Dachbodenausbau und eine Treppenhalle. Das Geschäftsgebäude mit mehreren Raubkopiererergänzungen beanspruchte zuvor die Hälfte des Grundstücks, überschritt die zulässige Grundfläche für das Anwesen und ließ nur wenig Freiraum. Um Platz für einen neuen Hof und die 60 Quadratmeter des ursprünglichen Hauses zu schaffen, wurden über 56 Quadratmeter der Geschäftsfassade abgerissen. Durch die Erweiterung geht das ursprüngliche Haus in den neuen Hof über, wobei das eine in das andere integriert wird. Es behält eine vom ursprünglichen Haus getrennte Identität, während die Grenzen zwischen innen und außen verdeckt werden.

Este complejo de vivienda y trabajo, antiguamente una propiedad muy concurrida con un bungaló y una tienda, alberga ahora la familia y el estudio del arquitecto. La expansión del recientemente remodelado bungaló incluye una nueva habitación familiar, un patio exterior y una cubierta, una conversión del ático y una sala de ocio. El edificio, con sus varias extensiones, ocupaba anteriormente la mitad del terreno, superando la superficie de suelo permitida para la propiedad y dejando poco espacio abierto. Con el fin de hacer espacio para un nuevo patio y los 60 metros cuadrados de adiciones, se demolieron más de 56 metros cuadrados de la antigua tienda. La expansión transfiere la casa original al nuevo patio quedando conectado con el otro más antiguo. Mantiene una identidad separada de la casa original mientras que oscurece los límites entre interior y exterior.

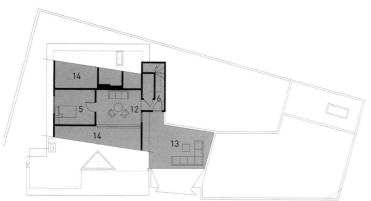

Second floor plan

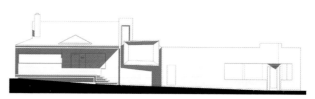

North elevation

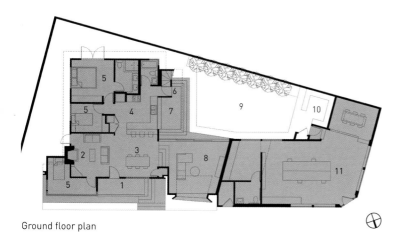

Ground floor plan

South elevation

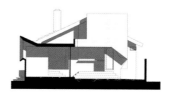

West elevation/section

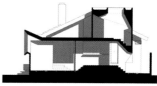

Section

1. Porch
2. Living room
3. Dining room
4. Kitchen
5. Bedroom
6. Stair hall
7. Deck
8. Family room
9. Yard
10. Sitting nook
11. Office
12. Den
13. Roof deck
14. Open to below

MORRIS HOUSE

HIGHLAND PARK, LOS ANGELES, CALIFORNIA

This project consists of an addition and renovation to an existing ranch house situated on a gently down-sloping lot with an exceptional view. To maximize light and space on a limited budget, the design was developed and modified in an improvisational manner by the architect and the owners over the course of construction. The living, dining, master bedroom, and bathroom were extended out from the back of the existing house within a contrasting wood-clad addition, forming a new carport underneath. The newly extended spaces have floor-to-ceiling glass walls, which let in an abundance of natural light and frame the expansive view. The roof of the main living area is punctured by a centrally placed operable skylight, which passively cools the space. Skylights also puncture the renovated kitchen, which is now continuous with the living and dining areas. Together, these spaces flow out onto the new outdoor deck. The addition hovers formally over the landscape, while casually integrating with the ground beneath it as a stair descends to an unfurling wood-clad runway.

Ce projet consiste en un agrandissement et une rénovation d'un ranch existant situé sur un terrain en pente douce avec une vue exceptionnelle. Afin de maximiser la lumière et l'espace sur un budget limité, le design en cours de construction a été développé et modifié de manière improvisée par l'architecte et les propriétaires. Le salon, la salle à manger, la chambre principale et la salle de bain ont été prolongés à l'arrière de la maison existante dans une annexe contrastée revêtue de bois, et en dessous formeformant un nouvel abri pour voiture. Les nouveaux espaces prolongés sont dotés de murs en verre du sol au plafond, qui laissent entrer une abondance de lumière naturelle et encadrent la vue étendue. Le toit de la zone d'habitation principale est percé par un puits de lumière central qui refroidit passivement l'espace. Les lucarnes percent également la cuisine rénovée, qui est maintenant en continuité avec le salon et la salle à manger. Ensemble, ces espaces nous améne sur le nouveau pont extérieur. L'annexe plane formellement au-dessus du paysage, tout en s'intégrant de manière naturelle au sol en dessous, alors qu'un escalier descend vers une piste en bois qui se déploie.

Bei diesem Projekt handelt es sich um eine Erweiterung und Renovierung eines bestehenden Ranchhauses, das auf einem leicht abfallenden Grundstück mit außergewöhnlicher Aussicht liegt. Um Licht und Raum mit einem begrenzten Budget zu maximieren, wurde der Entwurf vom Architekten und den Eigentümern im Laufe der Bauzeit improvisiert entwickelt und modifiziert. Das Wohn- und Esszimmer, das Hauptschlafzimmer und das Badezimmer wurden von der Rückseite des bestehenden Hauses aus in einem kontrastierenden holzverkleideten Anbau erweitert und bilden darunter einen neuen Carport. Die neu erweiterten Räume haben vom Boden bis zur Decke verglaste Wände, die viel natürliches Licht hereinlassen und die weite Aussicht einrahmen. Das Dach des Hauptwohnbereichs wird von einem zentral platzierten, bedienbaren Oberlicht durchbrochen, das den Raum passiv kühlt. Oberlichter durchbohren auch die renovierte Küche, die nun mit dem Wohn- und Essbereich verbunden ist. Zusammen fließen diese Räume auf das neue Außendeck hinaus. Der Anbau schwebt formal über der Landschaft, während er sich lässig in den Boden unter ihm integriert, während eine Treppe zu einer sich entfaltenden, mit Holz verkleideten Startbahn hinunterführt.

Este proyecto consiste en la adición y renovación de una casa de campo situada en un terreno ligeramente inclinado con una vista excepcional. Para maximizar la luz y el espacio disponiendo de un presupuesto limitado, el diseño fue desarrollado y modificado de manera improvisada por el arquitecto y los propietarios durante el curso de la construcción. El salón, el comedor, el dormitorio principal y el baño se ampliaron desde la parte trasera de la casa existente dentro de una extensión revestida de madera, formando una nuevo garaje en su parte inferior. Los espacios recién ampliados tienen paredes de vidrio de suelo a techo que dejan entrar abundante luz natural y enmarcan una generosa vista. El techo de la vivienda principal está perforado por un tragaluz central, que refresca el espacio de forma pasiva. Los tragaluces se encuentran también en la cocina, que, tras la remodelación, se abre a la sala de estar y al comedor. La ampliación se cierne formalmente sobre el paisaje, integrándose amablemente con el terreno a modo de escalera revestida de madera.

Section

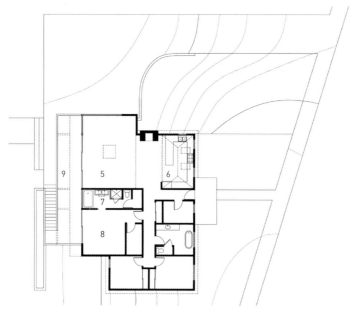

Upper floor plan

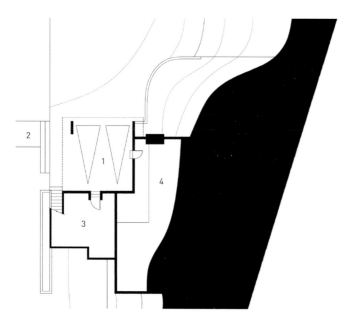

Lower floor plan

1. Carport
2. Runway
3. Storage
4. Crawl space
5. Living/dining area
6. Kitchen
7. Master bathroom
8. Master bedroom
9. Deck

ANGELUS HOUSE

SILVER LAKE, LOS ANGELES, CALIFORNIA

Lot size: 3,590 sq ft
Project size: 1,830 sq ft

The extensive remodel of an aging Spanish bungalow, nestled on a street lined with 1920s-era homes, resulted in a contemporary home. The original footprint and building envelope were maintained, keeping it consistent in scale with the surrounding homes on the street. Partitions were removed in the living, dining, and kitchen areas, creating a large open space that extends into the backyard with a large deck perched in mature trees. A cluster of skylights distributes natural light throughout the spaces, creating a bright and airy home. Circulation was also improved, adding Internal and external stairways to connect the upper and lower levels and the backyard. The smooth white plaster on the exterior walls and the new overhangs to shade the large glass surfaces minimize heat gain and echo the nearby work of Rudolph Schindler. In all, the remodel provides the house with the dual identity of old and new, resulting from a balance between careful preservation and radical alteration.

La rénovation complète d'un bungalow de style espagnol vieillissant, niché dans une rue bordée de maisons des années 1920, a permis de créer une maison contemporaine. L'empreinte au sol et l'enveloppe du bâtiment d'origine ont été conservées, ce qui lui permet de rester à la même échelle que les maisons environnantes dans la rue. Les cloisons ont été supprimées dans le salon, la salle à manger et la cuisine, créant ainsi un grand espace ouvert, qui se prolonge dans la cour arrière, avec une grande terrasse perchée dans des arbres matures. Un ensemble de puits de lumière illuminent tous les espaces, créant ainsi une maison lumineuse et aérée. La circulation a également été améliorée, avec l'ajout d'escaliers internes et externes pour relier les niveaux supérieurs et inférieurs et la cour arrière. Le plâtre blanc lisse des murs extérieurs et les nouveaux surplombs, pour ombrager les grandes surfaces vitrées, minimisent les gains de chaleur et font écho aux travaux de Rudolph Schindler, qui se trouvent à proximité. Au total, la rénovation confère à la maison la double identité de l'ancien et du nouveau, résultant d'un équilibre entre une préservation soigneuse et une modification radicale.

Die vollständige Renovierung eines alternden Bungalows im spanischen Stil, der an einer Straße lag, die von Häusern aus den 1920er Jahren gesäumt war, führte zu einem modernen Haus. Der ursprüngliche Grundriss und die Gebäudehülle wurden beibehalten, so dass sie im Maßstab mit den umliegenden Häusern an der Straße übereinstimmen. Die Trennwände in den Wohn-, Ess- und Küchenbereichen wurden entfernt, so dass ein großer offener Raum entstand, der sich bis in den Hinterhof erstreckt. Eine große Terrasse mit altem Baumbestand und eine Gruppe von Oberlichtern verteilt das natürliche Licht in den Räumen und schafft ein helles und luftiges Zuhause. Die Zirkulation wurde ebenfalls verbessert, indem Innen- und Außentreppen hinzugefügt wurden, um die oberen und unteren Ebenen und den Hinterhof zu verbinden. Der glatte weiße Putz an den Außenwänden und die neuen Überhänge zur Beschattung der großen Glasflächen minimieren den Wärmeeintrag und erinnern an die nahegelegene Arbeit von Rudolph Schindler. Alles in allem verleiht der Umbau dem Haus die doppelte Identität von Alt und Neu, die sich aus einem Gleichgewicht zwischen sorgfältiger Erhaltung und radikaler Veränderung ergibt.

La extensa remodelación de un antiguo bungaló de estilo español, situado en una calle bordeada de casas de la década de 1920, dio como resultado una casa moderna. La construcción original y la envoltura del edificio se conservaron, manteniéndolas consistentes en escala con las casas vecinas. Se eliminaron las divisiones en las áreas de la sala de estar, el comedor y la cocina, creando un gran espacio abierto que se extiende hasta el patio trasero con una gran cubierta rodeada de árboles maduros. Unos tragaluces distribuyen la luz natural a través de los espacios, creando un hogar luminoso y aireado. También se mejoró la circulación, añadiendo escaleras internas y externas para conectar los niveles superiores e inferiores y el patio trasero. El suave yeso blanco de las paredes exteriores y los nuevos voladizos para dar sombra a las grandes superficies de cristal minimizan la ganancia solar y hacen eco de las casas cercanas de Rudolph Schindler. La remodelación proporciona a la casa la doble identidad de lo viejo y lo nuevo, resultado de un equilibrio entre una cuidadosa preservación y una alteración radical.

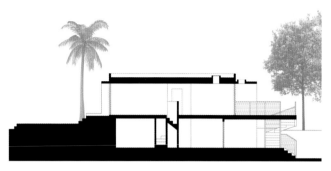

Longitudinal section

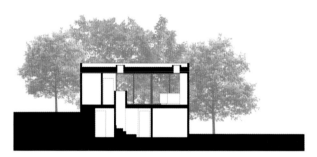

Cross section

Second floor plan

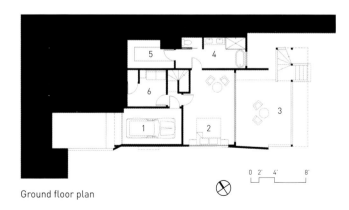

Ground floor plan

1. Garage
2. Master bedroom
3. Master deck
4. Master bathroom
5. Master closet
6. Laundry room
7. Entry
8. Living area
9. Kitchen
10. Upper deck
11. Dining area
12. Bedroom
13. Bathroom

OPA

SHAPESHIFTER

Landscape Designer: OPA

Planting: Delphine Huetz

Structural Engineer: Buro Happold

General Contractor: Mike Doherty Construction

Photographer: Joe Fletcher

DUNE

3D Visualizations: OPA

HIDDEN HOUSE

Landscape Designer: OPA

Planting: Delphine Huetz

Structural Engineer: Buro Happold

General Contractor: Forsythe General Contractors

Photographer: Joe Fletcher

At OPA, we believe in progressive built work, driven by ideas. We believe that architecture influences how we see the world and live in it. That architecture impacts our perceptions and emotions and acts as a physical framework for thought. By organizing our bodies and experiences in space, architecture can transform us. Our strength at OPA is identifying and crafting spatial experiences to make that possible. For us, every project is personal, whether private or public. Fundamental to our work is our close relationship with our clients and communities, whose use of our spaces gives life to the architecture. We see the design process as a joint exploration of expanding and choreographing what's possible. Together, we uncover what a project wants to be and make that desire a physical reality.

À l'OPA, nous croyons en un travail de construction progressive, motivé par des idées. Nous croyons que l'architecture influence la façon dont nous voyons le monde et dont nous y vivons. Cette architecture a un impact sur nos perceptions et nos émotions et agit comme un cadre physique pour la pensée. En organisant nos corps et nos expériences dans l'espace, l'architecture peut nous transformer. Notre force à l'OPA est d'identifier et d'élaborer des expériences spatiales pour rendre cela possible. Pour nous, chaque projet est personnel, qu'il soit privé ou public. La relation étroite que nous entretenons avec nos clients et les communautés, dont l'utilisation de nos espaces donne vie à l'architecture, est fondamentale pour notre travail. Nous considérons le processus de conception comme une exploration conjointe de l'expansion et de la chorégraphie de ce qui est possible. Ensemble, nous découvrons ce qu'un projet veut être et faisons de ce désir une réalité physique.

Wir bei der OPA glauben an eine fortschrittliche, auf Ideen basierende Arbeit. Wir glauben, dass Architektur Einfluss darauf hat, wie wir die Welt sehen und in ihr leben. Diese Architektur beeinflusst unsere Wahrnehmung und unsere Emotionen und fungiert als physischer Rahmen für unser Denken. Indem sie unseren Körper und unsere Erfahrungen im Raum organisiert, kann Architektur uns verändern. Die Stärke der OPA ist es, Raumerfahrungen zu identifizieren und zu gestalten, um dies zu ermöglichen. Für uns ist jedes Projekt persönlich, ob privat oder öffentlich. Grundlegend für unsere Arbeit ist unsere enge Beziehung zu unseren Kunden und Gemeinschaften, deren Nutzung unserer Räume die Architektur zum Leben erweckt. Wir sehen den Designprozess als eine gemeinsame Erkundung der Erweiterung und Choreographie des Möglichen. Gemeinsam entdecken wir, was ein Projekt sein will, und machen diesen Wunsch zu einer physischen Realität.

En OPA, creemos en el trabajo de construcción progresiva impulsado por las ideas. Creemos que la arquitectura influye en cómo vemos el mundo y vivimos en él; que la arquitectura impacta nuestras percepciones y emociones y actúa como un marco físico para el pensamiento. Al organizar nuestros cuerpos y experiencias en el espacio, la arquitectura puede transformarnos. Nuestra fuerza en OPA es identificar y crear experiencias espaciales y hacerlas posible. Para nosotros, cada proyecto es personal, ya sea privado o público. Fundamental para nuestro trabajo es la estrecha relación con nuestros clientes y comunidades, así como el uso de nuestros espacios que dan vida a la arquitectura. Vemos el proceso de diseño como una exploración conjunta de ampliar y coreografiar lo que es posible. Juntos, descubrimos lo que un proyecto quiere ser y hacemos de ese deseo una realidad física.

SHAPESHIFTER

RENO, NEVADA

Lot size: 28,574 sq ft
Project size: 5,900 sq ft

Two art collectors and dealers specializing in contemporary art and art of the American West wanted a house that would both reflect the contemporary moment and be explicit of the West. The American desert has a history of being understood as a place of lack and emptiness. Invoking the desert as a shapeshifter par excellence, the project began by treating the ground as a fluid material that allows different forms to emerge, which then dissolve into other forms. The project develops a synthetic ground to protect the house against its harsh desert landscape. Formally, the house is carved from a thick shell, composed either of the natural ground or a heavily insulated wall/roof assembly. Like a high desert creature, the house uses the ground (both real and synthetic) as a buffer against the harsh desert landscape. The result is a high-performance passive structure, which maintains a comfortable living temperature using only radiant heating and cooling. Outside, the landscape is populated exclusively by native plants—grasses, desert scrub, and wildflowers.

Deux collectionneurs et marchands d'art spécialisés dans l'art contemporain et l'art de l'Ouest américain voulaient une maison qui reflète le moment contemporain et qui soit orienté sur l'Ouest. Le désert américain a toujours été compris comme un lieu de manque et de vide. Invoquant le désert comme un métamorphe par excellence, le projet a commencé par traiter le sol comme un matériau fluide qui permet à différentes formes d'émerger, puis de vaciller ou de se dissoudre dans d'autres formes. Le projet développe un sol synthétique pour protéger la maison contre la rudesse du paysage désertique. Formellement, la maison est sculptée dans une épaisse coquille, composée soit du sol naturel, soit d'un ensemble mur/toit fortement isolé. Comme une créature du désert, la maison utilise le sol (réel et synthétique) comme tampon contre le rude paysage désertique. Le résultat est une structure passive très performante, qui maintient une température de vie confortable en utilisant uniquement le chauffage et le refroidissement par rayonnement. À l'extérieur, le paysage est peuplé exclusivement de plantes indigènes - herbes, broussailles du désert et fleurs sauvages.

Zwei Kunstsammler und -händler, die auf zeitgenössische Kunst und Kunst des amerikanischen Westens spezialisiert sind, wollten ein Haus, das sowohl den zeitgenössischen Moment widerspiegelt als auch explizit westlich geprägt ist. Die amerikanische Wüste hat eine Geschichte, in der sie als ein Ort des Mangels und der Leere verstanden wurde. Unter Berufung auf die Wüste als Gestaltwandler par excellence begann das Projekt damit, den Boden als flüssiges Material zu behandeln, das verschiedene Formen entstehen lässt, die sich dann in andere Formen auflösen. Das Projekt entwickelt einen synthetischen Boden, um das Haus vor seiner rauen Wüstenlandschaft zu schützen. Formal ist das Haus aus einer dicken Schale geschnitzt, die entweder aus dem natürlichen Boden oder einer stark isolierten Wand-/Dachkonstruktion besteht. Wie ein hohes Wüstentier nutzt das Haus den Boden (sowohl den echten als auch den synthetischen) als Puffer gegen die raue Wüstenlandschaft. Das Ergebnis ist eine hochleistungsfähige Passivstruktur, die eine angenehme Wohntemperatur nur durch Strahlungsheizung und -kühlung aufrechterhält. Draußen wird die Landschaft ausschließlich von einheimischen Pflanzen – Gräsern, Wüstenbuschwerk und Wildblumen – besiedelt.

Dos coleccionistas y comerciantes de arte especializados en arte contemporáneo y arte del Oeste americano querían una casa que reflejara el momento actual y que fuera explícita del espíritu del oeste; el desierto americano es a menudo entendido como un lugar de carencia y vacío. Invocando al desierto como el mutante por excelencia, el proyecto comenzó tratando al terreno como un material fluido que permite que las diferentes formas emerjan y luego se conviertan en otras formas distintas. El proyecto desarrolla un suelo sintético para proteger la casa contra su duro paisaje desértico. Formalmente, la casa está tallada en una carcasa gruesa, ya sea el suelo natural o un conjunto de pared-techo muy bien aislado. Como una criatura del desierto, la casa utiliza la base (tanto real como sintética) como barrera. El resultado es una estructura de alto rendimiento, que mantiene una temperatura cómoda utilizando calefacción y refrigeración radiante. En el exterior, el paisaje está poblado exclusivamente por plantas autóctonas —hierbas, matorrales y flores silvestres.

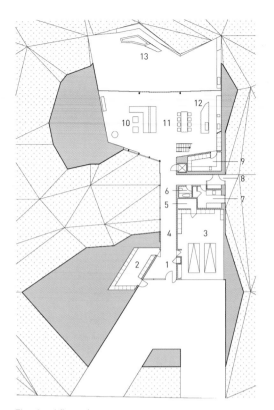

First level floor plan

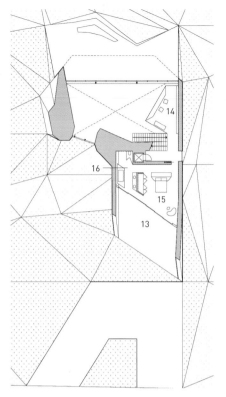

Second level floor plan

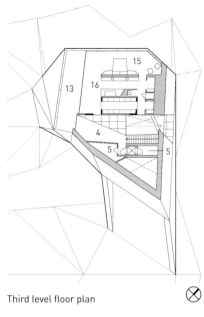

Third level floor plan

1. Entry
2. Cellar
3. Garage
4. Gallery
5. Mechanical room
6. Powder room
7. Utility room
8. Kennel
9. Pantry
10. Living area
11. Dining area
12. Kitchen
13. Terrace
14. Study
15. Bedroom
16. Bathroom

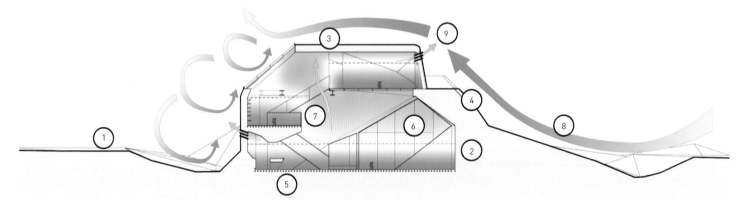

Sustainability diagram

1. NATIVE LANDSCAPE: A native species xeriscape provides a much needed return of habitat for local wildlife. This landscape mirrors the natural landscape visible in the distance rather than the artificial landscapes typical of the urban sprawl

2. EARTH BERMS: Like a natural cave, the house is buried below sculpted earth mounds which provide extensive thermal mass aiding both heating and cooling

3. THICK ASSEMBLIES: Both walls and roof are two-foot thick assemblies. This allows for thermal insulation of R-50+ throughout, extending the cave strategy above grade

4. ZINC CLADDING: Zinc rain-screen provides 100% recyclable moisture barrier while providing a zero toxicant rain water run-off

5. RADIANT HEATING AND COOLING: Highly ecient systems for delivering interior conditioning with large capacity to absorb and oset drawmatic swings in the outside environment. This system requires low energy consumption and eliminates duct loss. The high desert is an ideal climate for radiant cooling because of the relatively low humidity

6. HIGH PERFORMANCE WINDOWS AND SHADES: Thermally broken window frames with

performance glass (SFGC 0.23) minimizes heat gain. All openings have sensor activated roller shades to reduce energy demands

7. GREEN ROOF: The planted roof provides excellent thermal performance similar to the earth berms at the perimeter walls. (At front of project, beyond section)

8. NW PREVAILING WIND: Natural landform building does not disrupt existing wind patterns

9. OW PRESSURE ZONE: Three story open section allow for passive stack effect cooling

DUNE

PAJARO DUNES, CALIFORNIA

Lot size: 10,890 sq ft
Project size: 3,400 sq ft

Deeply embedded in the context of a coastal landscape, this weekend retreat is a synthetic dune, thematically and morphologically integrated into its site with its tilting floors and roof constrained by the angle of repose of the local sand drifts. These continuous, hummocky hills of sand, held together by beachgrass and other vegetation, provide specialized habitats and protect the beach from erosion. The project begins by remediating a previously developed lot and combines strategic architectural interventions that restore and conserve natural processes while creating conditions for new ones. In broad strokes, the house form was designed using a generative growth strategy that embeds a variety of specific behaviors. One of the primary behavior controls manages the potential slope of a wall or roof as it meets the adjacent dune. This form-finding approach is reinforced with 'soft techniques' of dune stabilization, including the planting of erosion-control vegetation, and the construction of dune walkways.

Profondément ancré dans le contexte d'un paysage côtier, cette retraite de week-end est une dune synthétique, thématiquement et morphologiquement intégrée dans son site avec ses planchers et son toit basculants, contraints par l'angle de repos des dunes de sable locales. Ces collines de sable continues et bosselées, maintenues ensemble par l'herbe de la plage et d'autres végétaux, fournissent des habitats spécialisés et protègent la plage de l'érosion. Le projet commence par la remise en état d'un terrain déjà aménagé et combine des interventions architecturales stratégiques qui restaurent et conservent les processus naturels tout en créant les conditions pour de nouveaux processus. Dans les grandes lignes, la forme de la maison a été conçue en utilisant une stratégie de croissance générative qui intègre une variété de comportements spécifiques. L'un des principaux contrôles de comportement gère la pente potentielle d'un mur ou d'un toit à la rencontre de la dune adjacente. Cette approche de recherche de forme est renforcée par des « techniques douces » de stabilisation des dunes, y compris la plantation d'une végétation anti-érosion et la construction de passerelles dans les dunes.

Tief in den Kontext der Küstensanddünen eingebettet, ist dieses Wochenendrefugium eine synthetische Düne, die thematisch und morphologisch in ihren Standort integriert ist, mit ihren kippbaren Böden und ihrem Dach, das durch den Schüttwinkel der lokalen Sandverwehungen eingeschränkt wird. Diese durchgehenden, hügeligen Sandansammlungen, die durch Strandgras und andere Vegetation zusammengehalten werden, bieten spezialisierte Lebensräume und schützen den Strand vor Erosion. Das Projekt begann mit der Sanierung eines zuvor erschlossenen Grundstücks und kombiniert strategische architektonische Eingriffe, die natürliche Prozesse wiederherstellen und erhalten und gleichzeitig Bedingungen für neue Prozesse schaffen. Die Hausform wurde unter Verwendung einer generativen Wachstumsstrategie entworfen, die eine Vielzahl spezifischer Verhaltensweisen einbettet. Eine der primären Verhaltenssteuerungen verwaltet die potenzielle Neigung einer Wand oder eines Daches, wenn sie auf die angrenzende Düne trifft. Dieser Formfindungsansatz wird durch „weiche Techniken" der Dünenstabilisierung verstärkt, einschließlich der Bepflanzung mit Erosionsschutzvegetation und dem Bau von Dünenwegen.

Profundamente asentado en las dunas de la costa, este retiro de fin de semana es una duna sintética, integrada temática y morfológicamente en el lugar, con suelos y techo inclinados, limitados por el ángulo de reposo de las derivas de la arena local. Estas colinas onduladas de arena, mantenidas juntas por la vegetación de la playa, proporcionan hábitats especiales y la protegen de la erosión. El proyecto comienza con la recuperación de un terreno previamente urbanizado y combina intervenciones arquitectónicas estratégicas que restauran y conservan los procesos naturales al tiempo que crean condiciones para otros nuevos. La forma de la casa se diseñó utilizando una estrategia de crecimiento generativo que incorpora una variedad de comportamientos específicos. Uno de los principales controles de comportamiento gestiona la pendiente de un muro o techo al encontrarse con la duna adyacente. Este enfoque que pretende encontrar la forma se refuerza con «técnicas suaves» de estabilización de dunas, incluyendo la plantación de vegetación para controlar la erosión y la construcción de pasarelas.

Sustainabililty diagram

1. RECLAIMED SHINGLES: Exterior to be clad in vernacular reclaimed redwood shingles

2. DAYLIGHT: Project is 100% daylit, including central "involution", which delivers natural light to the center of the house

3. SYNTHETIC DUNE: Roof slope constrained to less than 33°, the critical angle of repose of sand. The house is alternatively covered and exposed by the shifting sands.

4. DUNE WALKWAY: Walkway suspended above dune surface to minimize impact.

5. RECLAIMED FINISHES: Interior to be clad in recclaimed hemlock planking

6. NATURAL DUNES: These continuous, hummucky hills of sand, help together by beachgrass and other vegetation, provide specialized habitats and help protect the beach from erosion. The project is thematically and morphologically integrated into its site, reinforcing and stabilizing the dune environment

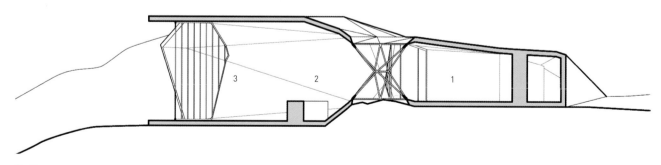

Section

1. Entry
2. Kitchen
3. Living area

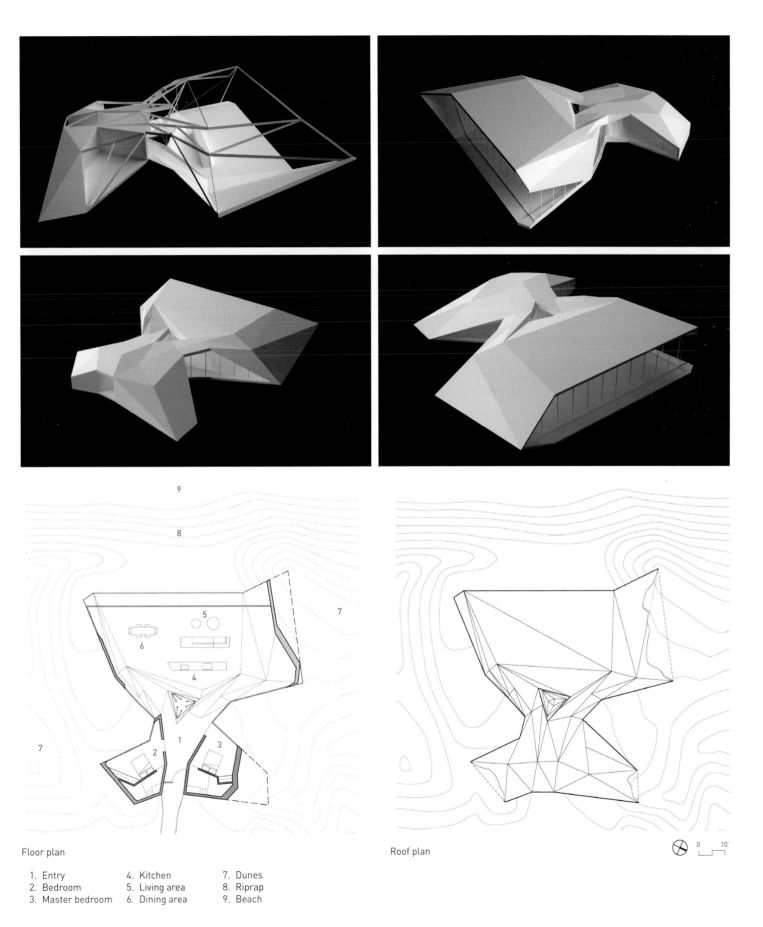

Floor plan

Roof plan

1. Entry
2. Bedroom
3. Master bedroom
4. Kitchen
5. Living area
6. Dining area
7. Dunes
8. Riprap
9. Beach

HIDDEN HOUSE

SAN FRANCISCO, CALIFORNIA

This house for an entrepreneur and an artist began with compromises. Impacted by powerful neighborhood groups that restricted its appearance, the house wears a mask to hide the architectural freedoms within. The mask achieves a blankness by abstracting the ubiquitous San Francisco bay window and covering the entire front face with a dense cedar screen. Behind the mask, vertical circulation is efficiently stacked on one side, opposing varied horizontal living on the other. A skylight emphasizes this split by creating a rift between these two zones, underscored by the use of raw materials on one side while the other side is drenched in pastel blue paint, which resulted from extensive color studies in collaboration with the artist client. The facets and fluctuating light conditions at the stair combine to make color perception unstable. Some amount of repression is essential to civilization—a compromise between the individual's instincts and society. In the Hidden House, the mask converts these disparate sensibilities into unified, civil behavior.

Cette maison pour un entrepreneur et un artiste a commencé par des compromis. Frappée par de puissants groupes de voisinage qui ont restreint son apparence, la maison porte un masque pour cacher les libertés architecturales qu'elle renferme. Le masque atteint une certaine blancheur en faisant abstraction de l'omniprésente baie vitrée de San Francisco et en couvrant toute la face avant d'un épais écran de cèdre. Derrière le masque, la circulation verticale est efficacement empilée d'un côté, opposant une vie horizontale variée de l'autre. Une lucarne souligne cette séparation en créant une brèche entre ces deux zones, soulignée par l'utilisation de matières premières d'un côté tandis que l'autre côté est imprégné de peinture bleu pastel, comme résultat d'études approfondies des couleurs en collaboration avec le client artiste. Les facettes et les conditions de lumière fluctuantes de l'escalier se combinent pour rendre la perception des couleurs instable. Un certain degré de répression est essentiel à la civilisation - un compromis entre les instincts de l'individu et la société. Dans la Hidden House, le masque convertit ces sensibilités disparates en un comportement civilisé et unifié.

Dieses Haus für einen Unternehmer und einen Künstler begann mit Kompromissen. Beeinflusst von mächtigen Nachbarschaftsgruppen, die sein Erscheinungsbild einschränkten, trägt das Haus eine Maske, um die architektonischen Freiheiten im Inneren zu verbergen. Die Maske erreicht eine Leere, indem sie das allgegenwärtige Erkerfenster von San Francisco abstrahiert und die gesamte Vorderseite mit einem dichten Zedernschirm bedeckt. Hinter der Maske ist die vertikale Zirkulation auf der einen Seite effizient gestapelt, während auf der anderen Seite ein vielfältiges horizontales Leben entgegengesetzt wird. Ein Oberlicht betont diese Trennung, indem es eine Kluft zwischen diesen beiden Zonen schafft, die durch die Verwendung von Rohstoffen auf der einen Seite unterstrichen wird, während die andere Seite mit pastellblauer Farbe getränkt ist. Die Facetten und schwankenden Lichtverhältnisse an der Treppe führen zu einer instabilen Farbwahrnehmung. Ein gewisses Maß an Repression ist für die Zivilisation unerlässlich – ein Kompromiss zwischen den Instinkten des Individuums und der Gesellschaft. Im Hidden House wandelt die Maske diese unterschiedlichen Empfindungen in ein einheitliches, ziviles Verhalten um.

Esta casa para un empresario y un artista comenzó con una serie de compromisos mutuos. Rodeada de poderosos grupos de casas vecinas que restringían su apariencia, la casa usa una máscara para ocultar las libertades arquitectónicas de su interior. Esta máscara logra un espacio en blanco abstrayendo la omnipresente vista de la bahía de San Francisco y cubriendo toda la fachada frontal con una densa pantalla compuesta de maderas cedro. Detrás de la máscara, la circulación vertical se apila eficientemente en un lado, oponiéndose a la vida horizontal en el otro. Un tragaluz enfatiza esta división creando una grieta entre estas dos zonas, un hueco subrayado por el uso de materias primas y pintura azul pastel, resultado de extensos estudios de color en colaboración con el cliente artista. Las condiciones de luz en la escalera se combinan para hacer inestable la percepción del color. En la Hidden House, la máscara convierte las sensibilidades humanas dispares en un comportamiento unificado y civilizado.

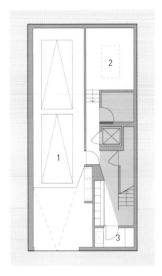

First level floor plan

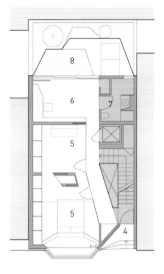

Second level floor plan

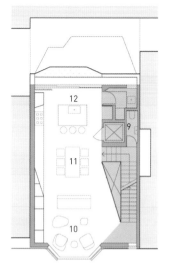

Third level floor plan

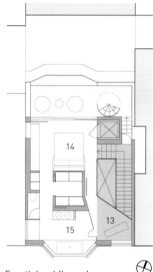

Fourth level floor plan

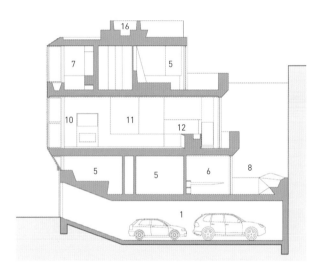

Sections

1. Garage
2. Arts studio
3. Utility
4. Entry
5. Bedroom
6. Office
7. Bathroom
8. Garden
9. Powder room
10. Living area
11. Dining area
12. Kitchen
13. Study
14. Master bedroom
15. Master bathroom
16. Roof spa

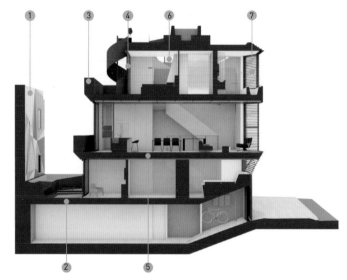

Sustainability diagram

1. SMALL HOUSE: Shallow 50' deep lot results in relatively modest house footprint, promoting increased urban density

2. GREEN ROOFS: Planted roof and planters at every floor minimize urban heat island effect

3. STEPPED SECTION: House steps back each level up at mid-block open space to maximize light and air at each level

4. HIGH PERFORMANCE WINDOWS: Thermally broken window frames with performance glass (SFGC 0.23) minimizes heat gain. All openings have sensor activated roller shades to further reduce energy demands

5. HYDRONIC HEATING AND COOLING: Climate regulated by highly efficient hydronic system in exposed concrete floors at all levels

6. DAYLIGHTING: Shallow footprint with large windows and stairwell skylight reduce artificial lighting loads. House is 100% daylit

7. SUN CONTROL: Wood louvers at bay window help regulate southern light. Automated shade screens provide additional granular control

Robert Nebolon Architects

RNarchitect.com

HERMOSA BEACH HOUSE

Architecture Team: Robert Nebolon, AIA-Design Principal and Charles "Chip" Moore AIA- Project Architect

Structural Engineer: Sarmiento Engineering

General Contractor: John Madison Construction

Photographer: David Duncan Livingston Photography

ART GALLERY HOUSE

Architecture Team: Robert Nebolon, AIA-Design Principal and Marc Newman, AIA -Project Architect/Project Designer

Interior Design Team: Pamela Lin/Urbanism Designs and Robert Nebolon Architects

Landscape Architect: Paul Harris/Imagine Sonoma Landscape Architects

Structural Engineer: Arnold Engineering

General Contractor: W.B. Elmer & Co.

Photographer: Bruce Damonte Photography

RIDGEBACK HOUSE

Architecture Team: Robert Nebolon, AIA-Design Principal and Charles "Chip" Moore AIA- Project Architect

Interior Design: Robert Nebolon Architects

Landscape Architect: Robert Nebolon Architects

Structural Engineer: Arnold Engineering

General Contractor: W.B. Elmer & Co.

Photographer: Gabriel Costa

California is distinctive for its blending of geographical, technological, cultural, and ecological influences in home design. Robert Nebolon Architects brings these sensibilities to their designs found amidst urban and rural setting on the West Coast. Solutions speak of that particular location and also to the character that suits the owners' lifestyle well. Site features such as views, sunlight, and climate can enrich the owners' daily lives. These features may be as simple as the changing play of sunlight in a room, on a terrace, or on the wall or fitting the entire project around a prized tree. Robert Nebolon best designs juggle many different nuances into one built work.

La Californie se distingue par son mélange d'influences géographiques, technologiques, culturelles et écologiques, dans la conception des maisons. Robert Nebolon Architects apporte ces sensibilités à ses projets qui se trouvent dans un cadre urbain et rural sur la côte ouest. Les solutions parlent de cet emplacement particulier et aussi du caractère qui convient bien au style de vie des propriétaires. Les caractéristiques du site, telles que les vues, la lumière du soleil et le climat, peuvent enrichir la vie quotidienne des propriétaires. Ces caractéristiques peuvent être aussi simples que le jeu changeant de la lumière du soleil dans une pièce, sur une terrasse ou sur un mur, ou encore l'installation de l'ensemble du projet autour d'un arbre précieux. Les meilleurs projets de Robert Nebolon jonglent avec de nombreuses nuances différentes dans une seule œuvre construite.

Kalifornien zeichnet sich durch die Vermischung geographischer, technologischer, kultureller und ökologischer Einflüsse im Wohndesign aus. Robert Nebolon Architects bringen diese Sensibilität in ihre Entwürfe ein, die inmitten der städtischen und ländlichen Umgebung an der Westküste zu finden sind. Die Lösungen sprechen von diesem besonderen Ort und auch von dem Charakter, der gut zum Lebensstil der Eigentümer passt. Standortmerkmale wie Aussicht, Sonnenlicht und Klima können das tägliche Leben der Eigentümer bereichern. Diese Merkmale können so einfach sein wie das wechselnde Spiel des Sonnenlichts in einem Raum, auf einer Terrasse oder an der Wand oder die Anbringung des gesamten Projekts um einen wertvollen Baum herum. Robert Nebolons beste Entwürfe jonglieren viele verschiedene Nuancen in einem gebauten Werk.

California se distingue por su mezcla de influencias geográficas, tecnológicas, culturales y ecológicas en el diseño de casas. Robert Nebolon Architects aporta estas sensibilidades a sus diseños que se encuentran en medio del entorno urbano y rural de la Costa Oeste. Las soluciones hablan de ese lugar en particular y también del carácter que se adapta bien al estilo de vida de los propietarios. Las características del terreno, así como las vistas, la luz del sol y el clima pueden enriquecer la vida diaria de esos propietarios. Estas características pueden ser tan simples como el juego cambiante de la luz del sol en una habitación, en una terraza, o en la pared o en basar el diseño de todo el proyecto alrededor de un árbol preciado. Los mejores diseños de Robert Nebolon consiguen malabares con muchos y diferentes matices.

HERMOSA BEACH HOUSE

LOS ANGELES, CALIFORNIA

Lot size: 1,500 sq ft
Project size: 1,832 sq ft

The "Upside-down House" best describes this California three-bedroom, two-bath home because communal and landscaped outdoor spaces are on the top floors instead of the ground floor. The unconventional home is built on a mere 30 feet by 50 feet back lot, entered off an alleyway where no gardens or yards are possible at ground level. This inverted planning gives the home optimal access to cooling sea breezes, views of the ocean only 100 yards away, and a garden roof deck. Committed to natural cooling methods, the stair is open on all sides, acts as the main natural ventilation space, and is topped by a huge operable skylight to help cool the house. The "floating" stair is designed to be an exciting focal point. The house is crowned with a garden roof deck with ocean views and private outdoor area. Colorful tile walls greet visitors and are reminiscent of the colorful beach towels found on the beach nearby. Part of a texturally varied and well-balanced composition, the steel cladding wraps the building protectively on its south and west sides, where sun and wind are harshest.

La « maison à l'envers » décrit le mieux cette maison californienne de trois chambres à coucher et deux salles de bain, car les espaces extérieurs communs et aménagés se trouvent aux étages supérieurs plutôt qu'au rez-de-chaussée. Cette maison non conventionnelle est construite sur un terrain d'à peine 9,1 x 15,2 mètres, accessible par une allée où il n'y a pas de jardin ou de cour au niveau du sol. Cette planification inversée donne à la maison un accès optimal aux brises marines, des vues sur l'océan à seulement 100 mètres et une terrasse de jardin sur le toit. L'escalier « flottant », ouvert de tous les côtés et conçu pour être un point d'attraction de la maison, est surmonté d'un énorme puits de lumière fonctionnel qui contribue à rafraîchir la maison. Un toit-terrasse avec vue sur l'océan et un espace extérieur privé couronnent la maison. Des murs de tuiles colorées attirent le regard des visiteurs et rappellent les serviettes de plage colorées que l'on trouve sur la plage toute proche. Faisant partie d'une composition de textures variées et bien équilibrées, le revêtement en acier enveloppe le bâtiment de manière protectrice sur ses côtés sud et ouest, là où le soleil et le vent sont plus forts.

Das „Upside Down House" beschreibt dieses kalifornische Haus mit drei Schlafzimmern und zwei Badezimmern am besten, da sich die gemeinsamen und möblierten Außenbereiche eher in den oberen Etagen als im Erdgeschoss befinden. Das unkonventionell gestaltete Haus befindet sich auf einem 9,1 x 15,2 m großen Grundstück, das über eine Gasse zugänglich ist, in der sich im Erdgeschoss keine Gärten oder Terrassen befinden. Diese umgekehrte Planung begünstigt einen optimalen Zugang zur Meeresbrise und bietet einen Blick auf das nur 100 Meter entfernte Meer sowie eine angelegte Dachterrasse. Die nach allen Seiten offene „schwebende" Treppe, die als Blickfang dient, wird von einem geräumigen und funktionalen Oberlicht gekrönt, das zur Kühlung des Hauses beiträgt. Eine Dachterrasse mit Meerblick und ein privater Außenbereich krönen das Haus. Die farbenfrohen Fliesenwände ziehen die Aufmerksamkeit der Besucher auf sich und erinnern an die farbenfrohen Strandtücher am nahe gelegenen Strand. Die Stahlverkleidung ist Teil einer Komposition aus abwechslungsreichen und ausgewogenen Texturen und umhüllt das Gebäude an der Süd- und Westseite, wo Sonne und Wind am stärksten sind, schützend.

Una «casa al revés» es lo que mejor describe esta vivienda de tres dormitorios y dos baños, donde los espacios exteriores comunes y ajardinados están en los pisos superiores en lugar de la planta baja. La casa, de diseño poco convencional, se alza en un terreno de 9,1 por 15,2 metros al que se accede por un callejón donde no se encuentran jardines o patios a nivel del suelo. Esta planificación invertida favorece un acceso óptimo a la brisa marítima y ofrece vistas al océano a solo 100 metros así como una terraza ajardinada en el tejado. La escalera «flotante», abierta por todos sus lados y diseñada para ser un punto de atracción, está coronada por un amplio y funcional tragaluz que contribuye a la refrigeración de la casa. Una terraza en el tejado con vista al mar y un área privada al aire libre corona la casa. Las paredes de azulejos de colores llaman la atención de los visitantes y recuerdan las coloridas toallas de playa que se encuentran en la playa cercana. Parte de una composición de texturas variadas y equilibradas, el revestimiento de acero envuelve de manera protectora el edificio en sus lados sur y oeste, donde el sol y el viento son más fuertes.

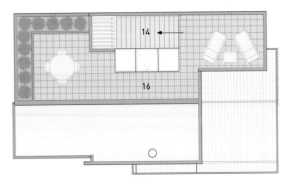

Roof plan

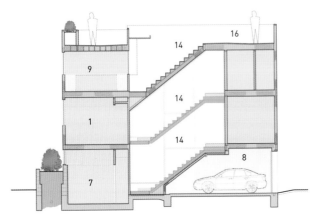

Section B

Third floor plan

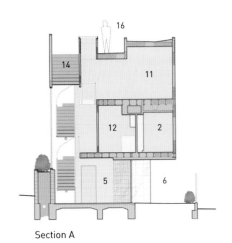

Section A

Second floor plan

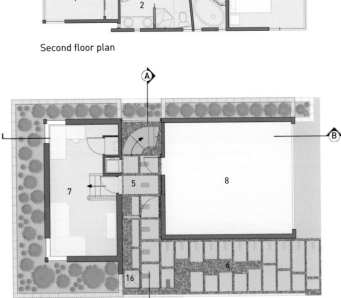

Ground floor plan

1. Bedroom
2. Bathroom
3. Closet
4. Dining area
5. Entry
6. Entry court
7. Family room
8. Garage
9. Kitchen
10. Living area
11. Master bedroom
12. Laundry room
13. Master bathroom
14. Stair
15. Powder room
16. Roof deck
17. Outdoor shower
18. Terrace

0   5'   10'

ART GALLERY HOUSE
HILLSBOROUGH, CALIFORNIA

Lot size: 29,800 sq ft
Project size: 4,880 sq ft

The house design is based on the East Indian planning principle called Vastu Shastra—which was then modified to adapt to California outdoor living for an "East meets West" fusion. The wooded site is triangular-shaped and is squeezed between the street and a creek. To fit on the site and address Vastu Shastra, the final building form evolved into a three-wing solution; the wings skew at a 15-degree angle to each other thus allowing gardens and daylight to penetrate the house in unexpected ways; the center wing, orientated on the cardinal compass points for excellent Vastu Shastra, has large folding glass doors on two opposite sides which allows the terrace to flow thru the house from south to north. Inside, high light monitors provide natural day lighting for optimal lighting for the modern East Indian art collection.

La conception de la maison est basée sur le principe de planification des Indes orientales appelé Vastu Shastra - qui a ensuite été modifié pour s'adapter à la vie en plein air en Californie pour une fusion « East meets West ». Le site boisé est de forme triangulaire est coincé entre la rue et un ruisseau. Pour s'adapter au site et s'adresser à Vastu Shastra, la forme finale du bâtiment a évolué vers une solution à trois ailes ; les ailes sont inclinées à un angle de 15 degrés l'une par rapport à l'autre, ce qui permet aux jardins et à la lumière du jour de pénétrer dans la maison de manière inattendue ; l'aile centrale, orientée sur les points cardinaux du compas pour l'excellente Vastu Shastra, possède de grandes portes vitrées pliantes sur deux côtés opposés qui permettent à la terrasse de traverser la maison du sud au nord. À l'intérieur, des moniteurs à haute luminosité fournissent un éclairage journalier naturel pour un éclairage optimal de la collection d'art moderne des Indes orientales.

Der Hausentwurf basiert auf dem ostindischen Planungsprinzip „Vastu Shastra" – das dann modifiziert wurde, um sich dem kalifornischen Außenleben für eine „East meets West"-Fusion anzupassen. Das bewaldete Grundstück hat eine dreieckige Form und ist zwischen der Straße und einem Bach eingezwängt. Um auf das Grundstück zu passen und Vastu Shastra anzusprechen, entwickelte sich die endgültige Gebäudeform zu einer dreiflügeligen Lösung; die Flügel sind in einem Winkel von 15 Grad zueinander geneigt, so dass Gärten und Tageslicht auf unerwartete Weise in das Haus eindringen können; der mittlere Flügel, der sich an den Himmelsrichtungen für ausgezeichnetes Vastu Shastra orientiert, hat große Glas-Falttüren an zwei gegenüberliegenden Seiten, sodass die Terrasse von Süden nach Norden durch das Haus fließen kann. Im Inneren sorgen Oberlichter für natürliches Tageslicht und eine optimale Beleuchtung der modernen ostindischen Kunstsammlung.

El diseño de la casa se basa en un principio de planificación de la India llamado Vastu Shastra, que luego fue modificado para adaptarse a la vida al aire libre de California para una fusión «Oriente-Occidente». El terreno, muy boscoso, tiene forma triangular y está encajado entre la calle y un arroyo. Para poder ubicarse en el lugar y conseguir el concepto Vastu Shastra, la forma final del edificio evolucionó hasta un volumen de tres alas inclinadas en un ángulo de 15 grados entre sí, permitiendo que los jardines y la luz del día penetren en la casa de maneras inesperadas. El ala central, orientada a los puntos cardinales de la Vastu Shastra, tiene grandes puertas de vidrio plegable en dos lados opuestos que permiten que la terraza fluya a través de la casa de sur a norte. En el interior, puntos de luz permiten una óptima presentación de la colección de arte moderno de la India Oriental.

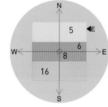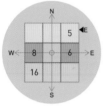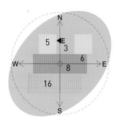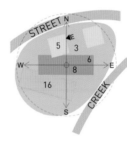

Adaptation of Vastu principles to the existing site

1. Driveway
2. Garage
3. Entry courtyard
4. Puja prayer room
5. Entry hall
6. Kitchen
7. Dining room
8. Living room
9. Office
10. Powder room
11. Den
12. Family room
13. Gym
14. Library
15. Laundry room
16. Guest bedroom
17. Patio
18. Staircase
19. Garden
20. Bedroom
21. Bathroom
22. Play/study
23. Terrace
24. Vastu Shastra site wall
25. Walk of Shiva

Floor plan

RIDGEBACK HOUSE

BERKELEY, CALIFORNIA

Lot size: 11,791 sq ft
Project size: 3,285 sq ft

The owners purchased a site located on a high ridge that overlooks San Francisco Bay and was once home to large redwood forests now long gone from logging. The clients are avid salt-water people—surfing and bodysurfing—and wanted their house to reflect their lifestyle and their collections of surf paraphernalia and ocean-inspired artwork. The house interior is reflective of the redwood forests and rocky topography and linked to outdoor stone terraces reminiscent of granite overlooks found in Yosemite. The roof is an independent structure supported by beams and steel columns under which walls are placed. Roofing is removed in places to reveal the roof structure that then acts as a trellis designed to shade the terraces below and from the afternoon sun in a manner much like sunlight filtered through the tree branches.

Les propriétaires ont acheté un site situé sur une haute crête qui surplombe la baie de San Francisco et qui abritait autrefois de grandes forêts de séquoias dont l'exploitation a disparu depuis longtemps. Les clients sont des passionnés d'eau salée - surf et bodysurf - et voulaient que leur maison reflète leur mode de vie et leurs collections d'accessoires de surf et d'œuvres d'art inspirées de l'océan. L'intérieur de la maison reflète les forêts de séquoias et la topographie rocheuse, est relié à des terrasses extérieures en pierre qui rappellent les vues en granit que l'on trouve au Yosemite. Le toit est une structure indépendante, soutenue par des poutres et des colonnes d'acier sous lesquelles sont placés les murs. La toiture est enlevée par endroits pour révéler la structure du toit qui agit alors comme un treillis, conçu pour ombrager les terrasses en dessous et du soleil de l'après-midi d'une manière similaire à la lumière du soleil filtrée par les branches des arbres.

Die Eigentümer erwarben ein Grundstück auf einem hohen Bergrücken mit Blick auf die Bucht von San Francisco, das einst große Mammutwälder beherbergte, die heute längst nicht mehr abgeholzt werden. Die Kunden sind begeisterte Salzwasser- und Body-Surfer und wollten, dass ihr Haus ihren Lebensstil und ihre Sammlungen von Surf-Utensilien und vom Meer inspirierten Kunstwerken widerspiegelt. Das Innere des Hauses spiegelt die Mammutwälder und die felsige Topographie wider und ist mit Steinterrassen im Freien verbunden, die an Granitausblicke aus dem Yosemite erinnern. Das Dach ist eine unabhängige Struktur, die von Balken und Stahlstützen getragen wird, unter denen die Wände platziert sind. Das Dach wurde an einigen Stellen entfernt, um die Dachkonstruktion freizulegen, die dann als Spalier dient, das die darunter liegenden Terrassen beschattet und der Nachmittagssonne entgegenwirkt, ähnlich wie Sonnenlicht, das durch Baumzweige gefiltert wird.

Los propietarios compraron un terreno situado en una alta cresta que da a la bahía de San Francisco y que una vez fue hogar de grandes bosques de secoyas, que ahora hace mucho que han desaparecido debido a la explotación forestal. Los clientes son amantes del agua marina —surf y bodysurf— y querían que su casa reflejara su estilo de vida y sus colecciones relacionadas con el surf y otras obras de arte inspiradas en el océano. El interior de la casa refleja los bosques de secoyas y la topografía rocosa con la que está vinculada a través de terrazas de piedra al aire libre que recuerdan a los miradores de granito encontrados en Yosemite. El techo es una estructura independiente sostenida por vigas y columnas de acero bajo las cuales se colocan las paredes. El techo se retira en algunos lugares para revelar la estructura del tejado que luego actúa como un enrejado diseñado para dar sombra a las terrazas del piso inferior y al sol de la tarde de una manera muy parecida a al efecto provocado por la luz solar filtrada a través de las ramas de los árboles.

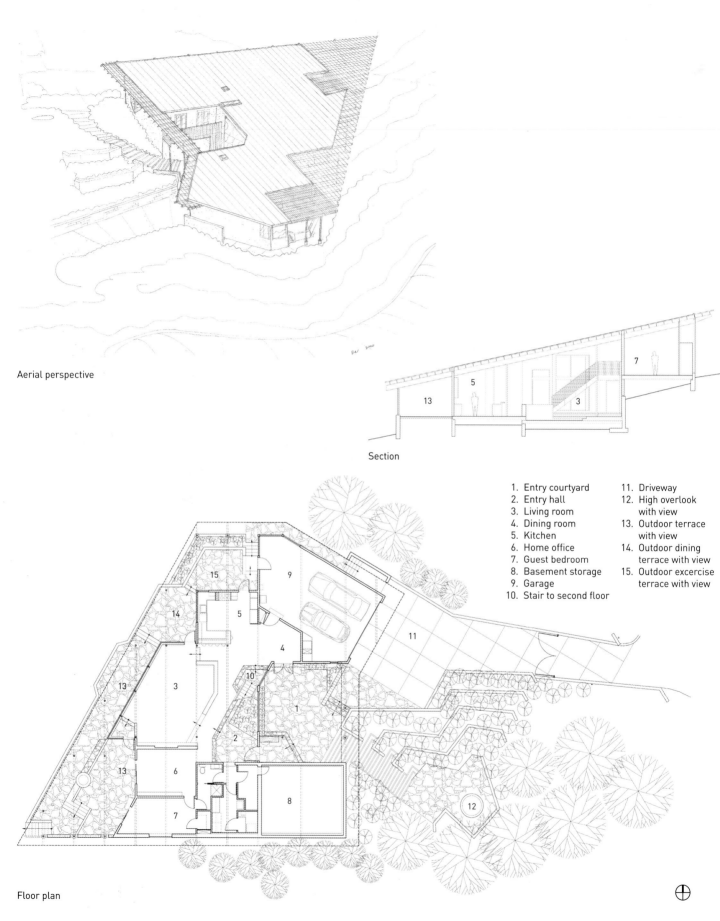

Aerial perspective

Section

1. Entry courtyard
2. Entry hall
3. Living room
4. Dining room
5. Kitchen
6. Home office
7. Guest bedroom
8. Basement storage
9. Garage
10. Stair to second floor

11. Driveway
12. High overlook with view
13. Outdoor terrace with view
14. Outdoor dining terrace with view
15. Outdoor excercise terrace with view

Floor plan

Turnbull Griffin Haesloop
Architects

tgharchitects.com

ELMWOOD COTTAGE

Architecture Team: Eric Haesloop FAIA, Principal;
John Kleman, and Amy Hu

Structural Engineer: Fratessa Forbes Wong
Structural Engineers

Energy Consustant: Loisos + Ubbelohde

General Contractor: Sawyer Construction

Photographer: David Wakely Photography

KENTFIELD RESIDENCE

Architecture Team: Mary Griffin FAIA, Principal;
Eric Haesloop FAIA, Principal; Jule Tsai, Project
Architect; John Kleman; Juliet Hsu; Evan
Markiewicz; Mayumi Hara; Tory Wolcott;
and Jerome Christensen

Landscape Architect: GLS

Living Roof Consultant: Rana Creek

Structural Engineer: Fratessa Forbes Wong
Structural Engineers

General Contractor: Redhorse Constructors

Photographer: David Wakely Photography

SKYFALL RESIDENCE

Architecture Team: Eric Haesloop FAIA, Principal;
Stefan Hastrup AIA, Principal;
and Sara Dewey AIA, Project Architect

Structural Engineer: I.L. Welty & Associates

General Contractor: Empire Contracting

Photographer: David Wakely Photography

Turnbull Griffin Haesloop is an award-winning architecture firm now located in Berkeley, California. We believe architecture is primarily concerned with establishing a "sense of place," inspired by the uniqueness of each site and each client. We listen carefully to the aspirations and requirements of our clients and together look for unique qualities to tailor the project. We are particularly attentive to topography, microclimate, water management, fire safety, vegetation, and solar orientation since the concept for each of our buildings is rooted in its environment.

Turnbull Griffin Haesloop est un cabinet d'architecte primé qui se trouve maintenant à Berkeley, en Californie. Nous pensons que l'architecture se préoccupe avant tout d'établir un « sens du lieu », inspiré par le caractère unique de chaque site et de chaque client. Nous écoutons attentivement les aspirations et les exigences de nos clients et recherchons ensemble des qualités uniques pour adapter le projet. Nous sommes particulièrement attentifs à la topographie, au microclimat, à la gestion de l'eau, à la sécurité incendie, à la végétation et à l'orientation solaire, car le concept de chacun de nos bâtiments est ancré dans son environnement.

Turnbull Griffin Haesloop ist ein preisgekröntes Architekturbüro, das jetzt in Berkeley, Kalifornien, ansässig ist. Wir glauben, dass es bei der Architektur in erster Linie darum geht, ein „Gefühl für den Ort" zu schaffen, das durch die Einzigartigkeit jedes Standorts und jedes Kunden inspiriert wird. Wir hören uns die Wünsche und Anforderungen unserer Kunden genau an und suchen gemeinsam nach einzigartigen Qualitäten, um das Projekt maßgeschneidert zu gestalten. Besondere Aufmerksamkeit widmen wir der Topographie, dem Mikroklima, dem Wassermanagement, dem Brandschutz, der Vegetation und der Sonnenausrichtung, da das Konzept für jedes unserer Gebäude in seiner Umgebung verwurzelt ist.

Turnbull Griffin Haesloop es una galardonada firma de arquitectura que ahora se encuentra en Berkeley, California. Creemos que la arquitectura está principalmente preocupada por establecer un «sentido de lugar», inspirado por la singularidad de cada sitio y cada cliente. Escuchamos cuidadosamente las aspiraciones y requerimientos de nuestros clientes y juntos buscamos cualidades únicas para adaptar el proyecto. Estamos particularmente atentos a la topografía, el microclima, la gestión del agua, la seguridad en caso de incendio, la vegetación y la orientación solar, ya que el concepto de cada uno de nuestros edificios está conectado siempre en su entorno.

ELMWOOD COTTAGE

BERKELEY, CALIFORNIA

Lot size: 50 by 140 feet
Project size: 432 sq ft

Located in a densely developed older neighborhood near the U.C. Berkeley campus with transit lines and a small commercial district, the project seeks to provide much needed car-free rental housing. The new accessory dwelling unit is an infill project sited to reshape and enhance an existing backyard, protecting views for both the new cottage and the existing main house. The 50' by 140' site was developed in 1908. The existing house is located near the front with some mature trees flanking the edges. The garage occupied a rear quadrant. The owners elected to take down and recycle the old garage, trading that lot coverage for the new cottage coverage. The design shapes the garden by creating a long gabled structure that edges the rear property line of the lot. The fenestration is concentrated on either end of the gable, maximizing views out, keeping the unit private from neighbors, and preserving the privacy of the yard for the front house. The structure is a design exploration for a compact, livable dwelling that is built economically and sustainably.

Situé dans un vieux quartier densément développé près du campus de l'Université de Berkeley, avec des lignes de transport en commun et un petit centre commercial, le projet vise à fournir des logements locatifs sans voiture, dont le besoin se fait cruellement sentir. La nouvelle unité d'habitation accessoire est un projet de construction intercalaire visant à remodeler et à améliorer une cour arrière existante, en protégeant les vues du nouveau cottage et de la maison principale existante. Le site de 15 par 43 métres a été développé en 1908. La maison existante bordée d'arbres matures est située à l'avant, avec un garage qui occupe un quadrant de terrain à l'arrière. Les propriétaires ont choisi de démolir et de recycler l'ancien garage, en échangeant la superficie de ce lot contre celle de la nouvelle maison. La conception façonne le jardin en créant une longue structure à pignon qui borde la limite arrière du terrain. La fenestration est concentrée à chaque extrémité du pignon, ce qui maximise les vues vers l'extérieur, garde l'unité privée des voisins et préserve l'intimité de la cour pour la maison de devant. La structure est une exploration de la conception d'une habitation compacte, habitable, construite de manière économique et durable.

Das Projekt befindet sich in einem dicht bebauten alten Viertel in der Nähe des Campus der UC Berkeley mit Transitlinien und einem kleinen Einkaufszentrum und zielt darauf ab, dringend benötigte autofreie Mietwohnungen bereitzustellen. Die neue Nebenwohneinheit ist ein Infill-Bauprojekt zum Umbau und zur Verbesserung eines bestehenden Hinterhofs, das die Aussicht auf das neue Cottage und das bestehende Haupthaus schützt. Das 15 mal 43 Meter große Grundstück wurde 1908 entwickelt. Das bestehende, von Bäumen gesäumte Haus befindet sich an der Vorderseite. Eine Garage nimmt einen Quadranten Land im hinteren Bereich ein. Die Eigentümer beschlossen, die alte Garage abzureißen und zu recyceln, indem sie die Fläche dieses Grundstücks gegen die des neuen Hauses austauschten. Das Design formt den Garten, indem es eine lange Giebelstruktur schafft, die an die hintere Grenze des Landes grenzt. Die Fensterung ist an jedem Ende des Giebels konzentriert, wodurch der Blick nach außen maximiert wird, die Einheit vor Nachbarn geschützt bleibt und die Privatsphäre des Hofs für das Vorderhaus erhalten bleibt. Die Struktur ist eine Erkundung des Entwurfs eines kompakten, lebenswerten, wirtschaftlich und nachhaltig gebauten Hauses.

Ubicado en un antiguo vecindario densamente desarrollado cerca del campus de U.C. Berkeley con bastante tráfico y un pequeño distrito comercial, el proyecto busca proporcionar la tan necesitada vivienda de alquiler. La nueva unidad accesoria consiste en un proyecto de remodelación y mejora de un patio trasero existente, protegiendo las vistas tanto de la nueva unidad como de la casa original. El terreno de 15 por 43 metros fue desarrollado en 1908. La casa existente está situada en la parte frontal del terreno, con algunos árboles flanqueando los laterales. El garaje ocupaba un cuadrante trasero. Los propietarios eligieron derribar y reciclar el viejo garaje, cambiando la cobertura de ese volumen por la de la nueva casa. El diseño da también forma al jardín creando una larga estructura a dos aguas que bordea la línea trasera de la propiedad. Ventanas en cada extremo de la parte frontal maximizan las vistas hacia el exterior, manteniendo la privacidad. La estructura es resultado de una exploración de diseño para una vivienda compacta y habitable construida de forma económica y sostenible.

Site plan

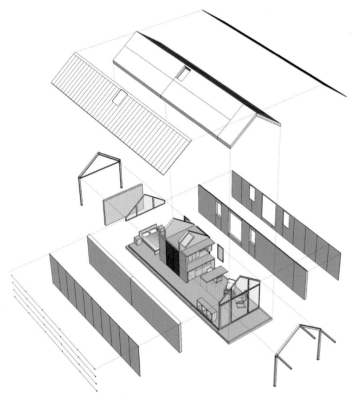

Exploded axonometric

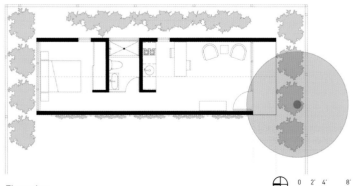

Floor plan

0 2' 4'   8'

322

The house is sited to engage the undulating hillside and capture the spectacular views of Mount Tamalpais and the San Francisco Bay. A curved retaining wall follows the contours of the hillside and anchors the house to the steep site. A living roof visually merges the house with the land. Growing out of the hillside, the roof is carved away to form a protected courtyard for the pool.
Three volumes housing the living room, kitchen-dining area, and master bedroom rise above the living roof with shed roofs angled to capture the sun for photovoltaic and solar hot water panels. The house incorporates passive and active heating and cooling systems, battery storage, and a cistern for water runoff management.

La maison est située de manière à s'engager sur le flanc ondulé de la colline et à saisir les vues spectaculaires du Mont Tamalpais et de la baie de San Francisco. Un mur de soutènement incurvé suit les contours de la colline et ancre la maison sur le site escarpé. Un toit vivant fait visuellement fusionner la maison avec le terrain. Le toit, qui pousse sur le flanc de la colline, est découpé de manière à former une cour protégée pour la piscine.
Trois volumes abritant le salon, la cuisine-salle à manger et la chambre principale s'élèvent au-dessus du toit de la maison. Les toits des hangars sont inclinés pour capter le soleil et permettre l'installation de panneaux photovoltaïques et de panneaux solaires pour l'eau chaude. La maison est équipée de systèmes de chauffage et de refroidissement passifs et actifs, de batteries de stockage et d'une citerne pour la gestion des eaux de ruissellement.

Die Lage des Hauses ist so gewählt, dass es den hügeligen Hang einnimmt und die spektakuläre Aussicht auf den Mount Tamalpais und die Bucht von San Francisco einfängt. Eine geschwungene Stützmauer folgt den Konturen des Hangs und verankert das Haus an der steilen Stelle. Ein lebendiges Dach verbindet das Haus optisch mit dem Land. Aus dem Hang herauswachsend, ist das Dach weggeschnitten, um einen geschützten Hof für den Pool zu bilden.
Über dem Wohndach erheben sich drei Volumina mit Wohnzimmer, Küche, Essbereich und Hauptschlafzimmer. Die Sheddächer sind so geneigt, dass sie die Sonne für Photovoltaik- und Solar-Warmwasserpaneele einfangen. Das Haus verfügt über passive und aktive Heiz- und Kühlsysteme, Batteriespeicher und eine Zisterne für das Wasserabflussmanagement.

La casa está situada junto a una ladera ondulante y captura las espectaculares vistas del monte Tamalpais y la bahía de San Francisco. Un muro de contención curvado sigue los contornos de la ladera y ancla la casa al empinado terreno. Una cubierta ajardinada fusiona visualmente la casa con el exterior, esculpiéndose para formar un patio protegido para la zona de la piscina.
Tres volúmenes que albergan la sala de estar, la cocina-comedor y el dormitorio principal se elevan sobre el techo del salón. Los techos de los cobertizos se sitúan en ángulo para captar luz solar para cargar los paneles fotovoltaicos. La casa incorpora sistemas pasivos y activos de calefacción y refrigeración, almacenamiento de baterías y una cisterna para la gestión del reciclaje del agua de lluvia.

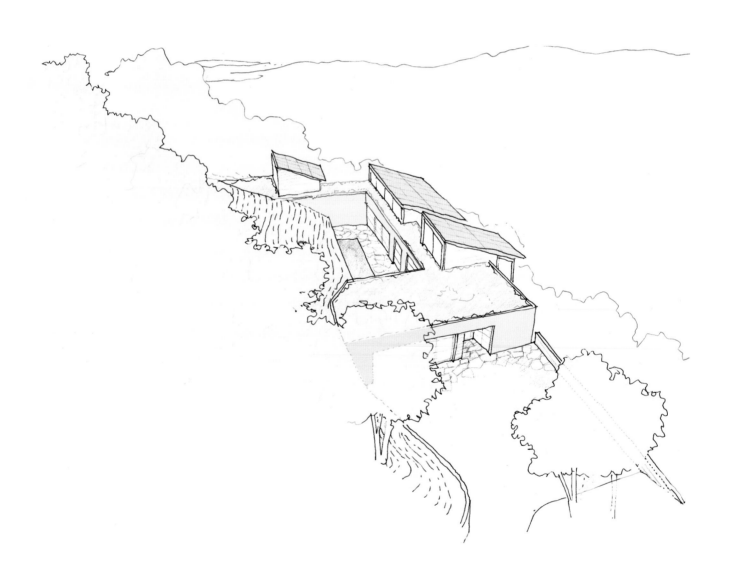

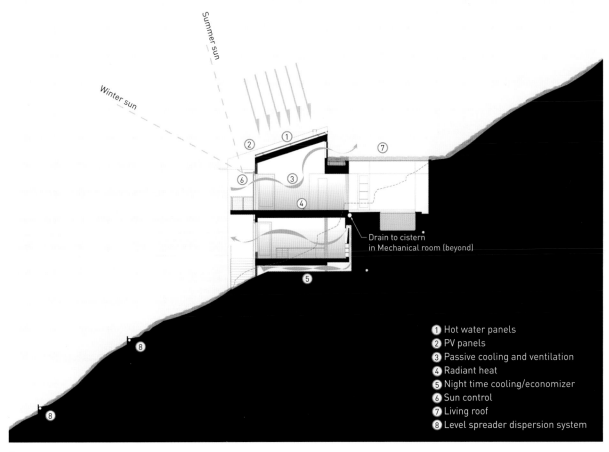

1. Hot water panels
2. PV panels
3. Passive cooling and ventilation
4. Radiant heat
5. Night time cooling/economizer
6. Sun control
7. Living roof
8. Level spreader dispersion system

Summer sun

Winter sun

Drain to cistern
in Mechanical room (beyond)

Environmental diagram

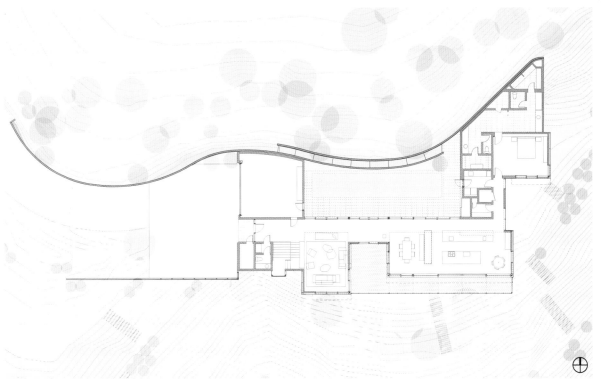

Site plan

SKYFALL RESIDENCE

THE SEA RANCH, CALIFORNIA

Lot size: 0.39 acres
Project size: 1,683 sq ft

Skyfall has a unique setting at the Sea Ranch. This cul-de-sac property is bordered by golf links on two sides. In contrast, a dense stand of cypress trees anchors the southern edge of the parcel. To the west, broad views sweep across the fairways to the Pacific and bluff houses, and north to the stands of trees along the Gualala River. The design utilizes simple barn-like forms to create a private courtyard as the central focus of the house. The courtyard functions as an outdoor living room, nestled against the cypress stand where it is protected from the wind and screened from the golf course. The gateway into the compound aligns with a framed view across the fairway to the Pacific Ocean beyond. Ribbed cement panels for both wall and roof surfaces and cedar wood accents on window surrounds and entry porch reference the early Sea Ranch use of wood planks and the original barn structures. This strategy also satisfied the owners' request for fire-safe alternative cladding materials that would complement the Sea Ranch vernacular but require minimal maintenance and age well.

Skyfall a un cadre unique au Sea Ranch. Cette propriété en cul-de-sac est entourée de terrains de golf sur deux côtés. En revanche, une grappe dense de cyprès ancre la bordure sud de la propriété. À l'ouest, les vues s'ouvrent sur le Pacifique et les maisons sur les falaises, et au nord sur les masses d'arbres le long de la rivière Gualala. La conception utilise des formes simples en forme de grange pour créer un patio privé comme point central de la maison. Le patio fonctionne comme un salon extérieur, niché à côté des cyprès où il est protégé du vent et des vues du terrain de golf. L'entrée de la propriété est dans l'axe avec la vue encadrée de l'océan Pacifique à travers la route d'accès. Les panneaux nervurés de béton sur les murs et les plafonds ainsi que le bois de cèdre sur les cadres de fenêtres et le porche d'entrée font référence à l'utilisation de planches de bois et de structures de grange d'origine à Sea Ranch. Cette stratégie a également répondu au désir des propriétaires d'utiliser des matériaux de revêtement ignifuges qui complètent le language vernaculaire de Sea Ranch mais nécessitent un entretien minimal et vieillissent bien.

Skyfall hat eine einzigartige Kulisse auf der Sea Ranch. Diese Sackgasse ist auf zwei Seiten von Golfplätzen umgeben. Im Gegensatz dazu verankert eine dichte Gruppe von Zypressen den südlichen Rand des Grundstücks. Im Westen bieten sich Ausblicke auf den Pazifik und die Klippenhäuser sowie nach Norden auf die Baummassen entlang des Flusses Gualala. Das Design verwendet einfache, scheunenartige Formen, um eine private Terrasse als zentralen Mittelpunkt des Hauses zu schaffen. Die Terrasse fungiert als Wohnzimmer im Freien, eingebettet neben den Zypressen, wo sie vor Wind und Blick vom Golfplatz geschützt ist. Der Eingang zum Grundstück befindet sich auf einer Achse mit dem gerahmten Blick auf den Pazifik durch die Zufahrtsstraße. Die gerippten Betonplatten an Wänden und Decken sowie das Zedernholz an den Fensterrahmen und der Eingangshalle verweisen auf die frühe Verwendung von Holzbrettern und originalen Scheunenstrukturen auf der Sea Ranch. Diese Strategie entsprach auch dem Wunsch der Hausbesitzer, alternative feuerfeste Abstellgleismaterialien zu verwenden, die die Umgangssprache der Sea Ranch ergänzen, jedoch nur minimale Wartung erfordern und gut altern.

Skyfall tiene un entorno único en Sea Ranch. Esta propiedad situada en un callejón sin salida está rodeada por campos de golf en dos lados. En contraste, un denso grupo de cipreses ancla el borde sur de la propiedad. Hacia el oeste, las vistas se abren hacia el Pacífico y las casas del acantilado, y hacia el norte hasta las masas de árboles a lo largo del río Gualala. El diseño utiliza formas simples parecidas a un granero para crear un patio privado que funciona como una sala de estar al aire libre, ubicado junto a los cipreses donde está protegido del viento y de las vistas desde el campo de golf. La entrada a la propiedad se encuentra en eje con la vista enmarcada del océano Pacífico. Los paneles acanalados de hormigón en las paredes y los techos así como la madera de cedro en los marcos de las ventanas y el porche de entrada hacen referencia al uso temprano de las tablas de madera y las originales estructuras para graneros en Sea Ranch. Esta estrategia también respondió al deseo de los propietarios de usar materiales de revestimiento ignífugos que complementaran el lenguaje vernacular de Sea Ranch pero que requirieran un mantenimiento mínimo y envejecieran bien.

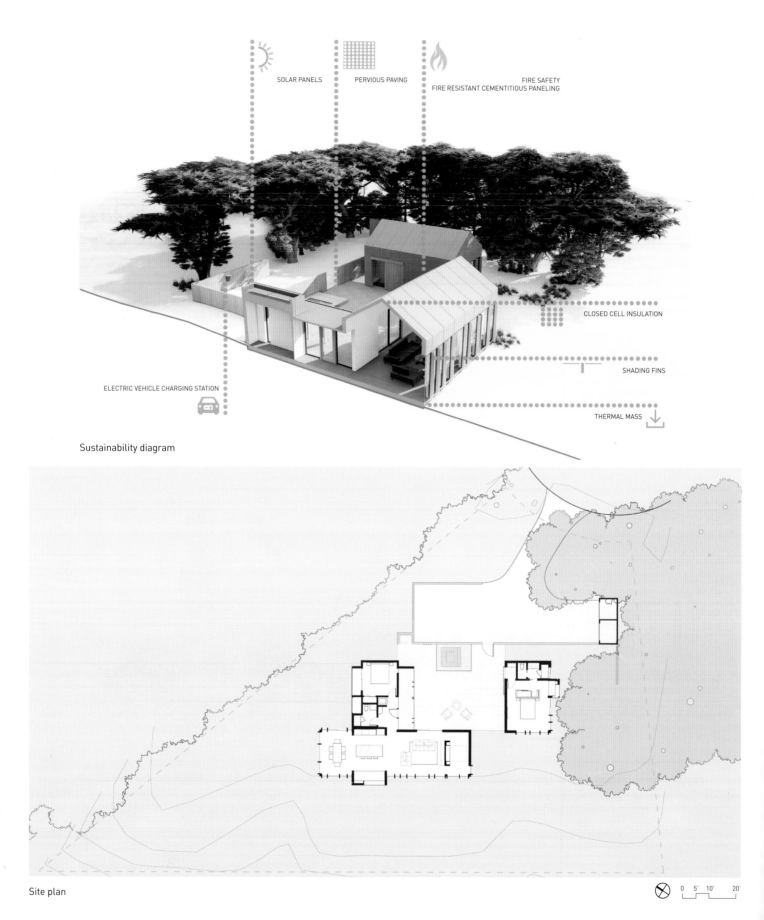

SOLAR PANELS   PERVIOUS PAVING   FIRE SAFETY
FIRE RESISTANT CEMENTITIOUS PANELING

CLOSED CELL INSULATION

SHADING FINS

ELECTRIC VEHICLE CHARGING STATION

THERMAL MASS

Sustainability diagram

Site plan

0 5' 10' 20'

Emerald Bay, Lake Tahoe, California. Photo courtesy of Francesc Zamora